SHORT-TERM THERAPY WITH CHILDREN
By Lawrence E. Shapiro, Ph.D.
Design by Charles Brenna

Published by:
The Center for Applied Psychology, Inc.
P. O. Box 61587
King of Prussia, PA 19406 U.S.A.
Tel. 610/277-4020

The Center for Applied Psychology, Inc. is publisher of Childswork/Childsplay, a catalog of products for mental health professionals, teachers and parents who wish to help children with their developmental, social and emotional growth. For a free catalog of books, games and toys to help children, call 1-800-962-1141.

Copyright ©1994 by The Center for Applied Psychology, Inc.
Printed in the United States of America

ISBN 1-882732-13-8

SHORT-TERM THERAPY WITH CHILDREN

Lawrence E. Shapiro, Ph.D.

Formerly
The New Short-Term Therapies for Children

The Center for Applied Psychology, Inc.
King of Prussia, Pennsylvania

Other books by Lawrence E. Shapiro, Ph.D.

*All Feelings Are OK: It's What You Do With Them
  That Counts*
Face Your Feelings!
Games to Grow On: Activities to Teach Children Self-Control
How to Be a Super-Hero
How to Find Buried Treasure
*Jumpin' Jake Settles Down: A Workbook to Help Impulsive
  Children Learn to Think Before They Act*
*Sometimes I Drive My Mom Crazy, But I Know She's
  Crazy About Me: A Self-Esteem Book for ADHD Children*
Take a Deep Breath: The Kids' Play-Away Stress Book
The Book of Psychotherapeutic Games
*The Building Blocks of Self-Esteem: A Skill-Oriented Approach
  to Teaching Self-Worth*
The Very Angry Day That Amy Didn't Have
*Tricks of the Trade: 101 Psychological Techniques to
  Help Children Grow and Change*
What Color Are Your Family's Dreams?

Table of Contents

Introduction

THE BIRTH OF A SHORT-TERM THERAPIST

Nearly twenty years ago, when I arrived in Colorado to be the school psychologist for a rural school district, I believed that open-ended, individual psychotherapy with children was the only way to have a significant impact on their problems. My psychoanalytic training in New York City had been very rewarding; I was fascinated with the slow unraveling of the Gordian Knot of the psyche that characterizes the analytic mode of therapy. Watching the human mind unfold, delicately revealing its layers in the security of a therapeutic relationship, was a sublime experience, whether it was with children, adolescents, or adults. My training had also taught me the rewards of patience and empathic caring built on an unhurried acceptance of the way children reveal themselves.

But in Colorado, I inherited a caseload of 150 children identified as having significant emotional and learning problems. For a year, I bemoaned the insufficient resources, and I felt that I was providing only stopgap services. Since I was responsible for providing psychological services in six different schools, I rarely had more than ten children in individual therapy: these I saw only once a week for a half hour, and usually for no more than three or four months at a time. Believing that intensive individual therapy was the only legitimate form of psychotherapy, I assumed that this was merely crisis-intervention—putting out one fire while on the way to the next. I treated the most severe cases first, and when those problems had abated somewhat, I worked my way down the referral list to the less severe problems, hoping that the children I had just worked with, although obviously not "cured," would at least have their problems stay in remission. And oddly enough, many of these children did improve, although I wasn't sure why. Watching them improve their behavior, feel better about themselves, or adjust to difficulties at home without having gone through months or years of therapy had a profound effect on me.

With limitations of time and space, I had to completely reconceptualize my ideas about therapy. While completing my doctoral work, I had become interested in the applications of developmental psychology to psychotherapy with children, and began devising my own games that focused on their specific developmental/emotional problems (see Chapter 2, "The Use of Games in Short-Term Therapy"). Since I worked in empty broom closets and in the back of gymnasiums, instead of well-equipped play therapy rooms with two-way mirrors, I usually carried all my materials in a large box. Fortunately, either the clean Colorado air or my youth made me much more open to experimentation. I even flirted with behavioral techniques, although I didn't admit this at the time to my mentors and colleagues back in New York.

But I still never felt that I had enough time to do things right; this made me feel insecure and defensive about my work. I always felt on the verge of exhaustion, and although I had hardly begun my professional career, I began to show the signs of "job burnout," a syndrome familiar to many therapists who work in schools, public clinics, and other institutional settings. Nevertheless, I persevered, always convinced that the system could be changed to provide more resources for children and to give therapists who worked in the public field more time to do their jobs.

Then, after many more years of griping about inadequate resources in several different jobs, I finally began to accept the truth that had escaped me: there will never be enough time and resources to give the large majority of children long-term individual therapy. There are an estimated seven million children in the U.S. with significant psychological problems, and only a fraction of these get adequate treatment, much less the long-term psychotherapy that many of us were trained to provide.

But there are other ways to help children change. We can create new techniques or modify old ones so that they are more effective, more quickly. We can use other people—parents, teachers, or paraprofessionals—to fulfill many of the therapeutic needs of children. We can develop a highly creative system of diagnosis and treatment that focuses precisely on the nodal change points of a child's life and stimulates development far beyond the time the child will spend with the therapist.

THE ESSENTIAL INGREDIENTS
OF A SHORT-TERM THERAPIST

First and foremost, a good short-term therapist needs a personality trait or temperament that he or she will never learn from a book or a course. The best word for this trait is elaborated on in a song from the musical comedy, *Damn Yankees*. This is a story about a hapless baseball team, the Washington Senators, who can barely win a game, much less a pennant. Amid their griping, their coach admonishes them that no matter what the odds, no matter what they may lack, they have to have one thing that will make them winners—heart. He sings,

Ya gotta have heart.
Miles and miles and miles of heart.
When the odds are saying, 'you'll never win'
That's when the grin should start.
Ya gotta have heart.

"Heart," as defined by the lyrics of Richard Adler and Jerry Roth, is courage, and *chutzpah*, and daring, and willfulness, all rolled up together. It is strength of character and determination. For the therapist, it is the *charismatic will* to help the child or adolescent get better. It is the force that preachers of every faith exude over their congregations; it is the force that mothers and fathers muster when they sit by their infant's sickbed. It is a belief in one's own strength and ability to help, no matter what the odds might be.

Therapists must bring *heart* to their work with children, for it is the curative force of therapy, but this does not mean that it is the therapist's job to "cure" the child, any more than it is the preacher's job to cure the ills of his congregation, or the parents' job to cure their infant. They, like the therapist, can only provide a guiding light. A light of hope and spirit.

This light is an inner light, a human light, which as Dr. Richard Gardner suggests, must not be confused with the light of the torch in the hand on top of the Statue of Liberty. Gardner notes in his introduction to his book *Conduct Disorders of Childhood* (Gardner, 1994), that therapists too often have grandiose fantasies about their abilities to help everyone they encounter. He calls this *The Statue of Liberty Syndrome*. Gardner notes that therapists also too often believe that the Emma Lazarus poem at the base of the Statue of Liberty applies specifically to them:

Give me your tired, your poor,
Your huddled masses yearning to breathe free,
The wretched refuse of your teeming shores,
Send these, the homeless, the tempest-tossed to me.
I lift my lamp beside the golden door.

Gardner warns child therapists—and I think that this warning is particularly relevant to short-term therapists—that they were not put on earth to save the world. Therapists have many limitations. They cannot help everyone. And a therapist who understands his or her limitations may ultimately be the most helpful. Rather than trying to accomplish a goal which cannot be accomplished, the therapist may serve children best by leading them to the resources that will be more likely to provide the help that they need. Understanding this, the therapist becomes the child's advocate (with all the wisdom and responsibility that this term implies), and finding the child the right help becomes the very legitimate goal of the short-term therapy.

Another important trait which makes an exemplary short-term therapist is his or her ability to synthesize information and techniques. This book reflects my interest and willingness in synthesizing more than twenty years of training, reading, and experience. I present the techniques in this book from my own very opinionated viewpoint, and I am sure in many cases I have done some disservice to their original authors and to practitioners who specialize in one set of techniques. Similarly, I make no attempt to give each school of therapy equal time, for I give some techniques much more weight in my practice than others and frankly find that some techniques are just more interesting to me than others.

The subjectivity of this book, like the subjectivity of any therapist, may be its greatest strength. The majority of books on therapy techniques are anthologies, collections of the works of dozens of specialists. Each chapter gives the reader a valuable in-depth presentation about a particular theory or technique, but typically the chapters are written with the implication that these are the only techniques that the author uses. In fact, almost all therapists who work with children and adolescents use a wide variety of techniques, and these techniques are further filtered through the therapist's particular blend of skills, interests, and prejudices. And this is certainly not a bad thing. One hopes that in borrowing different elements and theories, there will be a synergistic effect: that the whole will be greater than the sum of its parts.

I believe that this book, in reflecting the way that I practice therapy, reflects the way that most therapists help children. There are very few child therapists, in my opinion, who practice a single technique with the same degree of intensity or thoroughness that the anthologies suggest. Certainly child therapists will be drawn to, and will be more comfortable with, one or more clusters of techniques. But if they have a typical varied caseload, they will undoubtedly be challenged to use many other techniques as well. It is unlikely that the therapist will become an expert in all the techniques mentioned in this book (and I do not claim to be one), but he or she must learn the techniques and practice them "well enough." It is the therapist's responsibility to understand and be able to apply the fundamental ingredients and principles of the research and theory to use each technique effectively.

The effectiveness of any treatment program will always lie in the ingenuity, intellect, talent, and capacity for caring in the therapist, rather in the techniques themselves. If I can inspire any therapist to think about the ways that he or she chooses and applies the vast number of interventions that are available, I will have accomplished my purpose in writing this book

It is toward this end that I hope this book can be useful.

ON LANGUAGE

For some time the field of psychology has been criticized for using language that clouds the issues rather than clears them up. Although there has been little revision of the language in existing theories, there has been a tendency for newer therapies to be discussed in plainer English. But still it seems inevitable that each new therapy will introduce a few dozen new terms and redefine a few dozen old ones. This presents a particular problem for therapists who use the multiple-treatment approach that this book advocates.

As much as possible I have tried to avoid the use of esoteric psychological language and tried to present concepts as simply as possible. However in many therapies, particular words carry a richness of meaning that is difficult to define outside the theoretical constructs of that school of thought. The reader can assume that when I am talking about a particular technique or therapy, I am using the language as it exists in the context of that theory, unless otherwise noted.

—Lawrence E. Shapiro, Ph.D.
August, 1994

CHAPTER 1

THE BASIC ELEMENTS OF SHORT-TERM THERAPY

This is a book for people who help kids. It is aimed primarily at professional therapists, such as social workers, psychiatrists, psychologists, nurses, and counselors, but it can also be a valuable resource for regular classroom teachers, parents, and grandparents. Anyone who spends time with children can be part of their learning and growth and can provide therapeutic advice, guidance, experiences, and structure.

As the reader will see, there are many ways to "do therapy" with children, from reading books, playing games, drawing, and listening to music, to using sophisticated behavioral techniques and even electronic technologies. While some of these techniques require both natural ability and specialized training, many others require only that the person working with the child be sensitive, caring, and know the basic principles of helping children learn to help themselves.

For years it was assumed that the only people who could do therapy with children were the ones working in a private practice or clinic with a room full of therapeutic toys and games and years of experience in psychoanalytically-oriented play therapy. This kind of treatment often took one or more years. But while this method of treatment may still be appropriate for children with certain types of problems, the reality is that most children who get help from a therapist receive it in a relatively brief time period and in much less therapeutic situations. I arbitrarily define short-term therapy as lasting 16 hours or less, over a period of six months or less. Sometimes the goals of therapy can be accomplished in an hour or two with a professional; sometimes the child need not see a professional therapist at all. Therapy can take place virtually anywhere.

There are many reasons why children are commonly seen for a period of weeks or months rather than a period of years: some negative and some positive. The obvious reason is economics. Even with health insurance, long-term psychotherapy can cost thousands of dollars a year. The expense of long-term therapy makes it inaccessible to all but the wealthiest members of our society or to middle-class families who must make untold sacrifices in order to provide this type of therapy for their children.

A second unfortunate reason why short-term therapy has become the rule rather than the exception is the sheer number of children who seem to need help. For better or worse, we live in a society that is good at identifying children who need emotional help outside the normal parameters of the family. (It is worth noting that the US is unique in the world in this respect. No other country shows the same interest in the psychological health of children, but then again no other country may need to). But as a society, we are not as good in providing help to those children who are identified to need it. In most schools, hospitals, and community clinics around the country, you will hear the same complaints of too many children to see and not enough time or resources.

A more positive reason for the upsurge in interest in nontraditional approaches to psychotherapy with children is the proliferation of mental health professionals who are trained to work with children. Child development and child psychology courses are now standard in scores of undergraduate and graduate programs that train people for work in schools, hospitals, day care centers, community-based health centers, churches, and so on.

But perhaps the most important impetus for the changes in how we help children is the changing attitudes of parents. Through the news media, books, and workshops, mothers and fathers have been educated to recognize the early signs of problems their children are having, and the stigma of seeking help has lessened considerably. Life is tough for both children and their parents these days, and we are all beginning to see that there is no need to suffer in silence.

MULTI-MODAL APPROACH TO SHORT-TERM THERAPY

Accepting the fact that most children who are seen in psychotherapy will receive treatment over a relatively short period of time, how can we make sure that every moment of therapy is as effective as it can be? There are dozens of theories to choose from and seemingly hundreds of techniques, but which ones will work most efficiently for each child? What is the best way to help a child get over recurrent nightmares? What do you do with a child who is angry all the time or one who fights with his or her sister so much that the family can't even eat a meal together? What about the child who is fearful or shy and has no friends? Ask these questions to three different therapists and you may get three different answers. Unfortunately, while there is a book that helps us with very specific criteria for diagnosing the problems of children, the Diagnostic and Statistical Manual IV (DSM IV), published by the American Psychiatric Association, there is no equivalent volume to tell us exactly what to do once the problem has been identified.

Many therapists today deal with the overabundance of psychological theories and techniques by explaining that they have an eclectic point of view. They may say that they concentrate on a particular school of thought (e.g., Psychodynamic, Family Therapy, Client-Centered Therapy, etc.), but that they also take into account the immediate needs of the patient.

But as Lazarus (1980) has pointed out, this often means that the therapist chooses techniques largely on the basis of a subjective judgment operating on the premise, "I use whatever makes sense to me and whatever I feel comfortable with." Quoting Eysenk (1970), Lazarus argues that this intuitive approach to therapy ends up being "a mish-mash of theories, a hugger-mugger of procedures, a gallimaufry of therapies...incapable of being tested or evaluated."

To deal with this confusion, Lazarus promotes a "systematic eclecticism," called Multi-Modal Therapy, which defines seven areas in which patients express their problems and draws upon a variety of techniques to address each area in turn. Lazarus notes that while theories may be basically incompatible (e.g., Behaviorism vs. Psychoanalysis), techniques are not. He advocates that a thorough diagnosis be translated into a treatment plan which can use several techniques simultaneously, depending on the needs and style of the patient. This plan should take into account seven modes—behavior affect, sensation, imagery, cognition, interpersonal skills, drugs, and health—that form the acronym BASIC I.D.

Over the last 10 years, I have come up with my own acronym for six different modalities which I prefer simply because it is easier to remember and explain. I call these modalities the A,B,C,D,E'S of short-term therapy: Affect, Behavior, Cognition, Developmental Level, Education, and Social System. These modalities will be elaborated upon in Chapter 2 and will be used to present an organization of the techniques I feel are best suited to short-term therapy in Chapters 4 to 8.

The use of multiple techniques is particularly appropriate in short-term therapy where the object is to maximize the therapeutic effect in the least amount of time possible. One successful therapist has explained his use of a multiple-method therapy as a "shotgun" approach—firing many pellets simultaneously at the target, hoping that at least one will hit the bullseye. But this analogy assumes that the pellets are independent of each other, and that while one or two may hit dead center, most will miss. I prefer to think that the use of multiple techniques has a synergistic effect, with each technique working interdependently with the others, so that the total therapeutic impact is even greater than the sum of its parts.

While I agree with much of what Lazarus has to say about the need for a systematic eclecticism, I would never call myself a Multi-Modal therapist. Coming from a Behaviorist background, Lazarus rightly emphasizes exacting diagnostic assessment to determine which techniques should be used with each individual client. But he then assumes that once the techniques have been identified, any well-trained therapist can carry them out. Here I disagree. This assumption undoubtedly originates in Lazarus' experience in Behaviorism, a school of therapy which de-emphasizes the personality and intuitiveness of the therapist.

But other therapies emphasize certain innate characteristics of the therapist, such as creativity, warmth, and spontaneity, which we do not all possess in equal amounts. While Lazarus urges that the individuality of each patient be respected in accordance with his or her language and style, he neglects to acknowledge that the therapist's individual training, experiences, tastes, interests, and personality must also be accounted for in the therapy. Every therapist is different, just as every patient is different, and we must use the uniqueness of both in the therapy. To be effective therapists, we must know our strengths and weaknesses, as well as those of our clients.

The short-term therapist is a consummate craftsman, sharing characteristics with at least three other professions. First, short-term therapists are like premier detectives. They consider every nuance, not only of the child's personality, but also of the "personality" of the child's world. They understand all aspects of their client's development, and how it may be impeded by the presenting problem. They understand how the child's family system has contributed to the problem, both positively and negatively, and how children's problems affect their time in school, where they spend more than a quarter of their waking hours.

Second, short-term therapists are like brilliant chemists, always searching for the right ingredients to catalyze change and growth in the child's life. And like chemists, they combine the creativity of art and the precision of science, always searching for the nodal points where just the right additions or subtractions will make the difference. And finally, they are four-star chefs, preparing a course of therapy nearly perfect in its attention to detail. Thoroughly trained to heighten their perceptions, they never throw together just what is at hand, but prepare for each step well in advance. They use assistants, naturally, to help in the preparation and to serve what has been prepared.

And the final product is almost like a work of culinary art—appealing to every sense, nutritious, easy to digest, and of course, delectable.

THE DIFFERENCE BETWEEN SHORT-TERM AND LONG-TERM THERAPY

The difference between short-term and long-term therapy is more than a matter of time. They are two distinct models of psychotherapy with some similarities, but more differences.

The therapist and the child are usually best served when short-term therapy is most broadly defined. The aim of short-term therapy is not to "cure" children, but rather to simultaneously stimulate their internal resources for growth and development and make their environment more responsive to their needs. Short-term therapy is rarely an end in itself, but rather a transition point in a child's journey towards adulthood.

While long-term therapy is usually open-ended and deliberately ambiguous about its purpose, short-term therapy seeks to define the child's problem in terms as concrete as possible. Through thorough diagnostic assessments, the therapist formulates hypotheses about the change points in the child's inner and outer lives. A written plan is used to conceptualize the entire course of the therapy, including not only the specific goals and objectives to be accomplished, but also the specific techniques that will be used to achieve them. Because the therapy is time-limited, the techniques that the therapist will choose to achieve each goal will contain as much therapeutic power as possible.

Long-term therapists typically use nondirective and reflective techniques which allow children to reveal their conflicts and their solutions at their own rates. They create a nonjudgmental and accepting atmosphere where the children can explore the underlying unconscious issues that created their problems. However, the short-term therapist, with only a finite period of time for treatment, takes a more systematic approach. With a creative battery of standardized and nonstandardized measures and with information provided from the child's family and other correspondents, the therapist identifies the most important problems to be solved. These in turn are ranked hierarchically and become the major focus of the treatment.

A major difference in short-term therapy is its approach to the treatment of symptoms. A long-standing psychoanalytic premise, which began as a response to the Behavioral movement of the 1950s and 1960s, has been that if one treats the surface manifestation of a problem without resolving the underlying conflict, then another symptom, a potentially more serious one, will promptly take its place. But after more than two decades of treating the overt behaviors of children, this caveat has not been supported by clinical practice. Moreover, the concept of "symptom removal" is itself a misnomer. A psychotherapist is not a dentist extracting parts of a personality that are no longer useful as if they were rotted teeth. No form of therapy is so powerful that it can change a child in ways that are incompatible with his or her basic needs. The goal of psychotherapy is to give children choices where before they had none.

Short-term therapies seek to do this in the most expedient way possible by showing children how to use their inner resources more adaptively and how to make their external world more receptive to change. If a symptom functions in an adaptive way for the child that the therapist does not foresee, then the child will maintain that symptom until he or she can see that another way of functioning will serve better. While short-term therapy may occasionally fail to change a child in the direction that the therapist would like, it is highly unlikely that it will make a child worse. Some specific exceptions, where short-term therapy is contraindicated, will be considered later in this chapter.

Moreover, many systems therapists have rejected the medical model of symptoms and diseases altogether. Jay Haley (1976), who uses a directive approach to family therapy, considers all psychological problems to be a repeating sequence of acts between several people, maintaining the particular way that they relate to each other. He states that what we refer to as a symptom, such as phobia or depression, is simply a "label for the crystallization of a sequence in a social organization." The child's behavior is seen as a metaphor for larger problems within the family, usually between the parents, and when the dynamics of the family system change, the child's "symptoms" disappear.

TRANSFERENCE AND COUNTERTRANSFERENCE

While this book emphasizes the new techniques available to the short-term therapist for promoting effective change, some issues and techniques of more traditional therapy, including the roles of transference, countertransference, and resistance, can also play a role in short-term therapy.

Transference, the projection of the client's inner feelings, images, and representations onto the therapist, occurs in every type of psychotherapy whether recognized and interpreted or not. As in long-term traditional therapy, the recognition and use of the transference phenomenon as a specific technique will vary according to the training and orientation of the therapist. Therapists who have been schooled in psychoanalytic methods will pay more attention to this technique than humanistic therapists who have a "here and now" orientation. Some of the techniques described in this book, such as Hypnotherapy and Transactional Analysis, rely heavily on the transference phenomenon because the techniques are built on a psychoanalytic tradition. But other methods, such as Reality Therapy or Biofeedback, ignore the phenomenon altogether.

Countertransference, the projection of the therapist's needs and conflicts onto the child, is an issue which must be dealt with no matter what the orientation of the therapist is or what techniques are being used. To be effective, therapists must recognize when their objectivity is colored by their needs and prejudices. This is certainly not to say that the therapist shouldn't have all the feelings and foibles of the human condition, but rather that these must be recognized and kept out of the therapy, unless it serves some therapeutic purpose to reveal them. Certain methods, such as Reality Therapy and Values Clarification Therapy, encourage therapists to be self-disclosing as part of the therapeutic process. However, even with these methods, the therapist's personal thoughts, feelings, and experiences are not revealed randomly as in social conversation, but are selectively chosen and judiciously used as in any other treatment technique.

The issue of countertransference is important in defining the limits and limitations of the short-term therapist. In this book and in my lectures, I have always advocated that the short-term therapist "do whatever has to be done." I am, above all else, a pragmatist and realist, and believe that the most important task of the short-term therapist is to get the child and the system "unstuck" from a dysfunctional pattern and moving in a more positive direction. There are not too many things that I would not do if I thought they were in the best interest of the child and moved the therapy in the direction of the therapeutic goal; however, *this attitude can only exist within the strict boundaries of the therapist's role.* In other words, the therapist's "power" is a perceived one. Although it may sometimes be necessary, a therapist must not step out of a very clearly delineated role lightly, for it is the role of the therapist that defines his or her wisdom.

I learned this lesson early in my career, at a dinner party given by some friends a few years older. I was very eager to impress the group, who seemed at that moment to be more advanced in their careers and life experience, and when the subject came around to children I thought my moment in the spotlight had come. One parent was particularly concerned about whether or not her child should be moved from kindergarten into the first grade. Coincidentally, I had just completed a comprehensive literature review on that subject and was in charge of drawing up the criteria for kindergarten placement for the school district for which I worked. I eagerly offered my informed opinion to her question, confident in my correctness and authority. But then the person next to me (an accountant) gave his opinion. And then the person next to him (a salesperson) gave her opinion, and although these opinions were "wrong" in my view, they were just as valid as mine in the context of dinner party conversation. That evening I realized that the authority of the therapist is entirely contextual. When a therapist steps out of that context, he or she loses a good deal of the "power" of therapy.

I frequently hear of therapists who leave their offices to reward children for improved behaviors. Therapist A takes a child to the ice cream store; therapist B takes a child to buy baseball cards. I often hear these stories from therapists who want to make a point about how they motivate children. Clearly the intentions of these therapists are admirable, but I believe their procedures are misguided. It is not that I object to the therapist leaving the confines of his or her office (see section on the technique of On-Site Therapy in Chapter 4), but in these examples, these excursions are not necessary to further the therapeutic goal, and in fact subtly diminish the authority of the therapist in the child's as well as the parent's eyes.

Why? Because these are activities that parents, not therapists, do with their children. Therapist A might reply, "But you should hear the conversations that we have over ice cream!" And I would still say, "Those conversations are important. But they should take place in the therapy room where you can maintain your therapeutic stance and objectivity. You are intruding into the child's world by your presence, innocent and well-meaning though it may be, and this should not be taken lightly, for the sake of an ice cream cone." (See the section on Intrusion later in this chapter).

RESISTANCE TO THERAPY

Resistance is commonly defined as the various defense mechanisms that the client uses in order to protect himself or herself from self-awareness. Psychoanalysts more narrowly refer to resistance as the unwillingness of the client to make unconscious material conscious.

But I prefer to use the expanded definition of this concept, as suggested by Dr. Richard A. Gardner (1975) to include anything that prevents the client from participating in the therapeutic process. Gardner explains, tongue in cheek, that the child therapist must rightly be concerned with the deductive and inductive thinking that goes on in the therapy process, but allowance must also be made for the *seductive* thinking of the therapist: the seduction of the child into the therapeutic process. As Gardner explains his use of games, magic tricks, jokes and riddles, and verbal bantering, he adds, "And you see the levels that we will stoop to in child psychotherapy!"

Unlike the psychoanalytic therapist who limits his or her intervention to the *interpretation* of resistance, the short-term therapist meets obstacles to therapeutic change more directly. But as Gardner notes, directness does not necessarily mean confrontation. From the inception of the therapy plan, the therapist seeks to ally himself or herself with the child by choosing techniques which are compatible with the child's interests and style. The desire of the therapist to have the child accept the treatment process rather than fight it is one of the major determinants by which therapy techniques are chosen.

For example, a child interested in video games and technology might be drawn to the electronic gadgetry used in Biofeedback. Children who have difficulty expressing themselves in words might be more open to the nonverbal techniques of Art or Music Therapy. Psychologically sophisticated adolescents, who want to compete with the therapist in dealing with their problems or the problems in their families, may be introduced to Transactional Analysis, which has translated sophisticated psychological concepts into concrete terms and which emphasizes the ability of clients to be their own therapists.

Due to time limitations, the short-term therapist must tackle children's resistance to therapy as quickly as possible, engaging them by whatever means are necessary.

PARTICIPATION OF OTHERS IN THE THERAPY

Most short-term therapists are more social than their long-term traditional counterparts. At every stage of the treatment the short-term therapist interacts with other adults in the child's life to achieve therapeutic goals. Since the short-term therapist depends on other people in the child's life to do much of the therapeutic work, simple and precise communication is essential. With the information to be shared and by his or her language and demeanor, the therapist seeks to demystify the treatment process. Efforts are continuously made to engage the parents and teachers as colleagues in the treatment of the child and to respect them as experts in their own right. In many cases, the role of the therapist is intentionally downplayed in order to focus the responsibility for change on the significant adults in the child's life.

Communication begins with the written plan or therapeutic contact that clearly states what the therapist expects to achieve and how he or she expects to do it. The specifics of writing a therapeutic plan are discussed in Chapter 2.

The second level of interaction consists of an ongoing dialogue in which the therapist methodically communicates with parents, teachers, or other significant adults about their roles in the implementation of the therapy. This interaction is most intense and effective when it is in the form of family therapy. Within the therapy session, the therapist communicates on many different levels with the child's "system," providing opportunities for the family members to not only hear about how they might change, but to actually experience the change. Another form that this interaction might take is when the therapist identifies a person in the child's life to act as "cotherapist" in the treatment. In this instance the adult, usually a parent, is trained to carry out a therapeutic technique that is part of the overall therapy plan. Cotherapists may be chosen not only for their ability to implement the specific technique, but also for their strategic placement within the child's social and family system.

The third level of interaction puts the therapist in a consultative role. She or he may advise the teacher on specific techniques to help the child in the classroom, or may provide information to the family on such matters as the books they can read, support groups that are available, and so on. The consultative role of the therapist may involve a full range of therapeutic techniques. The teacher who cannot provide limits for the child may be asked to come in for assertiveness training. The father who cannot control his anger may be invited to see the therapist for treatment.

The fourth level of communication is directed toward other professionals. The multidisciplinary approach will be familiar to most therapists who have worked in a hospital or school setting, but there is no reason why this same approach cannot also be used in a community setting with complex or difficult cases or in private practice. A multidisciplinary approach draws selectively from a host of specialists including: speech/language therapists, pediatricians, pediatric neurologists, occupational therapists, specialized tutors, and so forth. The approach will include diagnostic assessments by each specialist, a plenary meeting to present the initial findings and draw up an interdisciplinary treatment methodology, and ongoing follow-up meetings to evaluate the progress being made.

Finally, therapists may be called upon to act as advocates for the child as part of the short-term therapy process. While this may be beyond what we usually refer to as therapy, getting the child the appropriate educational, medical, or social services that are needed can sometimes be the most significant intervention therapists can use. To be effective advocates, therapists should familiarize themselves with federal and state laws regarding the rights of and services available to children, and they should not hesitate to represent children before the agencies who are delegated by law to serve them.

In each of these circumstances, the therapist should not forget his or her role as a short-term therapist. In Solution-Oriented Therapy, as taught by William Hudson O'Hanlan at the Hudson Center for Brief Therapy in Omaha, Nebraska, emphasis is placed on the varied ways that the therapist can move adult patients toward finding his own solution through specific forms of communication. I might add that communication with everyone in the child's life—parent, teacher, grandparent, other professionals—needs to be considered. *Every time therapists speak to someone in the child's system, they have the opportunity to move that system toward achieving a therapeutic goal.*

Some of the many communication techniques that Hudson O'Hanlon suggests include:

- Acknowledge the person's point of view to develop rapport
- Create an expectation for change with solution-oriented language
- Identify the first signs that will indicate movement towards the therapeutic goal
- Cast doubt on suggestions or actions which close the possibilities for finding a solution
- Listen for things that support change for the better and reinforce the understanding that change will occur in small steps

CONFIDENTIALITY

In trying to interact forcefully and directly with children and their environment, we also create some difficult problems and questions about our roles as therapists. Two issues amplified by short-term therapy are the child's right to privacy about his or her treatment, and the intrusion or disruption that the treatment causes in the child's life.

The problem of confidentiality is usually of most concern to children in regard to their parents. One child is afraid that the therapist will report to his parents that he has been stealing again. Another thinks that the therapist will spill the beans on how angry she is with her father, causing him to leave the home. A third thinks that the therapist will tell his parents about his sexual feelings toward his teacher. Every stage of childhood has its secrets, and every child must be assured that the therapist respects these secrets. But often the right to privacy is overshadowed by the need for open and direct communication about the child's problems.

Dr. Richard Gardner (in *Conduct Disorders of Childhood*, 1994) suggests that the issue of confidentiality in the treatment of younger clients is not a significant issue:

> I believe that such therapists are placing too much weight on confidentiality. The patient is coming primarily for treatment, whether the patient is a child or an adult. The patient is not coming primarily for the preservation of confidentiality. I believe that to the degree that the preservation of the confidential relationship serves the ends of treatment, to that degree it should be respected. If it is a choice between confidentiality and doing what is in the best interests of the patient therapeutically, then, I believe, the therapeutic indications should be given priority over confidences.

Dr. Gardner goes on to explain that most child patients have the expectation that what they do or say will be shared with the adults who care most about them. If a child is brought to a therapist for stealing, then the child should certainly assume that his or her parents know about the stealing. It goes without saying that a child who perceives a parent or other caretaker as *not* caring, because they are either negligent or abusive in some way, will have different confidentiality issues. My general rule of thumb is that thoughts and feelings are usually the sole province of the therapy room, but a child's actions are often shared with other adults. It is sometimes surprising how easy it is for children, even very young children, to comprehend this, and in fact this distinction is often very helpful in their treatment.

Children are used to being talked about by people who care for them; it happens all the time with their parents, and they can accept this as a part of life. They do not necessarily distrust the therapist who also talks to their parents, as long as the therapist's intentions are made clear from the beginning of the treatment.

INTRUSION

Therapy, in and of itself, is an intrusion into the child's life. One argument for using short-term therapy techniques is that children should be spending most of their time with family and friends in age-appropriate activities rather than spending it with a therapist. Consequently, any technique that disrupts the child's normal day-to-day life is an intrusion, but certain techniques used in short-term therapy are inherently more intrusive than others. The general premise of short-term therapy is to minimize the disruption of a child's life by treating the problem as efficiently as possible, and the same rule of minimal intrusiveness applies in selecting specific techniques. Sometimes use of an intrusive therapy is unavoidable because of the crisis nature of the problem.

The issue of intrusion is more commonly a problem in school than at home. Children are very sensitive to their status with their peers, and having a therapist is rarely considered something to brag about. Even the children who seem to enjoy therapy and are deeply attached to their therapists are often embarrassed to be in therapy and do not want the therapist to visit their school and be seen by their friends.

The issue of intrusion in a child's life may manifest itself in subtle ways to which the therapist must be attuned. If a child is asked to wear a counter to record the frequency of a behavior, the therapist must also realize that this will be observed by other children in the class. If a teacher is asked to create special workspace for a child with a learning disability, the therapist must consider how the child's status in the class will be affected and whether this intervention will do more harm than good. Any change in children's lives, no matter how appropriate it may seem to the therapist, can make them so self-conscious that the therapy will be undermined.

Ideally, therapeutic interventions should be designed to have a maximum effect while being minimally intrusive, but realistically there appears to be an inverse relationship between the power of therapy to effect change and the disruption of the child's day-to-day life.

In some instances, such as problems that involve dangers to the child, the issue of intrusiveness must be put aside, and the most powerful techniques available should be used. In most other circumstances the therapist must weigh the power of the technique (that is, its predictable outcome as supported by research or experience) against the extent to which the technique can have a deleterious effect on the child (what I call intrusiveness). This trade-off is most readily apparent in the administration of psychostimulant medication to children diagnosed with Attention Deficit Disorders (ADD). Over the last 20 years, I have watched the pendulum of opinion on the administration of these drugs swing back and forth, propelled by the need to have these children function and learn in school and considerations about both short- and long-term physical side-effects. The opinion now seems to be more strongly in favor of the drug therapy for ADD, supported, I might add, by a considerable body of research literature.

But the power vs. intrusiveness issue is not so evident with many other techniques, and yet it is perhaps the most significant concern for short-term therapists choosing treatment strategies. As I have mentioned, if possible, the therapist should choose techniques which are maximally powerful and minimally intrusive. The use of psychotherapeutic games is one of the techniques that fulfills this criterion, which is one of the reasons I recommend it so highly as a treatment of choice in short-term therapy. Most other techniques will fall somewhere along the continuum of power vs. intrusiveness, and it is incumbent upon the therapist to choose a technique which provides just the right amount of therapeutic power to effect a change.

Consider, for example, the continuum of behavioral techniques available to the therapist:

- **Operant Conditioning and Behavioral Shaping:** Rewarding positive behavior with verbal praise
- **Behavioral Contracting:** Establishing a written contract between the child and significant adults to improve his behavior in exchange for a designated reward
- **Token Economy:** A system of winning points for improved or new behaviors
- **Contingency Management:** A system where rewards are both given *and* taken away; negative contingencies can include punishments like the Time-Out procedure
- **On-Site Therapy** (see Chapter 4): A treatment which involves therapy to occur in the context in which the problem occurs, such as the treatment of certain phobias

The experienced practitioner can easily perceive that these behavioral strategies are listed in order from least to most intrusive, and, inversely, from least to most powerful. Other techniques and strategies may not be so obvious. For example, when I lecture about the continuum just described, I frequently save the "most powerful technique and the one most feared by children" for last. My voice lowers and I hold the podium firmly for dramatic effect, as I describe, "the most horrible, the insidious, the most dastardly, and yet sometimes necessary intervention with children...taking away the TV!"

While this always get a laugh from the audience, I then point out the gravity of the problem. On the one hand, television is an extremely powerful force in a child's life, and one which the vast majority of children could do without (the average American child watches 24 hours of TV per week—one day a week!). On the other hand, I am amazed at how rarely limiting TV time is recommended as part of a behavioral program. Why is this? Because therapists know, consciously or unconsciously, that television is such an important factor in the lives of many children as well as their parents, that altering the viewing habits of a family will have a profound effect on family dynamics. In other words, although it seems that controlling a child's TV watching would be a fairly innocuous strategy, in fact, in some cases it is perceived as very intrusive.

CONTRAINDICATIONS FOR SHORT-TERM THERAPY

Although I have spent a good portion of my professional career advocating the development of effective brief therapy techniques for children, I have always recognized that short-term therapy is *not* the treatment of choice for some children. There are certain children, in specific situations, for whom short-term therapy can do more harm than good.

One example is the treatment of the traumatized child. I am not simply referring to children who have experienced a trauma, for often these children can be treated with time-limited techniques. I am referring rather to children who have been *traumatized;* those children who have been profoundly influenced by one or more traumatic events, to the extent that they have developed significant symptomatology or are otherwise dysfunctional. The traumatic event may range from experiencing a hurricane or flood, to the sudden loss of a parent or sibling, to the more common trauma of child abuse. In each of these events, the child may need an open-ended treatment, as opposed to a time-limited one, so that he or she will have the opportunity to work through the affective states associated with the trauma fully, as well as any potentially hidden memories.

Another category of children for whom long-term therapy is preferred is those children who have not completed the bonding process that normally takes place between the parent and child in the first two years of life. Typically, these children manifest severe personality disturbances such as autism, childhood schizophrenia, severe anxiety disorders, or chronic depression. What is most important for these children is to develop a relationship with an adult they can trust and care about, one who will meet them with nurturance and empathy. While this can certainly happen in short-term therapy, these children deserve to know the full benefit of a complex and rich relationship with another human being without the limitations of time and expediency.

A third category of children for whom short-term therapy is contraindicated will have had at least a partially successful experience in bonding and will be proceeding along the road toward individuation. However, they remain vulnerable because they have had a substantial number of adult figures come in and out of their lives as a result of frequent moves, changes of teachers, and most commonly, divorce. These children will be best served by a therapist who can see them for an extended period of time if at all possible.

Unfortunately, there is no hard-and-fast rule as to when short-term therapy can harm these children by presenting still another important person in their lives who comes, establishes a relationship, and then goes. Certainly many therapists treat children and their families for adjustment problems related to divorce or other types of loss in a relatively short time with effective results. But other times, brief therapy for these children has only a palliative effect, and significant conflicts remain unresolved for many years, sometimes with irreversible psychic damage.

The only sure way I know to avoid the error of inappropriately treating children with short-term techniques is to proceed with therapy only after a comprehensive diagnostic workup. In particular, the decision of whether or not to use short-term therapy on these children may rest on their ego development—how much they have formed an individuated sense of self; how they have developed a sense of their independence and mastery skills; the developmental stage of their peer relations; and, in particular, the structure of their ego-defense mechanisms.

If, in fact, their developments have proceeded more or less along normal lines and if their personalities tend to be adaptive, then short-term therapy, focused on building support for children in their natural environment might be indicated. However, if children have not successfully completed many of the appropriate developmental tasks expected at their ages, or if they have had difficulty in meeting many of the demands and stresses of the maturational process, then long-term therapy might be indicated. In an open-ended, non-directive therapy, these children would have the opportunity to regress and return to unresolved issues which might be triggered by the immediate circumstances of their lives.

In some cases, the question of whether or not to use short- or long-term therapy has a simple solution—*use both*. On several occasions, I began using short-term therapy only to realize that more intensive, longer-term treatment was needed. In these instances, the brief therapy became an extended period of diagnosis and helped determine important information about the exact kind of services that the child needed. In other instances, short-term therapists may work adjunctively with a child who is also in open-ended long-term therapy. A short-term therapist might be used to implement a behavioral program for a specific problem in the home or school, to alleviate a particular dysfunctional symptom, to move a child through a specific developmental task, or to deal with a specific life crisis.

A NOTE TO PARENTS

Although this book is primarily written for practitioners of psychotherapy and students, it can also be useful as a guide to parents in helping them choose a therapist for their child. Finding a therapist involves some of the most important and difficult decisions a parent must make, and should be done with both caution and knowledge. There are several factors, however, that make this difficult process even more difficult. Parents are understandably in a hurry to get help for their children. Usually the situation has become fairly serious by the time a professional is sought and the whole family feels a need for immediate relief. The parents may want to hand the problem over to the first therapist they meet, but this can be a big mistake.

Therapists are not all alike. They have many different views, theories, and practices, some of which will suit the child and the parents better than others. Sometimes any therapist will be able to help a particular child, but more likely this will not be the case. Some therapists will be better suited to the child's needs than others.

Another problem that parents face is the mystique surrounding psychotherapy, implying that the decisions about a child's treatment should be left to experts. This attitude is misleading and potentially harmful. Parents are experts in their own right. They are the ones who have acknowledged their child's problems, and undoubtedly they will be part of the solution. The informed opinion of experts should certainly be taken into consideration, but it can never supersede the responsibility of the parents to make the final decisions.

A third problem that parents face is where to look for a child psychotherapist. The child's pediatrician, the school principal, a clergyman, or a friend will often offer a name of a therapist, but I usually advise parents to consider at least three choices. If the parents cannot obtain three referrals through their own social network, they can contact local or state mental health agencies, which maintain lists of both public and private therapists. Finally, there are national professional organizations that maintain lists of their credentialed members across the country, including the American Psychological Association, the American Psychiatric Association, and the National Association of Social Workers. The phone numbers and addresses of these organizations are located in the Resource section in the back of this book.

Once the names of three therapists have been obtained, the therapists should be contacted by phone for an interview. Some therapists will charge for the first interview and others will not; this should be discussed in the initial phone contact.

During the interview the therapist will want to find out as much as possible about the child and his or her family, but parents should also use this time to find out about the therapist. Parents should feel free to ask whatever comes into their minds; however, these are some of the most important issues that I think should be pursued:

• What is the experience, orientation, and training of the therapist?
• How many children with similar problems has he or she seen, and what have been the outcomes?
• How often will the therapist see the child?
• Will other members of the family be present or be seen separately?
• How long might the therapy take?
• How will the therapist communicate with the parents?
• Does the therapist provide written reports, periodic meetings, regular phone calls?
• Is the therapist willing to visit the child's school if necessary?
• How will the therapist and parents know if progress is being made?
• How will the success of the therapy be judged?
• Does the therapist provide a written contract which says what to expect and when?
• How much will the therapy cost?
• How are payments to be made?
• Does the therapist accept payments from insurance companies or other sources?

Most therapists will easily be able to answer these questions to the parent's satisfaction, for they involve issues that are a part of every therapeutic practice. But the parents should also pay attention to the *way* they are answered: the responsiveness and warmth of the therapist, the tone of his or her voice, and how patient he or she appears to be, for these are important clues as to how the therapist will interact with the child.

Although these suggestions are primarily directed at parents who are choosing a private therapist, many of them will also apply to therapists who are assigned to a child either in school or at a clinic. Most parents don't realize that these assignments are often made as much for practical reasons as for therapeutic ones, and that parents can and should have a voice in what will be a very important relationship for their child.

If you take your child to a public or private clinic for treatment, you will probably first be interviewed by an intake therapist who is responsible for assessing the problem and directing you for appropriate treatment. This person can answer the questions that I have listed.

Often clinics will use students or trainees to treat a many of their clients; however, the fact that a therapist is relatively inexperienced has advantages as well as drawbacks. Usually therapists in training make up in enthusiasm and energy what they may lack in expertise, and children can be particularly responsive to the excitement and sense of adventure these new therapists bring. Still, you should rightfully be interested in just how student therapists are supervised, how often, in what format, and to whom they are accountable. If you are not happy with the answers to these questions, or with the therapists themselves, then you should make this known as soon as possible.

The main point to remember is that mental health personnel and systems are usually more flexible and more receptive to "consumers" than most people think. If you speak up, you are likely to be heard.

CHAPTER 2

A MODEL FOR EFFECTIVE SHORT-TERM THERAPY WITH CHILDREN

Developing the Model

When most practitioners think of child psychotherapy or play therapy, they think of long-term, open-ended models. But the model I use for short-term therapy assumes that the most comprehensive approach to a problem is also the most direct one. Since the intent of brief therapy is to maximize the impact on the child's conflicts while minimizing actual treatment time, the therapist may spend a considerable amount of time conceptualizing the therapy. It is my assumption that therapists with only a limited amount of time to see a child must act forcefully and directly, and only clear knowledge of both their clients and the effectiveness of their techniques will allow them to do so.

In developing a model for short-term therapy, I have naturally considered both historical trends and developments in the treatment of the emotional problems of children, as well as my own interests, experiences, and beliefs. Having originally been trained in analytic ego-oriented techniques in New York, I moved to Colorado, where the analytic method was viewed with a high degree of skepticism at best. Behaviorism, Developmental Theory, and Learning Theory were the preferred subjects of my professors, and my first job as a school psychologist reinforced my own perception of these theories as more practical models of working with children.

Behaviorism was in fact the first brief therapy, although it is not usually referred to in this way. Behavioral therapy is by definition a directive technique and in almost all cases is limited to less than 12 sessions with the client. My analytic training had taught me, however, to beware of the "quick fix." The analytic stance was that behavioral therapy techniques only treated symptoms, not the underlying causes of a problem. It was reasoned that if you only treated a symptom, a new symptom, perhaps a worse one, would quickly take its place.

But while this theory makes sense (particularly if you are an analyst), no significant research supports this proposition. More research suggests that when a particular symptom is treated, the symptom is transformed into a more functional way for the personality to express itself, and the transformation may have additional positive effects rather than negative ones.

Jay Haley (1976) and other influential family therapists have promoted the idea that treating the presenting problem is like throwing a stone in a pond; a ripple-effect spreads throughout the patient's system, which then reorganizes itself around the healthier functioning. Haley has promoted a short-term therapy, Problem-Solving Therapy, which focuses on the singlemost significant problem of a family rather than treating the multiple problems that may be displayed in the initial stages of treatment. Haley reasons that therapists are most effective treating one problem at a time, focusing the therapy on the problem which appears to the most significant impediment to healthier functioning by the family. When this problem is solved, therapy is over, although the therapist or family may renew the therapeutic contract to look at another problem in the same manner.

It is worth noting that Haley's practical strategy was influenced by one of the most creative therapists of our time, Milton Erickson. Erickson has sometimes been called the king of short-term therapy, because of his amazing ability to help people in just a few sessions. Erickson's methodology is described as Hypnotherapy, but his style went far beyond our conventional ideas of trance hypnosis. Anecdotes abound of Erickson's remarkable therapeutic successes (see *Uncommon Therapy*, Haley, 1973), many of which took place with only a few hours of treatment. For instance, there is the case where he treated a psychiatrist and his wife who had flown 1,500 miles to see him for just three sessions. Although they each had been in psychoanalysis for years, they remained unhappy in their marriage and unfulfilled in their careers. After a week, they returned home, and in a six month follow-up conducted by Erickson, they reported that for the first time in their adult lives they were making the kind of personal and job choices that brought them a sense of self-worth and fulfillment.

There was also the case of an eight-year-old boy brought kicking and screaming into Erickson's office. His parents had sought help from their neighbors for their son's bedwetting, had prayed publicly for him in church, and now, in desperation, wished to take him to the "crazy doctor." Erickson effected a cure of this overdetermined symptom in one short interview with the boy and one interview with the parents. An 18-month followup indicated that the symptom had not returned, and another had not come to take its place. These are just two examples of the hundreds of cases that Erickson treated in just a few sessions, at lectures with hundreds of people attending, by telephone and letter, and even by proxy, without even making contact with the identified patient.

Erickson worked through metaphor and suggestion, but if you look closely, many of his techniques have underlying behavioral components. However, few of us, if any, have Erickson's talents (which I believe are as close as one can get to extra-sensory perception), and I believe that his style and "magic" cannot really be taught. But what we *can* learn from Erickson is the *possibility* for quicker change for many patients, a possibility enhanced by innovation, directness, and a belief that people can seek direction for growth in their lives, given the right opportunities and guidance.

This philosophy is shared by advocates of Solution-Oriented Therapy (see *Keys to Solution in Brief Therapy*, Steve de Shazer, 1985), a brief therapy system developed for adult and family therapy, but which has implications for work with children as well. Strongly influenced by the work of Erickson, Solution-Oriented Therapy does not dwell on the overcomplicated and multidetermined variables that define a particular problem. Steve de Shazer explains that patients have tried many different things to understand and improve their conflicts before seeking therapy, but the solution to their problems remains behind a locked door. He continues with this metaphor by suggesting that the therapist does not necessarily have to find the exact key which unlocks the door, but can use a variety of skeleton keys which will do the job. Rather than focusing on the problem, this school of thought believes that it is the role of the therapist to present conditions in which the patient or patients can spontaneously find new ways to live which will transform their symptoms into a more functional and fulfilling lifestyle.

I believe that the short-term therapist treating children can work in a similar manner in helping the significant people in a child's life find solutions. After all, in many cases, it is not the child who is coming to therapy with a particular problem, but the adult experiencing a problem with the child's behavior or emotional state. Similarly, in the vast majority of cases, an adult will define when a child is better, or when a solution has been found. It is in everyone's best interest when the therapist can help the adult who has brought the child into therapy and other adults who interact with the child to reframe their experiences of the child's problems and focus on where the road to the solution begins and where it leads.

This may be a particularly relevant philosophy for therapists and counselors who work in schools or institutional settings. In seeking an alliance with the child's teachers, the therapist frequently joins in informal discussion of the child's problems commensurate with the teacher's classroom trials and tribulations. At every school I have worked or consulted in, I have heard the faculty room jokes and imitations of children, and freely admit to having participated in them as well. It is human nature to poke fun at what is frustrating or difficult for us. The jokes, although frequently unkind, are a release for our frustration and arguably allow us to recharge our compassion and empathy for the child. But while this bonding with the teachers or other front-line professional is understandable, it is nevertheless antitherapeutic. Our job as a brief therapist or counselor does not end when we walk out of therapy room if we remain in the same environment in which the child's problems exist. Whenever we are with adults who are responsible for caring for or educating our clients, we are therapists, no matter how informal the setting. With every statement we make, we have an opportunity to help those adults become part of the solution for the child we are treating (see Chapter 8, Communicating Solutions).

Having discussed some of the more elegant roots of the model of short-term therapy that I am proposing, I must now turn to the mundane. The final influence on my work as a short-term therapist derives from the most dreaded acronym in the mental health profession: I.E.P. (Individual Education Plan to those working with special needs children in schools) or I.H.P. (Individual Habilitation Plan to those working in hospitals or mental health centers). The requirements of federal and state laws for mental health professionals to write plans of accountability even now affect the private practitioner as more insurance companies and state licensing boards require such plans. For the most part, therapists hate them. Most professional training programs in psychology, counseling, and social work teach either from a medical or a humanistic model, neither of which emphasizes the need for writing a treatment plan. On the contrary, psychotherapy has always been held up to be as much art as science. Would you ask an artist to commit himself to a detailed plan before he picks up the brush? Hardly.

But although it may be an unpopular position, I believe that treatment plans are a good thing to use in short-term therapy. With a limited amount of time to actually do the work, it is incumbent on the therapist to think his or her treatment approach through thoroughly. This is not to say that a treatment plan should be viewed as a prescription; certainly it should not be represented as a scientific methodology (a discussion on writing objectives follows). But a plan can act as a road map towards a therapeutic goal. It can be a general contract between the therapist and significant adults in the child's life to each carry out through on specific procedures. Like using a road map, you may not need to rely on it all the time. A good therapist has his or her own sense of direction and surely pays attention to signs along the road. But if you get lost, there is nothing like a map to figure out where you went wrong and the direction you must take to get you where you want to go.

The Multi-Modal Approach:
The A,B,C,D,E'S of Short-Term Therapy

Using a multi-modal approach allows the therapist to borrow from the best of short-term therapy models as well as many of the techniques embedded in the models.

In most cases, short-term therapy should cast the therapist in the roles of teacher, expert, and facilitator. The therapist takes the lead in developing a treatment plan and provides techniques which will help the child achieve the therapeutic goal *with the guidance and cooperation of the significant adults in the child's life.* It is the responsibility of these adults, to a large extent, to participate in the therapeutic plan and to take responsibility and accountability for the implementation of many aspects of the therapeutic program.

The therapist must put together a plan that takes into account every possible inroad into the child's psyche, and in doing so he or she should consider at least six modalities: Affect, Behavior, Cognition, Developmental, Education and Social System. In some cases, it seems that just one modality quickly takes hold over the others. Frequently the behavioral aspect of the program predominates, and this becomes the most important area of intervention. But in other cases, it seems that the totality of the program is responsible for the change, rather than the particulars; a synergistic effect in which the sum of the parts is greater than the whole. Unfortunately, we never know exactly which technique or combination of techniques will be right, but generally speaking we know from both research and theory that certain problems are amenable to certain kinds of psychotherapeutic techniques.

The **Affective** modality refers to those problems which have a strong emotional element as a primary component. These problems may relate to the inability to express one's affect, as is characteristic of depression; the inability to control one's affect, as exemplified by children with excessive anger or prone to tantrums; and the inability to cope with affect, as in disorders characterized by fear or anxiety.

Children who have experienced trauma also have strong affective components to their problems, whether the trauma is long-standing as in familial sexual abuse, or acute, such as is experienced when a natural disaster occurs. These children certainly have to learn to cope with the affect associated with the trauma, but just as importantly need to be able to integrate it into their self-images in a positive and accepting way.

The inability to communicate feelings and understand the feelings of others can also be considered an affective problem. Although learning these skills have certain cognitive elements, it is primarily the intuitive part of the personality which expresses and understands feelings. The ability to communicate and understand feelings is so basic that it can be a factor in almost any problem of childhood and can also be considered a preventive factor in the development of problems or conflicts.

Another general affective issue common to all children with problems is the feeling associated with self-esteem. Although self-esteem is a much more complicated construct than most people realize (see *The Building Blocks of Self-Esteem*, Shapiro, 1993, and *Self-Esteem Problems of Children,* Gardner, 1992), at its root it is an affective state associated with contentment and well-being. It is unlikely that all children will experience a high sense of self-esteem as a result of short-term therapy, because so many factors in our culture make it difficult for even the most functional of children (or adults, for that matter) to feel really good about themselves. Rather, self-esteem should be thought of as a continuum ranging from children whose self-esteem is the hallmark of a diagnosable problem, including children whose self-esteem inhibits their functioning to some degree (even though they are not necessarily symptomatic), to children whose self-esteem is high enough, at least most of the time, for them to behave with confidence and self-assurance, and have the capacity to take risks without inordinate fear that failure will damage their self-image.

Behaviors that should be considered in developing a multi-modal plan will usually be the most evident, for inappropriate or dysfunctional behaviors are the primary reason that most parents seek therapy for their children. These behaviors can range from ones which disrupt the family, like resistance to following family rules, excessive sibling rivalry, or disrespect for parental figures, to more serious behaviors associated with breaking social rules and which encompass the diagnostic categories of Conduct Disorders, anti-social personality, and Defiant Disorders.

In addition, behaviors which interfere with learning stigmatize the child (such as tics or unusual habits), may also be a primary focus of short-term therapy.

As we shall see Chapter 5, problems in **Cognition** have taken a particularly prominent role in the development of short-term therapy techniques, particularly for the cognitive/behavioral problem of impulsivity, a hallmark of children with Attention Deficit Disorders. Other common problems associated with cognition include the myths and misconceptions that children may have: such issues as divorce, death, or other life events; negative thinking; dysfunctional or irrational thinking; bizarre ideation or obsessive thoughts; and the more general lack of problem-solving ability associated with a variety of social problems with both adults and peers.

The **Developmental** issues considered in multi-modal short-term therapy are perhaps the most significant and yet are difficult to define. A large body of research tells us that all children pass through very predictable developmental stages, and we expect them to achieve particular tasks or resolve certain conflicts at each of these stages. Problems can occur when children are unable to resolve the particular developmental tasks at hand and become fixated at that stage, or when they regress to an earlier stage in the face of extreme stress or anxiety. For example, Harry Stack Sullivan has suggested that children need to find a best friend and a bonding peer group, like a club or team, during their latency years. He suggests that children who are not able to accomplish this may have difficulty with relationships throughout their lives.

We also know that many children who experience conflicts or problems go through a different set of predictable stages related to these issues. For example, if a child has a significant loss through death or separation, we may expect that child to go through the well-known phases of denial, anger, depression, and eventual acceptance. Although these stages are not as predictable as the so-called normal developmental stages, as a whole they present a series of developmental challenges for children to meet. Children who are not able to meet the challenge of these tasks, may be vulnerable to a variety of problems related to their original life circumstances at a later point.

Education is a modality frequently overlooked by therapists. Sigmund Freud cautioned the student of psychoanalysis, "Above all, do not teach!" But few therapists who work with children and their families would agree with this dictum. In short-term therapy, one *must* teach, for the therapist needs to have not only the child be aware of the variety of options and resources that can be available to address a particular problem, but the significant adults as well.

Education in terms of short-term therapy generally falls into three areas: providing information, correcting misinformation, and teaching values. Each of these areas is important, but in my opinion, the third is most neglected. The issue of values gets a lot of attention in political rhetoric, but it has still not found a comfortable niche in the homes or in the schools of many children. It is our hope that children will learn positive values inductively, as if by osmosis; frequently they do. But they learn other values in the same unspoken ways, from TV, the newspaper, and their peer group, and these values may be far removed from the ones we want to accomplish our therapeutic goals. It is my opinion that the issue of *how values are taught* needs to be addressed in every treatment plan.

The **Social System** is the sixth modality which a treatment plan should consider and addresses problems that occur in the home, school, and community. Most children with psychological symptoms have social problems related to those symptoms or to the cause of the symptoms. In many cases the social problems, which can range from isolation, or the inability of the child to form friendships, to defiance of authority figures, will be more significant in the child's development than the actual symptom or referring problem. For example, children with Attention Deficit Disorders with Hyperactivity frequently have difficulty with their peers. They may be ostracized because of their overactivity, aggressiveness, or developmental immaturity. As a result, they may spend more and more time by themselves, becoming more enmeshed in family dynamics rather than meeting the developmental challenges inherent in age-appropriate activities with peers. This in turn may affect their self-images, which will affect their motivation to overcome their learning problems, and they will move in a downwards spiral of self-defeat.

Stages of Short-Term Therapy

As in other forms of psychotherapy, most children go through distinct stages in short-term therapy. These four stages—Working Alliance, Diagnostic, Implementation, and Generalization—are conceptualized as discrete and sequential, but in reality they may blend together with considerable overlap.

Building a **Working Alliance** is the first step in any psychotherapy. In most cases this alliance is built on a feeling of rapport between the child and the therapist, but although a rapport is helpful, it is not necessary to achieve it with every child. There are many techniques that will help build rapport with children and develop a trusting relationship. Psychotherapeutic games, discussed later in this chapter, are one of the quickest methods of building rapport, because the game format is so familiar to children. When children come into my office, after a brief discussion, I invite them to play a game, and they are immediately put at ease. The child may be thinking, "Oh boy! I'm *not* going to get a shot from *this* doctor!" or "'I thought he was going to make me tell him things I don't want to!" Most children are visibly relieved at the prospect of "just playing a game," since this is a safe format of social interchange.

As we play the game, whether it is one designed for therapeutic purposes or just a game of checkers, our conversation begins and therapy is in progress. By the end of the first session, we have laid the foundation for a shared experience, built on mutual disclosures and enjoyment of the game.

Although establishing a therapeutic working alliance is certainly a good prognostic indicator, short-term therapy does not *require* rapport with the child. Children who are diagnosed as defiant or to have a Conduct Disorder will make their distaste at being brought to therapy readily known, and the therapist may at best have a "working truce" with these children so that some progress can be made towards a therapeutic goal. It is particularly important with these children to choose a technique that can interest the children on some basic level to help reduce their resistance to therapy.

In some cases of extremely defiant behavior this can only be accomplished by creating a double bind for the child as part of the therapeutic goal. In creating a double bind, the child has only two choices. One of these choices is more positive; the other may be seen as negative or even punitive, but still moves the child in the direction of developmental progress. These are the *only* two choices that the child has and both will lead towards a more acceptable mode of behavior and a higher level of functioning.

I once treated a child, let's call him Tommy, with extremely defiant behavior. At eight years of age, Tommy was not only disrespectful and uncooperative, but had missed a tremendous amount of school due to suspensions and truancy. I proposed to Tommy and his family that we could instigate a token economy system that would be in effect both at home and at school to motivate him to change. I met with Tommy and with both his parents and then with his teacher, and we discussed how the program would work and what the criteria for improvement would be. The other alternative I proposed was military school in a residential setting. Neither the child nor his parents wanted this to happen. But I insisted that this was the only other choice and made my treatment contingent on the possibility that this was a viable alternative. I explained to the child and his parents that Tommy *must* be in school and he *must* learn to behave respectfully and that this was the only legitimate goal of therapy. It was Tommy's choice as to how he wanted to accomplish this goal. If he chose to participate in a token economy system (along with other techniques), then we would all support him. And if he chose, by his behavior, military school, then we would support that decision. Either way, the therapeutic goal would be accomplished.

It is important to note that in using a double-bind strategy to further a therapeutic goal, the system must be prepared to augment either choice. In this case, I insisted that before we started the formal therapy, the parents investigate the possibility of sending Tommy to a military school, visit at least one school, and even set aside money in a separate bank account to pay for the school. I made it clear that I would not begin therapy until the family was fully prepared to carry out either therapeutic alternative.

Once a working alliance has been established, hopefully in the first few sessions, the therapist will begin a **Diagnostic Phase** of therapy. This diagnostic phase should not be confused with the formal assessment usually performed before the initial referral for therapy. The diagnostic phase of short-term therapy is primarily to determine which techniques will be most effective in working with the child, rather than just to classify a child in a specific category. During this phase the therapist will try a variety of techniques in different modalities to ascertain which techniques will be most effective.

In the **Implementation Phase** the therapist will apply techniques in the different modalities of therapy, having narrowed them down to just a few, or possibly using techniques in all six modalities. In some cases, it will be clear by this middle phase of therapy that just one or two techniques will be the instruments of change, and these should be pursued with vigor. In other cases, techniques from all six modalities may seem to be operating, forming a synergistic effect with the whole being greater than the sum of its parts.

It is important to note that in this phase the therapist is not necessarily doing all the work. The therapist may have the parents applying new discipline techniques, the teacher using positive reinforcement approaches, and even the child be practicing techniques such as stress reduction. As early as possible in the therapy, the short-term therapist will be looking for ways for other people in the child's system to apply therapeutic techniques, both during and *after* the therapy.

In the final stage of therapy, the **Generalization Stage**, the therapist seeks to transfer and generalize the therapeutic effects and techniques into the child's natural environment. Knowing there is only a limited amount of time to accomplish the work, the therapist must always be thinking about how a particular therapeutic effect can be translated into the child's social system. From the moment that the child walks in the door, the therapist must also envision him or her walking out the door at the end of the treatment. At every step, the therapist seeks ways that the child's environment can be adapted to support the child's change, but this concern is brought more clearly into focus during this final phase. As we shall see in Chapter 7, the techniques of therapist-made books and Video Therapy can be particularly effective in generalizing the therapeutic effects.

The Treatment Plan

Many therapists shudder at the suggestion that they write a treatment plan, but as I have suggested writing a plan has many merits. In each case, the plan must minimally:

- State an objective or therapeutic goal
- Determine the methods or techniques that will be used for treating that goal
- Determine the people who will be responsible for implementing each technique
- State the criteria that will be used to measure the success of the treatment plan

Many therapists see the requirement to write a treatment plan to be an undue burden, and I agree that it should not be a burden. This task shouldn't be done pro forma, to fulfill some bureaucratic requirement. Writing a successful treatment plan can be perceived as an aid to the therapeutic process if a few key principles are followed.

Conjoint Planning: Writing the therapeutic plan should first of all be a therapeutic experience. Rather than formulate the plan in isolation, the short-term therapist will do well to invite all the people who are available to help the child to participate in the initial plan. It is certainly the therapist's job to direct this process, but significant people in the child's system should have a maximum amount of input, for they ultimately will be accountable for any change in the child.

The issue of accountability is important in short-term therapy (as discussed in the introduction). It is the therapist's responsibility to provide the direction and impetus for change in the child's life, but the change must ultimately come from the child, with guidance from the caretakers and educators who see the child most of the time. Most of the techniques that I discuss in this book require effort from people outside the therapy room, and it is imperative that they understand and agree to this effort from the onset of therapy. Involving them in the writing of the therapy plan is tantamount to establishing a contract between the therapist, the child, and the significant people in his life, so that everyone will agree as to how the therapy will succeed and who will be accountable.

Dr. John March, the director of Duke University's program for Childhood Mental Illness and Anxiety Disorders, involves parents throughout his short-term treatment program for children with Obsessive Compulsive Disorders (OCD). Dr. March even asks the parents' assistance in helping select a mixture of medications for their children, outlining the advantages and disadvantages of the different medications (first, of course, eliminating any medications which are clearly contraindicated). Dr. March explains (in *Child Therapy Today,* Chapter 2, 1994), that he lets the families help pick the medications because he feels that there is no reliable data on which medication is most effective for treating OCD. Involving the families in the selection of the medications in effect stresses that they will be at least partly accountable for the effects or possible side-effects of the medications on their OCD child. And why not? After all, the families are the ones who ultimately live with the improvements or lack of improvements in their child's functioning.

Reasonable Objectives: A second element of the treatment plan which therapists frequently see as an unfair burden is determining and writing the therapeutic objective. In many cases, therapists are correct; it *is* unfair to ask therapists to both predict and be responsible for changes in human behavior. Many institutions that require treatment plans with specified therapeutic objectives mistakenly require therapists to predict *quantifiable* behavior. They assume that therapists, trained in scientific methodology, can write objectives like:

By the end of therapy, Johnny will be able to stay in his seat and do independent work for a 20-minute period.

Or,

Jane will decrease her antisocial behavior as measured by behavioral charting at least 20% by the end of four weeks.

Although I have seen objectives similar to these written hundreds of times (and have written them myself), I have come to realize that it is totally unreasonable to ask a therapist to write quantifiable objectives as part of a treatment plan. *No one can predict human behavior with any degree of certainty.* Therapy is not a science, and predicting behavior is not consistent with the scientific method in any event as the scientific method is to *disprove* a null hypothesis. If a short-term therapist tries to predict the outcome of therapy in terms of how the child will change in quantifiable terms, he or she is virtually doomed to failure. So why should anyone try?

The short-term therapist can only be accountable for certain things, and behavioral change is not one of them. The short-term therapist *can* be held accountable as a teacher and facilitator of change. The short-term therapist *can* be accountable for providing a therapeutic experience for the child as well as the significant others who affect the child. The short-term therapist *can* be accountable for providing important information to the child and/or the significant people in the child's life. The short-term therapist *can* be held accountable for finding the appropriate resources and or people which will assist in the child's progress and development.

Understanding what the short-term therapist legitimately can and cannot do is the best way to approach the writing of the therapeutic goal. The therapeutic goal must be written in such a way that the short-term therapist is virtually assured that it can be accomplished. As the saying goes, "nothing succeeds like success." It is incumbent on the therapist to make sure that the treatment plan will lead to success if carried through.

To do this, one must accept the primary role of the short-term therapist as a teacher and facilitator. Objectives can be written which:

- Teach
- Provide alternatives
- Provide information
- Provide experiences
- Provide tasks to be accomplished

For example, instead of writing:

By the end of therapy, Johnny will be able to stay in his seat and do independent work for a 20-minute period.

Write:

Johnny will learn three techniques to help him stay seated when doing independent work.

Instead of writing:

Jane will decrease her anti-social behavior as measured by behavioral charting at least 20% by the end of four weeks.

Write:

Jane will learn alternatives to her antisocial behavior, including: expressing her feelings; earning token for positive behavior in the class-room; repeating positive self-statements; demonstrating cooperative behaviors with her peers; valuing other's opinions; and respecting social rules.

In the objective written for Jane above, you will notice that all six modalities are mentioned in a single objective. This objective was taken from an actual therapy plan that I wrote, and as it turned out, games were used to teach Jane these alternatives in each of the six modalities, and the objective was essentially met each time a game was played.

Multiple Techniques and
Key People to Help in Their Implementation

Figure 2.A shows a format that can be used to guide the writing of a multi-modal treatment plan. Normally the therapist will write a single therapeutic strategy for each modality, but more than one strategy may be written for each modality. In the third column, the therapist indicates the person, place, or thing that will be used to implement the strategy.

As I have said, the therapist can consider using any number of people to carry out the therapeutic plan. These people will be selected using primarily common-sense criteria and to exploit their vested interest in seeing the child improve. In choosing people to help implement the treatment plan, the therapist may wish to consider:

• Personality characteristics of the cotherapist
• Gender
• Availability
• Authority (I have used school principals and even police officers to carry out a particular strategy)
• Compatibility or interest in the particular strategy
• Identification of the cotherapist with the child's problems

The place or setting where a particular strategy will be carried out of course depends on the problem. As a general rule it is most help-ful if problems can be addressed at least in part in the setting in which

Figure 2.A
Treatment Plan

Name _____ Age _____

Date _____ Date of Birth _____

Presenting Problem _____

Plan Objective _____

Student Objective _____

Modality	Strategies	Person/Place/Thing	Done
Affect			
Behavior			
Cognition			
Developmental			
Education			
Social System			

they occur. Thus an Attention Deficit Disorder treatment plan should include at least have one strategy for the classroom; an anxiety treatment plan should include one strategy for where the anxiety occurs; and so on.

The "thing" referred to in the therapy treatment plan refers to a physical object or instrument which can be used in a particular strategy: a portable Biofeedback apparatus, a time-out timer, a therapeutic storybook, or a therapeutic game. Naturally it is the therapist's job to make sure that this object is available for the treatment and that practical considerations are considered. What happens if the child loses it? Does it draw undue attention to the child? Is there a safety issue that should be considered? And so on.

It is worth noting that the treatment plan is a *work in progress.* As strategies are implemented, it may become clear that one works well and another is too cumbersome. There are many reasons that a particular strategy might not work, but it is important for the therapist to investigate it thoroughly before giving up on a technique that should be effective. The therapist must recognize that he or she is always fighting a natural tendency for any person or system to retain homeostasis and not be deterred by initial problems with a particular strategy. Above all, the therapist must make sure that the principles underlying the technique are being adhered to. Many excellent strategies are undermined because they do not respect the underlying principles behind the technique and become so watered down that they are meaningless or self-contradictory. The therapist should also remember that change, whether it is within the child or in the system itself, comes slowly. The therapist should watch for small signs of improvement and focus on them.

Choosing Techniques

In teaching multi-modal therapy, one of the most difficult jobs is helping therapists choose the right combination of techniques for each child. On the one hand, I like to emphasize the need for a systematic consideration of techniques according to the individual needs and concerns of a child and the unique social milieu of that child. On the other hand, no system can take into complete account the all factors that make one therapist more effective using one technique than another.

Figure 2.B is a chart which can be used as a model in selecting short-term therapy techniques with a particular child. This chart shows 28 strategies or techniques I commonly use in working with children. On the top of the illustration are nine factors I consider to be integral in deciding which of these techniques might help a particular child.

Let me emphasize that these are techniques that *I* am comfortable in using with children; they may not be the same techniques that another therapist would use. In developing a systematic way to choose multi-modal techniques, I urge you to make a similar list of the techniques that you are comfortable using. There may be fewer or there may be more; the important thing is that these techniques are ones you believe in, have had training in, and have found to be effective.

Figure 2.B
Choosing Techniques for Short-Term Therapy

Child's Name _____

Presenting Problem _____

Age _____ Symptoms _____

Developmental Concerns _____

	Chron. Age	Dev. Age	Interests	Participation of others	Therapist compatibilty	Contra-indication	Motivation	Setting	Practical considerations	Total
The Affective Modality										
Creative Arts Therapy										
Self-Esteem Games										
Feelings Games										
Biofeedback										
Hypnotherapy										
Medication										
The Behavioral Modality										
Pro-social Learning										
Assertiveness Training										
Good Behavior Games										
Behavioral Shaping										
Token Economies										
Over-Correction Procedure										
Multiple Behavioral Programming with Severe Problems*										
On-Site Therapy										
The Cognitive Modality										
Cognitive Games										
Affirmations										
Cognitive Medication										
Cognitive Restructuring										
Transactional Analysis										
The Developmental Modality										
The Make-a-Game Technique										
Task-Oriented Therapy										
The Educational Modality										
Bibliotherapy										
Therapist-Created books										
Video Therapy										
The Systems Modality										
Reality Therapy*										
Social Skills Training										
Values Clarification*										
Communicating Solutions										

Once you have compiled this list, you should rate each technique against the nine criteria on the top of the chart, putting a plus in the appropriate square if the technique meets the criteria and a minus if it does not.

The first two criteria, Chronological Age and Developmental Age are the most important in this schema. If these criteria do not apply to a given technique with a given child, there is no need to go on.

The third column, Interests, refers to the child's broad interests. Does the child like computers? Techniques can be modified for some computer use. Does the child collect baseball cards? A token economy can take advantage of this interest; points can be earned to get cards. Does the child like rap music? Music or cognitive techniques might be of interest. If a technique can fit a child's interests, then it is more likely to at least have initial success.

The fourth column refers to how the technique is amenable to other people in the child's life that can be used as cotherapists. Certain techniques listed in my chart (like games, token economies, bibliotherapy, and values clarification) lend themselves more readily to implementation by others. But this may vary greatly from child to child.

The fifth column considers the therapist's compatibility with a technique. While it may seem that I am compatible with all the techniques on my list (since after all I chose them), this is not always true. Certain techniques require more time and energy from the therapist, and at least for me, these can vary. Equally important, I may feel more comfortable with a particular technique with one child (and family) than another. Ideally, there should be a match between the therapist, the technique, and the child, and there are many factors, some of them intuitive, that define a good match.

In the sixth column is a space for contraindications should be factored into choosing a particular technique. The fact that there might be a contradiction does not automatically rule out use of a technique, but it should certainly be a consideration. For example, suppose you wanted to have the child's teacher work on a problem-solving program to help the child deal better with his peers. But the teacher is overworked and doesn't even particularly like the child! This is certainly a contraindication for using this technique in the classroom, but may not rule it out. Perhaps there is an aide, or a resource room teacher, or a librarian who might be interested in working with the child. If there are other indicators that a particular technique will be successful, then you may often be able to work around the contraindications.

The next column, Motivation, refers to the variety of motivational factors that could be associated with a given technique. Certain techniques, like token economy systems, have the motivation for change built into them. Some techniques can motivate the child more because they are fun. Still other techniques can stimulate motivation within the family system, because they tap into conscious or unconscious processes. If a technique has the ability to motivate change, then you enter a plus. If it has no motivational value to the child or the child's system, then you enter a minus. Otherwise you leave it blank.

The setting required for a particular technique might also have positive, negative, or neutral value. In general, at least half of the techniques used in a short-term, multi-modal treatment plan should be able to be transferred into the child's natural environment. However, elements in that setting may be either conducive to a particular technique or not. Take for example the school-phobic child who lives with his or her mother and grandmother. An on-site therapy stressing systematic desensitization might seem appropriate, but the mother and grandmother, for unconscious reasons, cannot keep from interfering with your program. One day the grandmother is sick and can't leave the living room where you usually work. Another day, the mother mistakenly schedules house painters who cause chaos in the house. Everyone has the best of intentions, but the setting is simply not conducive to the therapeutic work that has to be done.

Finally, the therapist should consider the purely practical considerations of any given treatment technique. These can include, but are not limited to: time, cost, scheduling, other professional commitments, and so on. When the therapist is working with highly resistant problems or systems (which is often the case), he or she should carefully consider what can possibly undermine this treatment. When all the factors that can cause failure are considered, the therapist is much more likely to succeed!

The Use of Games in Short-Term Therapy

My interests in games and in brief therapies have always gone hand in hand. There are now more than 85 published psychotherapeutic games which are available to the therapist (see *The Book of Psychotherapeutic Games*, Shapiro, 1993), but these are only one type of game. Published board games are popular with therapists because they provide nearly instant gratification to the therapist. Open the box, read the instructions, play the game, and you are doing therapy. The experienced therapist will quickly see the strengths and applicability of a particular game to his or her clients. The novice therapist may not be attuned to all the nuances of the game, but if he or she follows the basic underlying principles of the game and acts in a way consistent with these principles, then a therapeutic interchange will almost always ensue.

It is worth noting, however, that published board games are only one of four types of therapeutic games available to the therapist. The therapist can also use commercial games available at any store; "naturalistic" games, which are adaptations of standard childhood games (like Simon Says; Freeze Tag; Mother, May I?; and so on), as well as "paper and pencil" games (adaptations of games like Mazes, Crosswords, Word Search, and so on). Examples of the latter two types of games, naturalistic games and pencil and paper games, will be given in each of the chapters discussing techniques. I particularly recommend these games because they can arise spontaneously out of a therapy session and require no financial investment by the therapist.

The major reason that I advocate the use of games in short-term therapy has to do with the many factors or variables that make this technique more accessible to therapeutic manipulation. These are discussed in following paragraphs.

Rules represent the structure of the therapy and the "reality principle" for the child. Many therapists like to adapt or change the rules of a therapeutic game to make it more suitable for an individual child. Adapting a game to suit a child should be encouraged; however once the rules are changed, they must be observed. The rules, by definition, form the underlying structure of the game and are the driving force of this therapeutic technique. More importantly, they represent the reality principle for the child, and must be respected as such. In other words, once the rules are decided upon, they should not be changed arbitrarily or too easily, for reality (problems, hurdles, handicaps, unfair life circumstances) can not be changed easily. If a rule needs to be changed, it should be changed only after you have finished playing a particular game, and then the rule and the reason for changing it should be discussed thoroughly. If possible, the new rule should be written out, and the game played again with the new rule in place.

I am frequently asked to comment about how to handle children who break the rules while playing a therapeutic game and cheat. I always answer decisively, "Don't let them cheat. It is counter-therapeutic." Sometimes the therapist feels that it is okay for children to cheat because they need the experience of winning for their self-esteem. But cheating is not winning, it is cheating, and the children know this. Cheating always detracts from a child's self-esteem.

I always call cheating to children's attention if they cheat during a game. If they argue that they are playing by some other set of legitimate rules, but I don't know about them, I reply, "Show me. If you can't show me the written rule, then you are cheating. You can't cheat in this game and you can't cheat in real life either. If you do, people will know it and think less of you and you will be known as a cheater."

This may sound harsh, but it is true. It is reality. It is not our job as therapists to cushion a child from reality. If a child cannot accept this, however, there may be other ways to deal with cheating which are more therapeutic. On a few occasions, I have simply made cheating a part of the rules. I write down a rule for the game, "It is okay to cheat." Then I can cheat too, and I do. Sometimes this is fun and helps build an alliance with a child. It can also provide an opportunity to discuss the issue of cheating in more depth, without causing a confrontation between myself and the child. Another way to approach a child who cheats is to play a cooperative game in which cheating is impossible. A cooperative game like *Gentle Winds,* described in Chapter 8, makes cheating impossible, because either *all* the players win or *all* the players lose. Players don't cheat, because there is nothing to be gained by it. Cooperative board games like *Teamwork* (published by The Center for Applied Psychology, Inc.) or *Harvest Time* (published by Family Pastimes) also work on this principle.

Cards represent an opportunity to individualize therapy. Sometimes a therapist criticizes a particular game to me because the cards seem inappropriate. For example, *The Talking, Feeling, and Doing Game* (Creative Therapeutics), the first published therapeutic board game and still one of the most popular, contains cards which may be too controversial for a school setting (e.g., "Your teacher is standing in front of the class with his fly open, what would you do?"). My answer to this is simple: "Take out the cards that you don't like or ones which don't move the therapy towards the therapeutic goal!" Cards can also be added to any game by simply cutting down an index card and writing in new questions. Sometimes I write my own cards, and sometimes I ask the child (or parents) to write cards. Once the appropriate types of cards have been selected or created, the deck can even be stacked so that the cards most relevant to the child's issues will come up early in the game.

Games provide an opportunity to observe and experience the child's conflicts or concerns and to create therapeutic experiences. Perhaps more than any other therapeutic technique, psychotherapeutic games allow us to step inside a child's world and see exactly why he or she is having difficulty. The game experience will reflect affective problems (e.g., low frustration tolerance, depressed affect), behavioral problems (e.g., difficulties taking turns, staying seated, following rules), cognitive problems (e.g. poor impulse control, difficulty in following directions) and so on. And if the child does not exhibit a particular problem, the therapist can choose a particular game or manipulate the situation to create that experience in order to observe it and hopefully change it.

Game play is a technique which can be manipulated on multiple levels. Game play can actually be manipulated on four different levels simultaneously: the *content* or surface issues; the *process* or dynamics of the problem; the social context or *system* where the problem is a concern; and the *metaphoric* level. The therapist can easily address the manifest content of a problem through his or her game selection. There are divorce games, games on anger control, self-esteem, and so on. The psychodynamic process can be addressed in the therapeutic stance of the therapist along with the selection of an appropriate game. The therapist can choose a game which requires self-disclosure, one where the therapist is cast in a nurturing or supportive role, a competitive game to challenge the child's assertiveness and so on.

The social context or system of the game will of course change with the players that the therapist brings into the therapy session. A specific parent, the whole family, a child of the same age, or an older or a younger child, can be brought in. In most cases, the therapist will bring another player into the game to act as a role model for the identified patient. In treating a depressed child, for example, the therapist may wish to bring in a child who is friendly and exuberant, and perhaps a third child who is quiet, but has a strong ego. In ideal cases, the child brought into the therapy session might be from the identified patient's class, and the therapist hopes that they may play the same game or share another experience spontaneously in class or on the playground.

Finally, the therapist should be aware of the metaphoric level of game play; the unspoken messages that the child receives when a therapeutic game is played. The active and directive therapist is necessarily focused on observable behavior in the real world, but the importance of unspoken messages should also be acknowledged. By playing a psychological game, the therapist gives the messages:

• I will take the time to work with you on your problem.
• We can enjoy this process.

• You will be rewarded for the new things that you learn and the behaviors that you change (in the form of chips won in the game).
• There is constancy and consistency to my approach (represented by the physical presence of the game).
• I will respect your rights and limits (as defined by the rules).
• I will be the director. I will guide you with these special tools.

Games can be helpful in motivating the child towards the therapeutic goal. Psychotherapeutic games are by definition a technique which motivates the child towards change. First, there are the aspects of the game which are intrinsically motivating. To be called a game it must be fun; if it is not fun on some level, then it will not be perceived as a game. Hopefully the appearance of the game and specific play elements of the game will also be appealing, interesting the child like any toy. If the game selected for an individual child is well-chosen, it will also stimulate the child's interest by its theme and developmental appropriateness.

The technique of using psychotherapeutic games can also be motivating because it presents opportunities to win chips or tokens. In most cases, these chips can be cashed in for small prizes. I know of one therapist who uses potato chips in her games (as opposed to the plastic kind), and the children eat them as they win them.

I like to tie chips won in the game with a comprehensive token economy system that can be used to motivate the child (or other people in the child's system) towards changing specific behaviors (see Chapter 4, Using Token Economy Systems).

Games allow for the repetition necessary to learning and behavioral change. Perhaps more than any other technique in child psychotherapy, games encourage the repetition necessary for learning and mastery. It is in the nature of children to want to play games over and over again, and in doing so they have the opportunity to continuously be exposed to the therapeutic principles that the game is promoting. It is often surprising to me when children *ask* to play a game like *Be Safe...Be Aware!* (Alternatives to Sexual Abuse), which has a theme of avoiding child sexual abuse, or a game like *My Two Homes* (The Center for Applied Psychology, Inc.), a game about the divorce process. But then I remember that all childhood play is motivated by children's needs to master their environment, which includes conflicts and emotionally-charged issues.

Some therapists have the misconception that a therapeutic game must be started and finished in a single therapy session. In fact, this is rarely the case. Playing a single game can take two sessions or more, depending on the child's interest and, of course, the relevance of the play. Sometimes a game is played for a part of each session throughout therapy; each time bringing the child back to a specific issue or skill to be learned.

Games allow for the transfer or generalizing of psychological principles. Undoubtedly the most important aspect of psychotherapeutic games is their ability to be used outside the therapy session. Ninety percent of the psychotherapeutic games that have been published, as well as games that you can make, can be used by others than the therapist. (Roughly 10% are restricted for use by trained therapists due to the emotional content that they are likely to stimulate during game play.) Games allow the therapist to solicit other significant people in the child's life to take part in the therapeutic process, including parents, teachers, teachers aides, siblings, babysitters, and so on. Many therapeutic games are simple enough that they only require brief training by the therapist with a reasonably nurturing caregiver.

Some games, or rather some situations, require more extensive training by the therapist to have a game used effectively as a technique by a person in the child's natural environment. This type of training usually takes place in the therapist's office, and consists of the therapist playing the game with the child and the cotherapist, while the game is videotaped. At the end of the session, the child is sent to a waiting area, and the therapist reviews parts of the videotape with the cotherapist, stressing the elements and reactions by the cotherapist which are beneficial to the child. The motivated cotherapist can also take the videotape home to review it again.

In using cotherapists in the therapeutic game play, not only will the therapeutic technique be extended, but by playing the game in the child's natural environment, usually where the problems or conflicts occur, you will be transferring the child's new abilities into that environment and generalizing those skills outside the game context.

Certain published board games, like The *Classroom Behavior Game* (The Center for Applied Psychology, Inc.), have the extension of therapeutic elements built right into the game. For example, *The Classroom Behavior Game* includes a behavioral contract, which lists the same classroom rules that the child learns during the game, and this chart is taped to the child's desk during schooltime. By checking off the rules as the child follows them, the child is following a token economy system which is directly tied into the game play. In my opinion, this is the best use of a therapeutic game: to teach skills which can effortlessly be applied to more functional behaviors in the child's natural environment.

Games allow for communication and controlled disclosure by the therapist. The first games used in psychotherapy with children were introduced as bridges to therapeutic communication. Analytically-trained therapists found that when children were too old to verbalize during doll play or other free play techniques but too young to respond to direct questions, they would talk more openly during a game of checkers, Parcheesi, or cards. Today, games specifically designed for a psychotherapeutic intent also share this basic function of serving as a platform where psychological issues can be discussed. The majority of therapeutic games use cards as a point of departure, and as many therapists know, a single card can take a whole session to discuss. The child may respond to a card, the therapist may comment on or ask a question about the child's response, the child begins talking in another related direction and so on.

Of course, not all children are this verbal; many children will respond with only a few well-chosen words. In these cases, the therapist may do more talking than the child. The technique of using psychotherapeutic games offers therapists the rare chance to self-disclose, to judiciously reveal aspects of himself or herself to the child. When responding to a particular card, most therapists reminisce about the way they were when they were the age of the child that they are working with. Self-disclosure is a therapeutic technique unto itself, and the experienced therapist will be able to disclose aspects of himself or herself which will interest the child, serve as a role model, and provide specific therapeutic messages.

Dr. Richard Gardner (in *Interviews with Experts in Child Psychotherapy*, 1994) describes a girl he worked with who refused to play *The Talking, Feeling and Doing Game* with him and so he simply played the game by himself, answering all the cards, while the child watched him from a corner with rapt attention. Gardner's answers, of course, acknowledged the presence of the girl and in some cases addressed her recalcitrance. Gardner even made asides to the video camera in his office, until the patient could stand it no longer. Finally, she played the game with him, but as you can see, therapeutic *communication* was taking place, long before therapeutic *cooperation*.

Games allow for the learning and reinforcement of social skills. Finally, we must acknowledge an element of psychotherapeutic game play that is so simple and basic that it is sometimes overlooked: the social experience of this technique. Some of us have vague recollections of times when families sat around on Friday evenings or rainy Saturdays on a regular basis, and played board games. No TV, no video games—just an hour or two of enjoyable human interaction.

Unfortunately this scene is now the exception rather than the rule, at least within the typical patient population. Parents and children are so busy these days that family leisure time is more likely to be spent in passive activities like watching TV. This is particularly true when there are problems or conflicts in the family which take an additional amount of time and emotional energy.

In this context, we can appreciate the therapeutic effects of game play as a social experience. Many of the children that come into treatment have a paucity of protected and quiet experiences with adults, in which they can just be themselves (by adults I refer not only to the therapist, but to selected cotherapists in the child's environment as well). Similarly, many children who come to treatment have peer problems related to their conflicts, and may lack age-appropriate developmental play experiences. The game can act as a magnet for the therapist to invite specific children into therapy, or to foster particular interactions between children outside therapy.

It may seem from this chapter that short-term therapy in general, and game play in particular, manipulate a child's life. In accordance with our definition of short-term therapy, it is our job as therapists to not only stimulate the child's inner resources, but to create an environment which is more receptive and health-promoting to the child. If this requires manipulation, then so be it. Short-term therapy is a directive technique, and there is one only person who can sit in the director's chair. When this chair is filled by a person with skill, wisdom, and heart, an incredible human drama will unfold.

CHAPTER 3

THE AFFECTIVE MODALITY

The Affective modality refers to what most people feel is the basic function of psychotherapy: to make people feel better. Freud, of course, was not so optimistic about the primary intention of therapy, which he described as "helping people to suffer less."

With children, however, I think that we can take a philosophical approach in the middle: children can be taught ways to have positive affect and to cope more effectively with negative affect. We can assume that children with positive affect will not only enjoy life more fully, but also fulfill more of their potential and have more successful relationships. There is no question that our society values positive people and that children who are perceived to be happier get more attention and concern from adults.

The therapist is concerned with various aspects of helping children deal with their emotions or affective states. In some cases, such as with depression, the therapist wants to help children *express* affect. In other cases, such as with Conduct Disorders and Opposition/ Defiantdisorders, the therapist seeks to help children *control* their affect. When treating children with anxieties or fears, the therapist helps children *cope* with these difficult affective states. And in cases where an acute or prolonged trauma occurs, the therapist wishes to attempt the difficult task of helping the child integrate affect related to the trauma of memories with current experiences.

In a more general sense, therapists are concerned about dealing with affective issues with nearly all clients, helping children understand their feelings and the feelings of others. We assume that when a child is able to speak and listen more clearly in the language of feelings, he or she will have more ability to relate to others and thus have richer life experiences at every age.

Finally, the therapist is concerned about helping children learn to have greater *feelings* of self-esteem. As I have written elsewhere (*The Building Blocks of Self-Esteem*, Shapiro, 1993), self-esteem is actually a multidimensional construct, but at its root it is an affective state which we associate with feelings of contentment and self-worth. It is certainly a legitimate therapeutic goal to help children (as well as adults) learn to stimulate and enhance these feelings.

I present the techniques in this chapter, as well as in the other chapters, from a very personal perspective. I am not attempting to give any particular technique a thorough examination, but rather to show how elements from a theory or technique can be woven into the individual style of a therapist and filtered through a systematic process of matching the most effective technique to the issues or problems of each individual child.

In this chapter and each succeeding chapter, I will present the techniques in a continuum from *least* to *most* intrusive (i.e., likely to disrupt the child's day-to-day life). As I mentioned in Chapter 1, the therapist should take into account that, generally speaking, the less intrusive a technique is, the less power it is likely to have in effecting a quick change. It is incumbent on the therapist to weigh these factors in considering the significance of the child's symptomatology, mental health, and safety, and choose the appropriate level of intervention.

I will also discuss the techniques I consider to stress affective issues in childhood psychopathology, the techniques that predominantly use a change in affect to move the child towards a therapeutic goal. Very few techniques are pure however, and most can arguably be placed in different modalities than I have chosen.

USING THE ARTS IN THERAPY

Art has been used as therapy since the beginning and through the development of every civilization. Cave drawings from the late Stone Age suggest that Art was used to treat physical and mental disorders; ancient Egyptian priest-physicians used chants as part of their healing process; the ancient Greeks used dance as a "means of achieving health in every part of the individual" (Feder and Feder, 1981). From the inception of modern psychology, artwork has been used in the diagnosis of emotional problems, but is was not until the 1940s, with the writings of Margaret Naumberg, that Art began to be recognized as a new form of therapy (Zswerling, 1979). Today the Arts are valued as potent tools in the treatment of both childhood and adult disorders.

It is unfortunate that relatively few therapists are exposed to Art as a therapeutic modality in their training. The Arts (Visual Arts, Drama, Music, Dance) can not only be effective in helping children express their feelings, but can help them to master and cope with experiences which are literally beyond words.

The arts also lend themselves to the imaginative use of concrete materials and experiences to teach abstract ideas. Neural immaturity makes it very hard for learning disabled children to grasp abstractions. They have to be introduced to them through their bodies, through objects and pictures, and then through symbols. The Arts offer opportunities to strengthen visual, auditory, tactile, and motor areas. Through the Arts, children can order their worlds, make sense of what they know, relate past experiences to the present, and turn muscular activity into thought and ideas into action (Smith, 1981).

Writing as Therapy

Like other Art Therapy techniques, writing can serve several diverse therapeutic functions. Diagnostically it can give insight into a child or adolescent's cognitive structures, use of language, verbal fluency, imagination, and so on. Writing can help articulate feelings, images, and vague thoughts that may otherwise remain out of the child's conscious awareness. It can break through inhibitions that may be present in verbal conversations with an adult, and it can add a new dimension in the therapy as a tool for self-awareness and interpersonal communication.

When I use writing as a part of a multiple-technique treatment program, it must originate with the interest of the child or adolescent. Writing is often perceived as work by students, and difficult work at that. I usually only introduce writing as a therapeutic technique when it is perceived as an enjoyable activity by the child or adolescent. Such was the case with Allen, a 13-year-old who had been diagnosed as a borderline personality with obsessive/compulsive character traits.

I worked with Allen when I was employed as a counselor by a psychoanalytically-oriented school for emotionally disturbed adolescents. Although many of the students had idiosyncratic behaviors and mannerisms, Allen seemed intent on standing out from the crowd. Allen had many obsessions and compulsive rituals that he liked to talk about because people found them strangely amusing and accepted Allen as an eccentric. One of his most complex and frequent obsessions was about the New York City subway system. Allen had memorized the entire subway schedule for all the boroughs. Not only could he tell you which trains stopped at which stations, but he knew where they all connected, which lines had the newest cars and the best efficiency ratings, where muggings were most likely to occur, and so on. He frequently rode the subways for hours on end to verify his wealth of facts. One time, when he decided to run away from home, he rode the subway all night for twelve straight hours.

When Allen talked about the subways, it was in excited run-on sentences, in the manner of an announcer at a racetrack. Once I overheard another student ask him for directions to a place in Queens.

Although I really couldn't follow what Allen said, not being familiar with the route myself, this is how Allen's reply sounded to me:

> You want to get to Flatbush Avenue? Great. I'll get you there in twenty-two and a half minutes. Now, first walk down to Ninety-Second Street and take the IRT down to Forty-Second. Then switch to the AA and go down to Sixth Avenue. That is, unless it's between four and seven o'clock, and then I want you to take the No. 6 down to Wall Street and change to the No. 8. Now you have to run very fast to the Express and hop on for three stops if it's exactly fifteen minutes after the hour and four stops if it's thirty past the hour, and then take the B train three stops and you'll be there. Of course, if you're traveling in the morning, or you miss the No. 6 at Forty-Second, then...

I saw Allen for about ten actual sessions. He was being treated by the milieu of this therapeutic school, and my job was to help him find more appropriate ways to express himself and to hopefully diminish his bizarre ideation and behavior. When I saw Allen in therapy, I discouraged him from talking about his obsessions, assuming that he used them as a magical shield to protect his real, but fragile self. This was very disappointing to Allen, but he seemed to respect the legitimacy of my decision. He asked, however, if he could keep a journal of the obsessions and rituals that I didn't want to hear about. This seemed like an odd request to me at the time, but no odder than the obsessions themselves.

I saw Allen twice a week and generally talked to him about a broad range of subjects, building on our relationship rather than trying to uncover deep unconscious conflicts. At the end of each session, Allen would hand me his journal, and I would read it and return it to him with comments.

Allen wrote primarily about his obsessions and compulsive rituals. He wrote about the Jewish dietary laws, about how he washed his hair, about the "state-of-the-art" of New York pretzels...all with the same excited and associative manner he used when he talked about the subways. Then, after about a month or so of this, he also wrote a poem:

> My life is like a loaf of bread
> Everyone takes a slice
> Some butter me up good
> Others put me in a jam
> I hope they don't let me go stale.

This short poem was a major breakthrough. For the first time, Allen had found a metaphor for his feelings other than his obsessive detailing and compulsive rituals. I interpreted the metaphor as Allen saying that he saw himself only in parts, parts manufactured for the tastes and pleasures of others. While some people responded to his "parts" by "buttering him up," others had no use for him, and he was in danger of going stale. I further assumed that Allen's obsessions and compulsions had something to do with this view of himself. Since Allen seemed so eager to communicate about his elaborate thought schemes and rituals, I hypothesized that each one was devised for intrapsychic and interpersonal reasons.

I wondered if Allen chose certain obsessions to communicate with certain people. Were some meant to please, some to anger and frustrate, and all to keep people at just the distance Allen wanted? Similarly, were the compulsions exclusively carried out at home ways to express his feelings toward his parents? The hair washing ritual that occurred every morning and night kept him in the shower for 45 minutes at a time, precisely at the periods of the day when his parents might also want to use the only bathroom in the apartment.

Of course, all of this was conjecture. Each hypothesis would have to be tested in the context of a relationship based on acceptance of Allen as a whole person and the presentation of myself in the same way. I answered Allen's poem using the same metaphor, trying to imitate his irony and humor:

> I like bread and butter
> It's nourishing and delish
> I'd rather spend an hour with a loaf of bread
> Than spend all day with a Brussels sprout.

As the weeks went by, Allen slowly stopped writing about his obsessive thoughts and ritualistic behaviors. We found many ways to communicate through his journal: word games, pictures, short stories, and more poems. As a result of continued individual treatment, the milieu therapy of the school, and family therapy, Allen was able to move out of his home and attend college on a part-time basis the following year.

Music as Therapy

It would be a misconception to think that short-term therapy techniques can only be applied to the simpler, more accessible cases. I have spent much of my career working with multi-handicapped children who will spend their entire lives dependent to some extent on the mental health system. Short-term interventions are frequently necessary to help these children make a variety of transitions in their lifetime: moving from their home to a residential setting, learning to work independently in the community, and diminishing inappropriate behaviors, so that the child or adolescent can have more community involvement. Although by some standards, the gains that these children or adolescents make may be small, in reality short-term treatment can make a tremendous difference in the quality of their lives.

Although Music Therapy initially grew from a more behavioral model than the other Art therapies, its application to the treatment of children has more recently been influenced by the developmental point of view. The developmental model extends from before the child is born to the prenatal influences of the mother and child's heartbeats and the intrauterine vibrations and rhythms. During the first year of life, there is a rich interchange of nonverbal "music" between the infant and his/her environment as the infant begins to cry, coo, hum, babble, and respond to the parents. By the second year of life words are added to the child's vocalizations, and soon simple song patterns are put together (Levick et al., 1979). While many of the songs of early childhood are used to teach basic cognitive concepts ("One, two, buckle my shoe...") or to stimulate the child's motor coordination ("Patty Cake, Patty Cake, Baker's Man") the primary function of these musical experiences is to augment the pleasurable bond between adult and child and to communicate on an emotional level.

Shawn, a ten-year-old moderately retarded boy with a severe language deficit had been a center resident for several years and had made consistent but slow progress with various therapeutic and educational approaches during most of that time. Although this speech consisted of one- or two-word phrases and echolalia of his teachers and counselors' speech, Shawn also had begun to use sign language as a means of communication and could express himself on a three-year-old level. Shawn's world suddenly seemed to fall apart, however, when his parents announced that they were going to separate. Even though he had not lived at home for several years, the conflict and anxiety that his parents generated in their frequent visits had a dramatic effect. Once an affable and outgoing child, Shawn suddenly became sullen and depressed. He rarely spoke, his appetite diminished, he slept more than normal, and he showed no interest at all in learning.

Although there were many people with whom Shawn had close relationships, including teachers, counselors, and his speech therapist, no one knew how to approach him now. Without a formal language to express himself, Shawn suddenly seemed to be enclosed in a glass case. The people who cared for him could look in and observe, but they couldn't get through.

Similar examples of the use of Music as a means to access the closed world of the nonverbal retarded or autistic child can be found throughout the case reports of music therapists. Children who have never smiled light up when they hear a rhythm they have tapped on a drum being repeated. Children who have spent years of their lives purposelessly manipulating the same objects have learned to say "Hello" by a particular strum on a guitar or "I'm angry" by the crash of a cymbal. Participation in a rhythm band can be the first interaction these children have ever had with others their own age, and their response to simple repetitive songs might be the first indication of a willingness to listen and learn.

In Shawn's case, his therapist found that his vocalizations increased in range and complexity as the sessions went on. Movement to accompany Shawn's vocalizations was added to enlarge his new affective language further. At the same time his therapist verbally acknowledged what he expressed: "You're going up, up, up! Strong, tall Shawn! Now, down, down, down!"

Although Music Therapy has made some important contributions to working with severely handicapped, nonverbal patients, these children are by no means the only types of children who can benefit from it. Music is entwined throughout the lives of all children and has a particular interest and meaning for children who can otherwise be impossible to reach. Once, I was asked by a private school to suggest a treatment for a nine-year-old boy named Jacob who had been placed in a class for learning disabled children with behavioral problems. Jacob had created a role for himself as the class clown; in a class of rambunctious, rebellious boys, establishing this role takes some doing. Whatever the teacher, Ms. B, asked of Jacob, he did the opposite. If she wanted him to raise his hand to be called on, he insisted on calling out. If she wanted him to ask permission to leave the room, he simply got up and did as he pleased. What really drove his teacher to distraction was Jacob's constant tapping. He tapped with his pencil, with his fingers, and with his feet. Sometimes he did it deliberately to fluster and interrupt Ms. B, but many other times he tapped for the sheer enjoyment of the rhythm.

Jacob and his teacher battled every day, but although he smiled and laughed when he thought he had gotten away with something, he was far from being happy. He lived at home with his mother and a baby brother and was, from his teacher's account, virtually ignored. Court proceedings were being held to remove Jacob from his home due to parental neglect and to place him in a foster home. Even at school, where he tried so hard to be accepted by his schoolmates, his lack of progress in learning made him feel like an outcast. A token economy program that his teacher had instigated at the beginning of school made it clear that while Jacob enjoyed clowning around, there was not much in it for him except for a few laughs from his buddies. When tokens were cashed in at the end of each week, Jacob rarely had any, and was unable to purchase treats or special privileges with them.

When I saw Jacob alone, he showed none of the recalcitrant behaviors his teacher had described, but on the other hand, he was not thrilled to see me. I questioned him about his interests and hobbies, trying to avoid topics that might make him more defensive, but he showed little interest in my attempts at conversation. It was evident that being circumspect wasn't getting me very far, so I decided to be blunt:

> THERAPIST: Well, I guess you know why you're down here seeing me, don't you? Ms. B says that you're not very happy about being in her class and she's not very happy about all the trouble you give her.
>
> JACOB: Yup, I know.
>
> THERAPIST: And she thinks that I might have some ideas to turn the situation around.
>
> JACOB: Humph.
>
> THERAPIST: Do you know what you do that really bugs the hell out of her?
>
> JACOB: (Interested) No...what?
>
> THERAPIST: This! (I tap out a complicated beat.)
>
> JACOB: (Giggles) Oh, that!
>
> THERAPIST: Yup. This! (Another rhythm.)
>
> JACOB: (Smiling) You mean this?
> (Taps out about 30 seconds of a syncopated beat.)
>
> THERAPIST: That's it! (I repeat the rhythm.)

We went on like this, tapping out rhythms back and forth like a duel between two hot-shot drummers in rival bands. Although the mood was competitive, there was also a feeling of mutual respect. We got into a pattern of copying each other's beat and then adding another flourish. When I couldn't quite get the rhythm that Jacob had given me, or vice versa, we showed each other how to do it. We kept this up for the remainder of the session, and at the end of our time, I said, "See you next week," and beat out the rhythm of the words. Jacob did the same.

After that session, I wondered whether the behavior that so annoyed Ms. B could be used as a bridge between her and Jacob. Jacob's tapping had always been termed disruptive, but is it was also something he enjoyed and obviously could communicate with. The next week, after greeting Jacob with a tapped message, I asked if he might be interested in learning to use his taps in the classroom in a way that Ms. B would accept and even enjoy! He looked at me suspiciously. I then talked to him about the Morse Code, about the ways that Native Americans used to send messages by drumbeats, and about the way blind people use their canes to tap the ground to determine what's ahead or if there are obstacles in the way.

I told him that we could make up our own tapping code to help him communicate with Ms. B in ways that would suit both of them, and that would help him earn some of the tokens that he was missing out on in class. I asked Jacob three things that he thought Ms. B would like him to be able to say to her. He offered: "Can I sharpen my pencil?" "Can I go to the bathroom?" and "I need help." We worked out a system of rhythmic taps that seemed to fit these phrases and that afternoon I presented them to Ms. B. She readily agreed, noting that she would try anything. We decided that Jacob could earn points from the class's token economy system every time he appropriately communicated with his taps. He would get points taken away, however, if he tapped on his desk inappropriately. At the same time, as part of a multiple-technique treatment plan, I suggested several other techniques for Ms. B to use in the classroom and made an immediate referral to a music therapist.

The Visual Arts as Therapy

Drawings are frequently used by mainstream psychotherapists (therapists without specific training in Art Therapy) as part of their diagnostic assessments of children. Common methods for using drawings to assess the personality makeup and conflicts of children include the Human Figure Drawing Test (Koppitz, 1968), the House-Tree-Person Test (Buck, 1948), and the Kinetic Family Drawing Test (Burns and Kaufman, 1970). Although considerable controversy exists about the validity of each of these techniques to add a differential diagnosis, their ease of use and richness of their product continues to ensure their popularity. Each technique begins with a simple direction:

Human Figure Drawing Test: "Draw a person for me on this sheet of paper. Now draw a picture of a boy/girl (the opposite sex of the first drawing) on the back."

House-Tree-Person Test: "Draw me a picture of a house, a tree, and a person, using this pencil. Now draw me another picture of a house, a tree, and a person, using these crayons."

Kinetic Family Drawing Test: "Draw me a picture of your family doing something."

Directions may vary slightly, but all advocates of these techniques emphasize to the child that the artistic quality of the drawings is not important and that everything they produce is of value. The drawings are then interpreted by specific symbols that the child uses (although interpreting a one-to-one correspondence between a symbol in a drawing and a universal meaning is frowned upon); the way that the child uses the writing instruments and the paper; the degree of the tension exhibited by the lightness or width of the line; the spacing of the drawing(s) on the page; the exaggeration of specific features (particularly in the body) and the absence of others; the use of color in the House-Tree-Person Test; and in the Kinetic Family Drawing Test, the choice of activity, relative size of the family members, style of the drawings, and so forth.

Although as Feder and Feder suggest (1981), the diagnostic use of Art cannot really be separated from its therapeutic use, there are specific functions of Visual Art techniques which make this modality distinct. They note that while there is a wide variation in the use of Art Therapy, the majority of therapists come from a Freudian or neoFreudian tradition, and define the benefits of Art Therapy in psychodynamic concepts. In this framework, the most basic benefits to be gained by Art Therapy are through catharsis, the release of emotional energy and tension. Clay, fingerpaints, Play-Doh®, water, and sand have always been standard equipment in the analytic playroom to promote the free expression of pent-up conflicts and inhibitions.

The choice of materials, colors, the manner in which these are used, and the verbalizations that accompany their use provide clues as to where a child's unconscious anxieties may be located and the particular ego-defense structures that may be either restricting or failing to bind libidinal or aggressive drives.

A second function of Art Therapy is to provide a channel between the patient's conscious and unconscious. Within the concept, Art may be seen as a sublimation of unconscious drives and conflicts, a symbolization of unconscious images such as we find in dreams, or an integration of thoughts, feelings, and behaviors, both conscious and unconscious, that leads to a sense of fulfillment as a whole person in the process of creating Art.

The most important contribution of Art to the therapeutic process, however, may be its capacity to act as a channel for nonverbal communication. The possibilities for communicating outside the limitations of words can open up new vistas to the patient and the therapeutic relationship. Through their artistic creations patients can explore issues that have been so emotionally laden that they have been prohibited from finding conscious verbal expression, or issues that are so basic in their origin in the first years of life that they predate the child's ability to use words.

An example of this communicative use of Art occurred in a family session where I was cotherapist with an analytic colleague. The identified patient was a four-year-old boy who had an older brother with a severe hearing loss and concomitant speech and language problems. Since birth the younger boy, Mark, had been relegated to the role of the "normal" child by the parents, whose marriage had nearly broken up over the difficulties in raising their older handicapped son. Now Mark was beginning to display his own set of serious problems. In the six months before they sought therapy, Mark had become increasingly belligerent toward his older brother as well as toward children his own age. He verbally and physically teased them and also expressed violent fantasies when he was the least bit annoyed.

His mother reported a recent incident that had occurred while Mark was riding with several other children to preschool. Another child had inadvertently bumped his shoulder, and Mark had turned in a rage and said, "I'm going to kill you for that. I'm going to take my Daddy's gun and shoot you in the head until you bleed and you're dead." As might be anticipated, Mark's behavior once again threw the family into disarray. Both the mother and father felt that they had somehow been cursed to bring up children who would be social outcasts.

In the fourth conjoint family session an incident occurred that demonstrated how an Art Therapy technique can be used in both a psychodynamic and a family framework. I was talking to the mother and father who were seated at opposite ends of the couch, when my colleague noticed Mark drawing in a corner of the room. The older boy was sitting in a chair close to his mother's end of the couch. I always keep drawing and other Art materials available during family sessions, but this was the first time that Mark had used them. Immediately prior to selecting some paper and a box of crayons, he had been jumping on and off the couch between his parents until his father angrily told him to stop it. When my cotherapist observed that Mark had completed his drawing, she asked him if he would bring it over to show her (she was positioned in the center of the room) and to also bring some paper and the box of crayons.

Mark's drawing showed four stick figures, three of about equal size in the middle of the page and one much smaller lying on its back in the corner. When Mark was asked who these people were, he indicated that he was in the center of the picture, sandwiched between his mother and father, and his older brother was in the corner. When he was asked what the people were doing, he replied that he and his mother and father were talking, and his older brother was going to his special school. My colleague replied that she liked the picture and she understood how children often wished to have their mothers and fathers all to themselves and not have to share them with anyone. She went on, "This is a wish that most children have, but it is only a wish. Even babies don't get their parents all to themselves. Parents must have time for each other and for other children in the family."

Mark and the rest of the family listened to this quietly. Mark was fiddling with the crayons and my colleague asked him if he wanted to color his picture in, but he replied, "No." (We assumed that this was because he was not yet ready to deal with emotional colorations of what he had just revealed. Note that his verbalization expressed none of his anger toward his older sibling, even though the prone positioning of the smaller figure suggested that the impulse was there.)

I then suggested that it would be interesting to see some more pictures of the family. I gave new sheets of paper to Mark and to his brother and asked the parents if they would draw a picture together on a single sheet of paper. I asked them to move together on the couch and gave them a clipboard and a box of crayons. My colleague and I positioned ourselves on either side of the two children, who were now seated much farther from the couch. Each child had his own box of crayons.

During the remainder of the session we used the pictures as a stimulus to talk about each person's wishes about the way the family could be. In each case, the therapists recognized the legitimacy of the fantasies and talked about some of the other ways besides wishing that children and adults can fulfill their needs. The session ended with an assignment for the family to go home and draw a joint poster showing everyone in the family doing what they like best. Specific directions were given to the parents on how to structure the task, how to intervene if the children began to fight, and how to set limits on the task.

LEARNING THROUGH THE ARTS

In short-term therapy, therapists must work to manipulate every aspect of the child's system in order to bring about a more supportive and adaptable environment in which the child can grow. For children who have been identified as having atypical learning needs and who are part of a school's special education program, the therapist frequently has resources within the school which can address the child's interlocked emotional/behavioral/learning needs.

The importance of using Art and Art Therapy in education has been recognized in federal legislation. Public Law 94-142, the Education for All Handicapped Children's Act, was passed by Congress in the mid 1970s to ensure that all children with disabilities have access to the appropriate services they need to fulfill their learning potential. Public Law 94-142 specifically mentioned the appropriateness of using Art and Art Therapy in the education of children with special needs. Although the spirit of this law was widely praised and was at the time seen as a coming of age for the application of mental health principles to public education, its implementation has in many ways fallen short of the expectations of special educators and the hopes of parents, children, and therapists in schools. Ambiguities in the law itself, the widely-varying perspectives of school boards across the country, changes in the structure of the federal bureaucracy, and most of all the realization of how expensive this program will be, have stifled the dramatic changes that many of us involved in the education of the handicapped had hoped for.

Still, some progress has been made, particularly in the private sector where government support in the form of tuition grants for handicapped children has encouraged creative educational experiments. One such program is the Kingsbury Lab School directed by Sally Smith. Ms. Smith, the mother of a significantly learning disabled child who did not read until he was thirteen, has won national recognition for her school. The school has worked with hundreds of severely handicapped children and 90 percent of her students return to regular classroom settings. Many have gone on to college.

The curriculum at the Lab School is built around the Arts. Half the day is spent in the classroom; the other half is spent in Woodwork, Music, Dance, Drama, Puppetry, and Filmmaking. Ms. Smith sees the artist/teacher as contributing to every phase of the child's treatment. Difficulties that the child has using an Art medium provide important diagnostic information about the way the child thinks and perceives. Attention to the Art forms in which the students excel provides information about what each child needs to learn to succeed in academic subjects.

The inherent structure of each of the Arts and the ability of artists to see the world in a purposeful, organized way are the keys to using Art to teach the learning disabled child. Labeling, discriminating, sorting, comparing, grouping, classifying, synthesizing, preparing, and planning are the basic building blocks of all learning. The Arts provide opportunities for children to experience all of these cognitive processes, whatever the developmental level they are working through, while holding their interest and motivating them to muster their resources in ways that traditional academic teaching doesn't seem able to elicit.

Several years ago I worked with a ten-year-old boy with a learning disability that prevented him from learning mathematics beyond the first-grade level, even though he performed at an above average level in many other areas associated with intelligence. His vocabulary, his memory for details, and his skill at solving visual puzzles all suggested that he should be able to perform at least as well as other children his age, if not better. Still, numbers didn't make sense for him and he avoided anything resembling math problems so he wouldn't appear and feel stupid.

This boy was also enrolled in a Filmmaking workshop. Each member of the class had been asked to make a ten-minute film about any subject, and he had chosen his passion: electronic games. His teacher asked him what the film would be about; he replied that some adults thought electronic games were dumb and even bad for kids, and he wanted to show them that games are worthwhile, not only because kids love to play them, but because they can help kids learn as well.

Before the project had even begun, the relationship of the teacher to the student had been defined in terms of the child's interests and emotional needs. Art, unlike traditional education, does not impose values on children, and so they are free to choose subjects that make them feel good about themselves and messages that affirm their pride in their achievements rather than their shame about their disabilities. In this case, the next step was to channel the boy's interest so that it could include instruction in basic skills.

The teacher began by explaining how the student must organize his film on paper before he began to use the camera. He suggested that a storyboard of the film should be made by drawing a sketch of each scene, noting how many minutes each scene should take, and arranging the scenes in a sequence that would tell the story most effectively. He gave the student a film book showing how a storyboard was made for a popular adventure movie. He reminded him that each student only had a limited amount of film to work with, the equivalent of 20 minutes, and that the edited version should be about five minutes in length. This is a complicated mathematical problem for a child who has trouble with simple subtraction!

The boy took the task to his math teacher for help and although theoretically the math involved was well beyond the child's level, involving the division of the total number of minutes by the number of scenes, the Filmmaking teacher had successfully concretized and organized the task so that the math teacher could break it down into manageable steps. The boy decided that he wanted to shoot five scenes: one of a video arcade; one showing two friends playing a hand-held game; one showing a child beating an adult at the same game; a fourth showing an interview of the science teacher explaining the relationship between electronic games and computers; and a fifth showing himself working at a computer. The student made one sketch for each scene.

Then, the math teacher took a large piece of poster board measuring exactly 20 inches across and drew a straight line at the top. She explained that the board that would hold the sketches was exactly 20 inches wide and then asked the student to take a yardstick and make a mark at each inch. When this was done, she explained that each mark would represent a minute of filming. She then asked him to number the marks up to 20. She also asked the student to make three sets of five cards: one set was to be three inches square, another four inches square, and the last, five inches square. She had him mark out the top of each card in inches.

She then explained the principle of division, the meaning of dividends and divisors, the symbol for division, and so forth. She knew that she was only introducing these concepts and did not imply that they should be mastered just yet. But she also let the student know that these concepts were the basic elements of his problem and were exactly what other kids of his age were learning.

She then asked him to take each set of cards and to see which set fit exactly on the storyboard. Only one set would fit, she explained, and the number of inches on the top of those cards would indicate the number of minutes for each scene of his film. She then directed the student to take the cards that fit the storyboard and paste his sketches on them. Finally, she sent him back to the Filmmaking teacher with the equipment for the storyboard completed. He could now discuss the best sequence of scenes to convey his message.

To review what happened: A child with no interest in math, who normally performed three years below his age level, excitedly solved a math problem at an age-appropriate level by having it broken down into concrete tasks that he could master. In doing so, he performed operations in measuring, in equating different systems of measurement (inches and minutes), in sequencing, in comparison, in numbering, and so on. In addition, he was introduced to the basic principles behind a mathematical concept presumed to be far out of his reach. Since the same basic task would be repeated several more times before the actual filming was underway (scenes would have to be divided into shots, dialogue would have to be added), the student would have the opportunity to repeat the process over and over again, strengthening each of the basic organizational tasks he had to learn. Most importantly, this child would find repeated success, strengthening his belief in his own powers to learn, and motivating him towards continued progress.

FEELINGS GAMES

There are many published feelings games available to the therapist (see *The Book of Psychotherapeutic Games,* Shapiro, 1993). My personal favorite is a game called *Face It!* (published by The Center for Applied Psychology, Inc.), which features a deck of 52 cards, each card showing the face of someone with one of 13 feelings, representing the 13 cards in a standard suit. The faces are divided into four suits, categorizing the feelings faces into four ages: children, teens, adults, and older adults. Using this deck, the therapist can play at least ten different games, from memory games like "Feelings Go Fish" to more sophisticated storytelling games.

Games can be used to teach a hierarchy of skills related to having children learn to express and understand feelings:

- Identifying feelings words
- Learning to appropriately express feelings in different situations

- Learning to handle two different feelings at the same time
- Identifying the feelings of others
- Empathizing with the feelings of others

Figure 3.A
Search for Feelings

In this word search, find these feelings words: Angry, Scared, Happy, Sad, Stressed, Upset, Worried, Loving, Jealous, Shy, Proud, Anxious, Guilty, Shocked, Embarrassed, Satisfied, Surprised, Affectionate, Irritable, and Confused.

```
K A D L W H K L M G S T P O R K J L D I
A E T A N O I T C E F F A W J K K Y E Z
N C O T A R L S W Y Y Z D E D A N G R Y
X W L A Y Z Y C O N F U S E D K W R A E
I X J K B T H S J Y W K S C O N R L C Z
O Z G H S Y D A S X L I E D W F F O S G
U Y I B S A R W P A R E Z E Y L W R E H
S G H W I S A T I P O Q D B Z H W N D J
W C D I F I R S R T Y Z E B L O V I N G
J S E D L L D U E F L L S R R Z W C O E
G Z K I Y O S W F E M B A R R A S S E D
C W C R U V Z P H M N L I B R O V T S T
B O O R R E L Q T W X E Y M R R G J Z A
R L H I Y W A E A H D T K I R P M X H Y
E T S T R E S S E D O W Y N T R Y R H T
Y J C A I P H W P X Z J E A L O U S W L
Z E R B U M C N Q B O T R V V U O S C I
H Y B L S X R S A T I S F I E D T U J U
F K Q E X W U T R F F E T L K R B C S G
```

Feelings games can be played between the therapist and the child, used within a family session, or be easily integrated into a classroom curriculum on "understanding ourselves and others."

Figure 3.A is a game that you can use right away called "Search For Feelings." The game is a word search; the object is to find the 20 hidden feelings words. To play, have a child find each of the words by circling it, and when each feelings word is found, the child has to tell of a time when he or she had that feeling. The 20 feelings words can also be copied onto individual 3 X 5" cards and the game played with a group of 2 to 4 children.

First, hide the cards around the room. The players have to hunt for the cards and when one is found, shout out "I feel angry, sad, etc.," saying the word in a voice which reflects the emotion. When all the words have been found, the group should get together, and each player should talk about a time that he or she had that feeling. In both versions of the game, the therapist can give out a chip each time a feeling is talked about, and the chips can later be cashed in for a small reward.

HYPNOTHERAPY

Hypnotherapy is a treatment technique that requires at least minimal cooperation from a child. Although resistant children may show initial interest in this type of treatment, this interest will quickly fade when they realize that Hypnotherapy is not some sort of magic or mind control technique like they see on television or in the movies, and they are not going to learn how to make other people cluck like chickens. A strong intractable prejudice against hypnosis, usually by the parents, is also a contraindication to using this technique.

It is important in all cases to dispel the mystique and fear of hypnosis by explaining that Hypnotherapy is really only a form of relaxation therapy. Hypnosis does not imply loss of control by the subjects, whether children or adults. The patients do not go to sleep, nor do they forget who they are, where they are, or what they are doing. In fact the vast majority of patients who are helped by hypnosis report they are completely aware of everything that is happening. Only a relatively small percentage, estimated at less than five or ten percent of the population, experience the type of trance state that is popularized by TV and drama, in which the subject appears to be asleep and is unaware of his or her immediate environment. The hypnotic state is a relatively normal and common experience for both children and adults. Daydreaming or becoming immersed in a TV show, story, or certain kinds of mechanical repetitive tasks to the extent that one is hardly conscious of what one is doing are all examples of trance-like states. They are different from what is called hypnosis only in that no suggestions are being made to the subjects from a therapist and the subjects are not consciously cooperating in a process aimed at helping them.

Adults, and to a lesser extent adolescents and children, can have specific fears about hypnosis. They can be afraid to undergo hypnosis because they are afraid they will not "come out" of it. This is a myth because the subject remains in control of himself or herself throughout the entire period of hypnosis. Another patient can feel that he or she will be made to do unethical or inappropriate things that would later be regretted. This is highly unlikely, if not impossible. The vast majority of clients state that they are aware through the entire process that they are being hypnotized and do not feel they are being manipulated.

When parents are worried about their children, they may need to be reminded or reassured that the therapist is working only in the children's interest. In some cases the parent may be so anxious that he or she should be invited to observe from behind a two-way mirror or watch a videotape of the therapist working with another client in order to demystify this type of treatment. If the right equipment is not available and there are no specific contraindications, the parent may be invited to remain in the room with the child and can even take part in the hypnotic experience if he or she wishes.

Since each person has individual misconceptions, the therapist needs to take the time to ask both the child and the parents what they know and think about hypnosis and to allay any fears and dispel any myths that exist. Strong fears and anxieties are a contraindication for using this technique.

There is a long-standing debate on what Hypnotherapy is. Most researchers and clinicians agree that Hypnotherapy is an altered state of consciousness in which the patient uses his or her abilities to concentrate and block stimulation that are otherwise present in the environment. In theory, this hyperconcentration makes the subject amenable to suggestion and motivated to change. The greatest difference of opinion comes in describing whether this state of concentration is actually different from any other type of concentration and boils down to whether or not a trance exists or whether the subject is simply experiencing something new and experiences a "trance" to please the therapist. In clinical practice the trance versus non-trance debate is not significant. Whatever kind of psychological phenomenon hypnosis represents, it is a technique that draws on universal human experiences and appears to have wide application.

Hypnotherapy can be divided into three phases: induction, the process whereby the patient goes into an altered state or a trance state; the treatment itself, when a specific set of suggestions is made to the patient; and a posthypnotic state, when the actual change in the patient's emotions, thoughts, and behaviors must occur.

Induction can be done in many different ways, both with children and adults. To be hypnotized, the patient must be in a relaxed, highly concentrated state and at least marginally receptive toward the suggestion of change. For very young children induction may take the form of a simple repetitive task such as putting blocks in holes and taking them out.

In more formal inductions the child is told to sit and relax and then is given the suggestion to form mental images as if he or she is watching a movie or TV. The therapist may suggest that the child close his or her eyes, but this is not necessary. The therapist then may describe a scene, emphasizing concrete visual aspects of the image and ideas that are multisensory to provoke images of sound, taste, sight, and touch. As the child enters a trance state, the therapist points out the natural occurring physiological responses *just as they begin.* The therapist notes: "Your eyelids are heavy and you want to rest" (as he or she observes the eyes beginning to blink and close). "You are breathing slowly and more deeply" (as this is observed). "Your arms are heavy, as if there are weights attached to them" (as it is observed that the child's hands are limp and resting heavily on his or her legs). As the therapist mentions physiological responses *that have actually already begun to occur,* the child develops a sense of trust that other suggestions, therapeutic suggestions, will also occur.

The therapist, once he or she has observed that the child is focusing inward and responding less to outside stimuli, may wish to test the child's suggestibility; however, this is not necessary. Suggestibility scales exist for children and adults. These scales typically test to see whether the patient will follow specific suggestions such as levitation of hand and arm, immobilization of limbs, inability to open the eyes and so forth, suggesting that the patient's unconscious mind can act without acknowledgment or even cooperation with the patient's conscious mind. While these scales are considered to be reliable and valid in measuring hypnotisability, there has been no research that correlates the degree of suggestibility with the success of Hypnotherapy treatment.

In other words, even though subjects may be highly suggestible and go into trancelike states very easily, this doesn't necessarily mean that this technique will be successful in helping them solve their problems. Conversely, *even though a child or an adult may not appear to be in a highly suggestible state, and may report feeling absolutely normal, the suggestion that is given may still have a significant therapeutic effect.*

One of the simplest techniques of induction is to have patients open their eyes on the count of one, close their eyes on the count of two, open them on the count of three, close them on the count of four, and so on, up to a hundred. The therapist comments: "At any time you may feel the need to keep your eyes closed and to let them remain closed." This suggestion has several components. First, it relies on the therapist's knowledge of the physiological certainty that the patient's eyes will tire of opening and closing before the therapist counts to 100. The therapist may speed up the count to speed up the patient's weariness. He or she may skip numbers in random order, thus confusing the patient and only allowing the patient to escape the confusion by accepting the suggestion that the patient's eyes "may soon wish to close."

The therapist should offer suggestions in the context of a choice that the patient can make ("Your eyes will close whenever you like.") The physiological and psychological dice are loaded so that the patient's eyes certainly will close; if they do not, neither the patient nor the therapist has failed, because the patient has simply chosen that they will not close and the therapist only presented the choice: he did not *dictate* that the eyes will close. In the event that the eyes close, the therapist may then wish to continue testing the patient's suggestibility by seeing if he or she will receive a suggestion that the eyes will open. The therapist comments:

> Your eyelids feel as if they are *stuck* together. As if they are *glued* shut...*heavy* as lead...Even though *you may wish* to open them, they would probably *stay closed.* The eyes want to stay closed...stay closed...closed. (Italicized words are emphasized.)

Because of the voice inflections, use of repetition, and emphasis on what the therapist is aiming toward, a division is made between the patient's conscious and unconscious motivation. In this instance, the patient knows that he or she can open his or her eyes, but wants to keep them shut to please the therapist (as some theories suggest) or perhaps because of the force of the suggestions themselves. If the patient does not take the suggestion and, in fact, chooses to prove that he or she can consciously control his or her eyes, this again is not taken as a failure, but rather a choice. The therapist may simply respond that "your eyes are not yet ready to stay shut but you may want to close them sometime later." By accepting all behaviors in this manner, the therapist does not fight the patient, but rather always remains on the side of the patient's desire to control his or her behavior and to use this control for therapeutic change.

As an experienced hypnotherapist will tell you, the method of induction is relatively unimportant compared to the second stage of Hypnotherapy where the treatment occurs. In this stage the children or adolescents receive suggestions that will help them cope with their problem in a new way. The treatment itself will vary according to the particular problem, the abilities and age of the child, and according to the interests and other idiosyncrasies that make each child an individual. Although a skilled therapist may have set ideas as to the specific type of suggestions that will be useful, he or she must also keep an open mind and a skilled eye to determine how the child is reacting and what effect the suggestions are having. The following paragraphs describe the types of suggestions that can work with children.

Using Hypnotherapy to Aid in Pain Control

There are many different types of suggestions for the control of pain, since this is one of the areas in which hypnosis is used most widely. Inductions may be used with transient pain as well as with intractable pain. Examples of both follow.

A hypnotherapist working at a sickle cell anemia clinic recently told me of a young child who came in experiencing extreme panic at the thought of giving blood. As in many types of anticipated pain or other medical procedures that children are afraid of, it is difficult to separate children's anxiety and panic from their actual physical experiences. In this case the therapist, after a quick induction, had the eight-year-old imagine that she was out in the snow building a snowman. As the child relaxed, she was given very concrete suggestions that she could feel, just as if she were really in the snow and could feel the coldness and the wetness and the wind and the taste of snow. She was delighted with the image as she saw herself tumbling and sledding down a snow-covered hill near her house. The therapist then suggested that she take a snowball and put it on her arm just where the needle was going to go. It was very cold: so cold, in fact, that it numbed the arm entirely. The arm could feel nothing but the cold. It could not possibly feel the pain. The therapist demonstrated that this was true by pinching the child's arm where the needle would go, and, in fact, the child had no experience of pain whatsoever. Minutes later the child, who had been hysterical at the thought of giving blood, confidently waved to the lab technician and held out her arm, much to the surprise of her parents and doctor.

In another case a hypnotherapist on an oncology ward was treating a child with cancer who had periods of very severe pain. The therapist explained to the child that the brain could control all sensations in the body and was, in fact, like a little computer sending out signals to various limbs, muscles, and organs. Each path that carried a message to the computer was described as a cable; each cable was a different color and led to a colored light in the brain. At the sites of the pain, particularly in the arms and feet, were switches; when the nerves were on, the switches were open and the lights were on. When the nerves were off, the switches were closed and the lights were off.

While the therapist was with the child, he suggested that the child experience some of the pain; the child was able to do this. The therapist then told the child to turn off the switch where the pain was; to *slowly* turn it off so that the light would grow dimmer and dimmer until it was completely off and the place that once hurt would have no pain and feel perfectly comfortable and perfectly natural. The child learned, through concrete images, to concentrate on turning off the pain, controlling the pain so that it was hardly experienced (no more than a very dull ache); and sometimes it was not experienced at all. Other people, including the child's nurses and parents, were also taught to use this hypnotic procedure to encourage the child with these suggestions to control the pain.

Using Hypnotherapy with Psychogenic Disorders

Olness and Gardner (1978) note that "Hypnotherapy has been found to be effective as an ancillary therapy in treating numerous problems connected with the autonomic nervous system including: asthma, nausea, vomiting, hypertension, hyperhydrosis, recurrent hives, bleeding, urine retention, globus hystericus and hiccoughs." They state that although these problems are often treated by other means, Hypnotherapy can be used to relieve symptoms. However, they also caution the secondary gains for these symptoms are important considerations and that the child who may learn to stop wheezing in a hospital room surrounded by friendly staff may not be willing to do so when he or she is at home craving attention.

The treatment techniques for these psychophysiological disorders will generally use the components of relaxation and imagery that were discussed in the treatment of pain, helping the child to use concrete images to dilate the vascular system, relax specific muscle groups, and so forth. Often the support and suggestions of the hypnosis itself can be enough to convince the child that he can control some of the symptoms. For example a nine-year-old enuretic learned to could control symptoms in two sessions by paying attention to body signals and by imaging controlling the bladder while sleeping.

Using Hypnotherapy with Habit Control Techniques

In working with habit disorders, which can include nail biting, thumb sucking, hair pulling, tics, insomnia, and eating problems, I have combined Hypnotherapy with the techniques developed by Azrin and Nunn's *Habit Control in a Day* (1977). These authors emphasize the following method:

1. Accurate records of habit episodes are kept.
2. The social effects of the habits are considered.
3. The patient is directed toward paying attention to the mannerisms and behaviors that precede the habit episode.
4. The patient is taught to identify situations, activities, and people that cause the habit to occur.
5. The patient is encouraged to practice and rehearse a competing habit which will interfere with the problem and yet be socially acceptable.

(Hypnosis is particularly helpful in steps 3, 4, and 5.)

For example, in the treatment of a ten-year-old girl who sucked her thumb both at school and at home, I began by having her put a check in a notebook each time she was aware that she was sucking her thumb. This data-keeping reduced the habit behavior simply by drawing her attention to it and making the child conscious of what she was doing. To raise the awareness of the habit, I put her into a light trance in which she was directed to imagine herself in a situation where she was perfectly comfortable sucking her thumb.

She was then told to imagine it would be even more comfortable with her hands relaxed on the desk (the substituting behavior). "Your poor thumb," I told her, "it really isn't so comfortable being wet and chewed on. The thumb, after all, is a part of your body and it likes to be comfortable too! Your thumb enjoys having the air circulate around it and feeling free to do what thumbs do: to press on the desktop, to twiddle the other thumb, to tap out a melody, to put in a thumbtack, to *do what thumbs do.*"

With these suggestions, the child was made to feel comfortable about disassociating the thumb as a mode of oral gratification. The competing, substitution behaviors included pressing the thumb against the table and twiddling the thumbs. The competing behavior was then practiced under hypnosis and in real life. The girl was directed to practice keeping her thumb out of her mouth and letting it "be free to be a thumb." In one session she decided to put a little face on her thumb and use it as a finger puppet to give the thumb its own "life," differentiating it from the need for oral gratification (which was addressed using other therapy techniques).

Another therapist might have used an aversive technique similar to one used with smokers, whereby the patient would be told under hypnosis that the thumb would have a noxious taste or a horrible smell and it would be so vile and disgusting that she could not possibly want to put it in her mouth. I avoid using these aversive techniques whenever possible, for although they may work, the implications of having a child become disgusted with part of her own body, even so small a part as a thumb, does not seem therapeutic.[1]

This is a good illustration of how Hypnotherapy can be used to facilitate behavioral principles. Suggestions given to the unconscious support the work with the patient's conscious motivation to effect a change.

The third phase of Hypnotherapy is the most important since it is during this phase that the patient changes life patterns. Sometimes the therapist will make tapes of the sessions for the child or adolescent to use at home, but more often he or she will use posthypnotic suggestions. Tape recordings of hypnotic sessions which are played back at home are usually only effective when the client is highly motivated to change. If there is no motivation, the child or adolescent may find it convenient to lose the tape or the tape recorder or to forget to practice this technique.

Contrary to popular opinion, posthypnotic suggestions are usually remembered by the subject and are done with his or her full cooperation. While the client is still under hypnosis, the therapist will suggest that with a given signal the client will experience comfort, relaxation, or some other appropriate affective state that he or she has experienced in hypnosis. The signal may be one under the client's control, such as clasping his or her hands together to feel more confident when going to the dentist. Or the signal may be an external cue, such as hearing the school bell ring and being motivated to concentrate on schoolwork. Usually the client is trained in the office to respond to a signal. For instance, in the example of the school bell, the therapist might ring a bell and have the client go into a state of relaxation; this is practiced over several days.

Gail Gardner (1974) suggests that aside from the alleviation of

---

1 Site or place substitution is another type of substitution sometimes used in Hypnosis. Here the symptom is not changed at all, but the *place* where the symptom resides is changed. A facial tic, for example, can be moved to a hand or foot where it is less noticeable and more easily treated.

symptoms, Hypnotherapy can be useful in ego-strengthening techniques, such as guiding the child toward such positive feelings as confidence, trust, and mastery in dealing with certain problems. In helping an older child or adolescent deal with a trauma, hypnotherapists will sometimes use the trance state to have the patient relive the experience in his or her imagination with gentle guided support.

There has been new interest in Hypnotherapy techniques in the last few years and this seems to slowly be expanding itself towards the treatment of children. The creativity and imagination inherent in this technique make it a particularly appropriate skill for the child therapist to learn and apply in short-term treatment.[2]

BIOFEEDBACK

Many people would argue that Biofeedback should be discussed in a chapter on behavioral techniques, rather than as an Affective modality. However, I have more frequently used Biofeedback to treat children with affective disorders than children with behavioral problems (although behavioral problems may be present as a result of the affective disorder).

Biofeedback can be defined as any organized way in which a patient is immediately shown the degree of his or her physiological responsiveness. A patient who takes his or her blood pressure daily because of a fear of heart attacks is utilizing a Biofeedback technique. A runner who judges his or her endurance by pulse rate is using Biofeedback. In the laboratory and clinic, the measurement of a wide variety of physiological changes such as muscle tension, skin temperature, skin electrical impulses, metabolic rate, and brainwave patterns are all examples of Biofeedback, when these changes are made known immediately and continuously to the patient. Biofeedback assumes that when patients have a continual knowledge of their physiological states, they may eventually learn to control this state to their own advantage, producing a physiological state associated with relaxation and health rather than tension and anxiety.

The use of "feeding-back" physiological information to children or adolescents is a relatively new technique. The benefits can be significant, however, and research has claimed success in working with such

---

2 For those therapists interested in training in Hypnotherapy approaches, an annual conference in Hypnotherapy techniques is presented by the Milton H. Erikson Foundation in December. This conference typically offers several seminars for practitioners working with children and adolescents. For information, write: The Milton H. Erickson Foundation, Inc., 3606 N. 24th St., Phoenix, AZ 85016-6500.

diverse problems as asthma, pulmonary insufficiency, migraine, and in the physical rehabilitation of stroke, cerebral palsy, and multiple sclerosis victims.

There are many different types of Biofeedback instruments. A well-equipped laboratory that can treat a variety of complaints can cost thousands of dollars, a cost that is prohibitive for most clinicians to whom this book is addressed. For that reason, I will primarily emphasize cases where I used relatively inexpensive instruments costing less than one hundred dollars.[3] There are currently four major psychophysiological processes that are measured by Biofeedback instrumentation although, as I mentioned earlier, any physical process that can be measured with the information immediately being sent back to the patient, can be deemed Biofeedback.

Electromographic feedback is considered to have the widest range of application (Brown, 1977). The electromograph, or EMG, tests the electrical activity of specific muscles or muscle groups. When muscles are tense, they are subject to more electrical activity, although people may not be aware of this until the tension actually becomes pain. Small sensors that can detect minimal amounts of tension are placed on the skin over the muscle. EMG Biofeedback may be used to either decrease muscle activity, as in controlling pain, or to increase muscle activity, as in the rehabilitation of muscles from partial paralysis. The relative accuracy of EMG Biofeedback depends on consistent placement of the electrodes on the appropriate muscles.

A second type of Biofeedback instrumentation relies on the measure of brainwave patterns: this instrument is called an electroencephalogram or EEG. The EEG measures microvoltages of electrical activity in the brain from eight or more electrodes placed on the scalp. The electrical activity is then converted into brainwave frequencies that have four (somewhat arbitrarily defined) components: beta, associated with alert behavior and concentration; theta, associated with passive problem-solving and creativity; delta, the predominant brain wave pattern exhibited during sleep; and alpha, associated with the meditative daydreaming sometimes called relaxed wakefulness.

The primary use of EEG Biofeedback has involved using the alpha frequency. The popularity of this method among the lay public as well as in clinical settings has led some scientists to begrudge the emergence of an alpha cult. Scientists are concerned that many people are misled into believing that the alpha state (or any of the other EEG states) is a true psychoneurological process, when in fact each state is

---

3 For a catalog of portable Biofeedback equipment contact Thought Technology, 2186 Avenue Belgrave, Montreal, Quebec CAH4A2L8, Canada; (514) 489-8255.

an oversimplified brainwave *component* that has questionable validity or reliability as a measurement tool. Still, there are numerous clinical reports that credit alpha training in reducing pain, epileptic seizures, and a variety of psychoneurotic disorders.

The third major type of Biofeedback instrumentation measures that peripheral blood flow that changes the temperature on the surface of the skin. The dilation or restriction of peripheral vessels can change skin surface temperature so that it fluctuates between 60 and 95° in a constant room temperature. Minute changes in skin temperature are measured by a thermistor, usually placed on the fingers. Temperature Biofeedback, sometimes abbreviated as TEMP, is typically used for general relaxation and stress-related disorders in which internal organs are predominantly involved.

The last major type of Biofeedback instrumentation uses the galvanic skin response (GSR) and measures changes in the sympathetic nervous system by recording the chemical change in the sweat response on the surface of the skin, usually the hand or fingers. When the patient is more tense or aroused, there are concomitant changes in the sweat response. GSR Biofeedback has been used in the treatment of anxiety disorders, asthma, and stuttering.

Whatever physiologic process the instrument is measuring, feedback can be either visual or auditory, sometimes both. Visually, the subject may be told to watch a needle that registers a higher number when there is more tension, a printout that registers an upward slope when there is more tension, or a digital readout where higher numbers indicate more tension. Auditory feedback is usually in the form of a pure tone that becomes louder and develops a higher pitch when tension is present and becomes softer and lower pitched when tension decreases.

The most basic use of Biofeedback with children and adolescents is to teach them relaxation. It should not be surprising that many very active children do not really know what we mean when we ask them to *calm down,* to *relax,* to *concentrate*, or to *pay attention.* These behaviors are simply not in their repertoires. When we ask a child to sit down and read, he or she may understand the request or command to stay seated and even be able to control himself or herself to begin the reading process. But the cognitive and affective states that are necessary for concentrated reading are the ones that we find hard to communicate. As a result, the child may sit down to begin a lesson, but then daydream, fidget, take toys out of the desk, or otherwise express activity without doing the assignment. This type of behavior is characteristic of many learning disabled children or children with Attention Deficit Disorder with Hyperactivity (ADHD) and can be extremely frustrating for their teachers and parents.

Teaching the child to relax enough to be able to concentrate on learning can be facilitated with the use of GSR Biofeedback.[4] Of course relaxation is only one of the skills needed to teach a child who has a hard time learning and other learning techniques must be taught as well.

Nine-year-old Benjamin was a third grader with a diagnosed learning disability. He had been receiving remedial tutoring and attending a resource classroom as part of his schooling since the first grade. While he had mastered many of the basics of reading, could sound out words, and even spell at an average level, Benjamin had great difficulty completing assignments because of his lack of concentration. He could work adequately with an adult on a one-to-one basis, but had not yet learned to work by himself in spite of the fact that he was reasonably well motivated and cared about getting good grades.

Before I attempted Biofeedback training, I asked Benjamin simply to sit in a chair and relax. He sat in a chair looking at me; however, he was far from relaxed. He crossed his legs, crossed his arms, put his head down and then up, rolled his eyes, laughed, smiled, and did a variety of other things to get my attention. Again I told him to try to relax and asked him if he knew what I meant. Smiling and giggling, he put his hands in his lap but kept his feet swaying. I then showed him a small Biofeedback machine and explained to him how it worked. If he placed two fingers on the palm-sized machine, the chemicals that came from the sweat on his fingers would make the machine buzz. The more he was excited, the more the chemicals would be excited, and the louder the machine would buzz. The more relaxed he was, the more relaxed the chemicals would be, and the lower the buzz would be, until the noise could not be heard. When he could hardly hear the noise, he would be relaxed, and he should stay like that for a period of five minutes.

I gave him the machine and let him try it. During this time I explained techniques to relax his body to him, including deep breathing and muscle relaxation. While his fingers were lightly touching the machine, I directed him to put his feet firmly on the floor with his hands resting on his lap. I told him that he should let all his muscles

---

4 This discussion involved the use of Biofeedback to teach general relaxation only, and should not be confused with the recent use of EEG Biofeedback to treat ADHD children. EEG Biofeedback training assumes that ADHD children have less electrical activity in the areas of the brain which are responsible for inhibition and attention. There is some evidence that shows that children can be taught to increase their electrical activity and thus improve their symptoms; however, there has not been enough evidence to make this a widely-practiced technique.

relax and feel very heavy. Then, beginning with his toes, he should make each small muscle relax: first in his left foot with his large toe, then his other toes, then his arch, his heel, his calf, and his thigh, all while breathing very deeply, and listening to the buzz as it became softer and softer.

After repeating this process with his left foot and leg, we proceeded to the tips of his right fingers, up through the wrist, the forearm, and the upper arm, and then proceeded to have him relax his left fingers, hand, wrist, forearm, and upper arm. By this time the Biofeedback machine reflected a significant change in Benjamin's body. No longer was he fidgeting and giggling, and his eyes were partially closed. His body was almost completely relaxed.

Next I asked him to relax the large muscles in his body: the stomach, chest, shoulders, and finally the forehead, the facial muscles, and the neck, and to continue breathing deeply and feeling relaxed. I asked him to think of someplace pleasant he had been recently, either a trip, a place near his home, or a playground, and just to remain relaxed for five minutes.

When this five-minute period was up, I told him that I would like him to complete a ten-minute reading assignment for homework and that I would leave the room and return when he was done. I knew that Benjamin could work for ten minutes at a time if he were motivated to do so. I also knew that the reading material was interesting to him and was at his level. Had I asked him to concentrate for a longer time than he was able to do or to attempt material that was over his head, this experiment in the effects of relaxation would have surely failed. When I returned, Benjamin had completed the assignment and was drawing a picture. He seemed to still be relaxed and calm and said that he felt so good he was able to work more quickly than he usually did.

The object of this therapy was to teach Benjamin to relax enough so that he could maximize his ability to concentrate. We worked for ten sessions, using Biofeedback to get him into a relaxed state and then letting him work by himself, gradually increasing periods of time until he was able to work up to half an hour. During these ten sessions I also videotaped Benjamin working and spent time after each session reviewing the videotape with him and commenting on how well he paid attention to the work and how well he was able to sit and relax, helping him observe distracted him from his work.

As Benjamin learned to identify when he was in a distracted state, I taught him how to use the same relaxation techniques he had used with the Biofeedback machine to calm himself down and continue working. When Benjamin found that his attention was wandering and that he was doodling or daydreaming, he knew that these were signs that he was distracted; he would instruct himself to sit down, to relax, to turn over a three-minute timer, to try to achieve a state of concentration for those three minutes, and then go back to work.

It may be useful to review the therapeutic variables that made this particular program a success. First, there are a variety of general psychological principles that formed the structure of the program:

1. Relaxation constitutes a readiness state for focused concentration.
2. Relaxation can be taught as a conditioned response to specific external cues.
3. Children who are able to sit quietly and work are regarded as better students by their teachers than those who are more active (in spite of the fact that they may have the exact same knowledge and abilities on objective tests) and get *significantly more positive attention and praise from their teachers.*

Following the logical sequence of these principles, we can see how a relatively straightforward intervention can promote a behavioral change that, in turn, promotes a systems change that will potentially benefit the child's overall development. This is brief therapy at its best.

This type of program can work, however, only when the needs, abilities and interests of the child and the resources available in his or her environment are taken into account. The Biofeedback instrumentation interested Benjamin and made him feel that he was receiving special attention (his interest in gadgets influenced the selection of this technique). The teacher and parents were kept informed of Benjamin's progress: what motivated and what distracted him. They were encouraged to expect progress at a realistic rate and helped to support him without being demanding. Benjamin was reinforced for success within the treatment sessions, the classroom, and at home. The reinforcement was frequent and positive.

Increasing a child's attention span is a slow process. The videotape was used as feedback to help everyone concerned with the program recognize the progress being made. When ten sessions were done, Benjamin was given a certificate of achievement, specifying all that he had learned and emphasizing that now he could study for half an hour without supervision. I later learned that he had the certificate framed and hung over his desk at home.

Biofeedback was used to teach relaxation to Ernest, a schizophrenic 14-year-old boy who attended a private special education school for the moderately handicapped. Ernest, who was undergoing a variety of psychiatric treatments, was having particular trouble in his classroom because he was the scapegoat for some of the older, more aggressive boys. They would tease him about his various mannerisms, whereupon he would compulsively throw something or strike out. He would then be so upset at his own aggression that he would shake and cry and be unable to work for the rest of the day. His teacher wondered if Ernest could be desensitized to the teasing of his classmates, and he was assigned to a psychologist under my supervision.

The psychologist designed a program that would pair relaxation with increasingly potent stimuli. Ernest would first be exposed to pictures of the boys who had teased him and then he would be told to relax. Then he would be exposed to the words the boys taunted him with (spoken by the psychologist), then to audiotape recordings of the boys' voices, and finally he would be exposed to videotape recordings of them in the classroom. (Ironically, the boys who teased Ernest were interested in helping him and fully cooperated in providing the necessary material for the program.)

But we soon found out that Ernest had no concept of what it meant to be relaxed. He sat rigidly, his eyes fixed, clenching his fists until his arms and upper body started to shake. He was taught deep breathing and progressive relaxation, but he was still so out of touch with his body that he could hardly relax for even a minute. At this time we decided to try using Biofeedback with Ernest. We used an instrument similar to the one used with Benjamin; this time, however, we used visual rather than audio feedback since the buzz seemed to annoy Ernest. The visual feedback was simply a needle that registered higher when there was more agitation and lower when there was more relaxation.

Rather than try to teach Ernest to monitor his own behavior, as we had done with Benjamin, we followed a more classical conditioning approach in which Ernest was hooked up to the Biofeedback equipment throughout the desensitization training. When shown the stimulus (for example, a picture of the boys who had teased him), Ernest would tense up and react usually with some phrases like "I don't like them. They tease me. They're bad boys." Then he would be told to relax and watch the needle go down, at which time he would be instructed to remain in the relaxed state while watching the picture.

This conditioning went on for approximately a month with two sessions a week. The teacher kept a record of the number of teasing incidents as well as the number of Ernest's explosive outbursts. When Ernest was teased, the teacher simply said, "You can relax now, Ernest," and instructed him to sit down in a relaxed position and ignore the teasing. As Ernest learned to ignore the teasing, the boys predictably lost interest in this game and treated him more like an equal, enabling Ernest to have much more appropriate peer interaction.

Janet's case is an example that demonstrates use of more sophisticated Biofeedback instrumentation. Eighteen-year-old Janet was suffering from a number of problems, including not being able to get along with her parents, sporadic drug and alcohol abuse, poor school achievement, and migraine headaches. The headaches occurred two or three times a week, usually on school days. Janet was referred to a medical clinic that specialized in Biofeedback and treating migraine headaches. Using a photoplethysometer to measure the pulse of the temporal artery, Janet watched a meter that showed the amount of blood volume in each pulse beat. Janet was told that without moving any muscles, she was to try and alternately constrict and dilate this artery for ten-minute periods. Constriction would be indicated by a lower pulse rate and dilation by a higher one. The program consisted of four weeks of treatment, two sessions per week, during which time Janet was taught how to practice this technique at home, using her finger to detect her temporal pulse.

Janet was also taught total body relaxation techniques on the assumption that these could help reduce the general tension that can bring on the headaches. By the end of the month the number of her headaches had been cut in half and the duration of the remaining headaches cut by two thirds. Over the next few months it was noted that Janet was able to do more homework and her grades began to improve. The successful treatment of this one symptom was a major factor in convincing her that she could learn to cope with all her problems and she became a motivated participant in individual psychotherapy.

If Biofeedback is selected as the treatment of choice for a child or adolescent, care must then be taken that the form of Biofeedback is appropriate. All four of the major Biofeedback modalities—GSR, TEMP, EEG, and EMG—can be used in reducing general tension; however, EMG Biofeedback may be the most accurate way to reduce specific stress since it can measure the tension in individualized muscle groups which vary from patient to patient.

TEMP modality may be most useful in the treatment of stress reactions where the patient is primarily manifesting visceral tension (certain types of cardiac arrhythmia, migraines, ulcers, colitis, diarrhea, and so forth); use of EMG feedback may be most useful when tension is manifested by external signs, such as bruxism (teeth grinding). Although there is more methodological controversy in using EEG Biofeedback, this still may be the method of choice when addressing problems associated with mental states such as sleep disorders, study problems, and severe anxiety disorders.

CHAPTER 4

THE BEHAVIORAL MODALITY

Most therapists working with children and adolescents will be more familiar with behavioral techniques than techniques in any other modality. Behavioral techniques are often the simplest to implement and yet, in my opinion, are also the techniques that fail most frequently. Too often in my work, I suggest a simple behavioral technique to a teacher or a parent and get the response, "Oh, I already tried that. It didn't work."

Although I try to refrain from being critical and making the person with whom I am consulting feel like a failure, in nine out of ten cases, I am sure it is not that the technique doesn't work, but that it wasn't administered properly. Behavioral techniques *don't* work when the principles behind them are not followed correctly or there are inconsistencies in carrying out the program. Sometimes I feel it is best to try a new approach altogether and teach the correct behavioral techniques for that approach more thoroughly so that I know it will be administered correctly. Other times I feel the failed approach was the correct one and I will help the adults I am working with to find out what went wrong.

I often use what I call "the salad dressing analogy." Research has found that people who go on a low-calorie diet often don't realize that they are taking in many more calories than they want to. The most common culprit is salad, very healthy and low in calories, but just as high in calories and fat as many types of fast food when dressing, croutons, cheese, are added. Dieters *feel* like they are dieting because they eat so many salads, but they are undermining their own best intentions. Eventually they see that they are not losing any weight, become discouraged, and go back to even unhealthier ways of eating.

So it goes with many behavioral programs. The adults *feel* like they are doing something different with the child, but they are unintentionally undermining themselves. Take for example the child who is earning tokens to go out for ice cream at the end of the week with his father. But it's a gruelingly hot day, and Dad is driving by the ice cream parlor, and he really would like some ice cream for himself, and so he says, "Why don't we give you the treat a little early this week? I am sure you are going to get your points, anyway. Let's stop and get some ice cream right now! But we won't tell Mom, okay? And then maybe you'll get ice cream twice!"

The father's conspiracy with his son is well-intentioned and to him, it seems only a very minor deviation from the behavioral program. He feels closer to his son, because they now have this little secret between them, and since he mentioned the behavioral program and expressed faith in his son's changing his behavior, he has done a good job all around. But the net effect of this stop for ice cream is to undermine the behavioral program entirely. The father broke every rule of the program himself, and ironically the behavior that the program was addressing with the child was...learning to follow rules!

Behavioral techniques, like other techniques in a short-term therapy program, must be selected judiciously (see Figure 2.B, *Selecting Techniques in Multi-Modal Therapy*). Once selected, they must be taught thoroughly and preferably rehearsed in front of the therapist or using a video camera. The rules and principles of the program must be carefully explained and presented to parents in ways that they are likely to remember. I particularly like simple rules that parents can remember easily or that define the program with a simple mnemonic. For example, there are two basic rules for using the time-out procedure:

> 1. Place a child in time-out for a period of time equal to one minute for each year of his or her age.

> 2. When placing a child in time-out, always choose a neutral nonstimulating place, and lead him or her to the time-out place within 60 seconds of the behavioral infraction, speaking six words or less.

Or, there is the "4:1 Rule" for behavioral shaping. Every time a child does something wrong and should be corrected, the adult should find four positive things that the child does or says which should be praised. The parent is much more likely to respond and act appropriately using the rule as a mnemonic, than if the therapist simply said, "I want you to look for more times when Mary acts appropriately and reinforce that behavior."

To be effective, behavioral techniques frequently take more time and energy than techniques in other modalities. As previously discussed, additional time and energy (whether expended by the child or the significant others in the child's life) is intrusive; it is incumbent on the therapist to make sure that this intrusiveness is justified by positive change. The techniques herein are ranked by intrusiveness: my sense of how much energy is required to carry out the technique effectively and how disruptive the technique will be to a child's life.

Prosocial Learning

Perhaps one of the simplest and most overlooked behavioral strategies is *teaching children to be good,* rather than preventing them from being bad. Many times therapists advise parents to reward good behavior, and yet there is no good behavior to reward! We tell parents not to dwell on the negative, and yet there is no positive in dealing with the child. My advice to parents is to teach children to behave in *exemplary* ways. Then, addressing the confused look on their faces, I explain that today's parents rarely ask children to stretch themselves in terms of altruistic and charitable behaviors. Rather than exclusively focusing on one child's being rude or another child's not doing homework, why not take at least as much time helping these children do things that will make everyone, including themselves, feel wonderful?

I recommend three books: *Kid's Random Acts of Kindness* (Conari Press, 1993), *The Helping Hands Handbook* (Random House, 1992), and *The Kid's Guide to Social Responsibility* (Barbara Lewis, Free Spirit Publishing, 1991). Each of these books suggests ways which kids can help others (e.g., reading books to people at a nursing home); help the environment (e.g., collecting cans for money and then giving the money to the National Wildlife Fund); or even change society for the better (e.g., writing letters to Congress; circulating petitions). Some churches urge their congregations to give 10 percent of their income to charity. I think children should spend 10 percent of the time that they would normally watch TV doing something for others. Since the average child in the US watches 24 hours of television a week, this is only about 2-1/2 hours that they will spend doing a selfless task.

There are many reasons why I advocate teaching prosocial behaviors as part of a short-term therapy plan. First, teaching prosocial behaviors redirects adults from the problem behavior (which is undoubtedly resistant to change) and towards a behavior that can be accomplished fairly easily. It is always easier to teach a new positive behavior than to extinguish a negative one. Secondly, it changes the child's system and can have important side effects for other family members. Maybe one or both parents will get involved in a cause as well, increasing their own self-esteem and distracting them from the problems of their child. And most importantly, the child will build a *platform* for his or her self-esteem. Every week will be filled with experiences that will inevitably make children feel good about themselves. In addition, adults will sincerely praise and appreciate the children for their good works. And, as the song goes, "the world will be a better place for you and me."

Assertiveness Training

Another teaching technique which can help children improve their behavior is assertiveness training. Assertiveness training is another indirect way of getting children to address their behavior problems. Assertiveness training does not just involve sticking up for your rights (although this is certainly important); it is defined more broadly in terms of getting what you need. And of course assertiveness training is always taught in a social context that respects the rights and needs of others. Assertiveness training assumes that a child's misbehavior is directed at meeting some need. The training, which involves the teaching of specific assertive skills, teaches the child to fulfill those needs in a more socially appropriate and functional way.

Sam, a learning disabled eleven-year-old from a broken home, was also overweight. Sam was not doing well at school, rarely completing his classroom work or his homework, and his teacher described him as "silly and inappropriate" in class. From Sam's point of view, his biggest problem was the fact that other children teased him about his weight problem. Although he was certainly aware that the adults were concerned about his learning and his behavior, to Sam, the teasing of his peers was what determined whether he would be happy or miserable on any given day. Since this teasing was Sam's overriding concern, it made sense that it was where his treatment plan should start.

I made a list of the assertiveness techniques that I thought were appropriate for a child Sam's age, and typed out each technique on a 5 x 8" card. The techniques were:

Broken Record: When you are sure you know what you want, just say it over and over again, like when a broken record.

Gentle Firmness: When you believe in something, be firm, but be polite as well. Say things like: "I'm sorry that you feel that way, but I have to do what *I* feel is right."

Be Patient: There is an expression "all things come to those who wait." Decide what it is that you want and decide that it is worth waiting for.

Stay Calm: Don't get rattled. Take slow deep breaths to help you stay calm.

Be Sincere and Serious: Don't let someone make a joke out of something that isn't funny.

Be Kind and Understanding Towards Others: Most people will treat you well when you are thoughtful and considerate.

Be Direct: Speak clearly and be clear about what you want.

Use Your Imagination: If there is something you want or need, think of a variety of ways to get it.

We began the assertiveness training by going over all the cards, applying them to Sam's being teased as well as to other situations where it might be important for Sam to be assertive. After discussing these techniques at some length, we took another set of 5 x 8" cards and Sam dictated exact scenarios of situations in which he could be more assertive when his classmates teased him. Sam was very animated during this time. Of course he was angry and hurt about the way he had been treated, and he started to go off on tangents about how he would hurt this child or burn that child's house down. But I redirected Sam to the task at hand: learning *new behaviors* which really could change his situation. His fantasies, which another therapist might have wished to explore, were counter-productive; the problem that Sam was encountering needed to be solved in the real world, not an imaginary one.

At the next session, we took the 10 scenarios out again, and I had Sam match one or more of the assertiveness cards to each scenario. We then role-played two or three scenes, first with me playing the "assertive Sam" and Sam the "teasers" and then we switched roles. After some practice we videotaped the scenes, edited them, and I sent them home for Sam to watch (see Video Therapy, Chapter 7).

We practiced these assertive techniques for three or four more sessions, and during the course of therapy, Sam reported a few instances of actually using them to deal with the teasing. But I was more struck with Sam's other behavioral changes. His mother reported that he was more cooperative at home. His teacher reported that he was doing more work at school. And naturally, I advised them on ways to reinforce these improved behaviors.

Nearly two years later, Sam asked his mother to allow him to see me again on an unrelated problem that he was having. I was struck by how much Sam had changed in those two years. He had slimmed down, gone through puberty, and he carried himself and spoke with an air of confidence befitting a young teenager. I asked him what he remembered from our earlier meetings, and he told me that he most remembered the assertiveness training. He still had the videotape, and he said with a smile, "I was kind of 'dorky' then."

Teaching Good Behavior Through Games

Games provide a unique opportunity to work on behavioral problems, because they can provide "corrective experiences" for children which can then be immediately reinforced. Certain behaviors are required to play any game: taking turns, following the rules, being a good sport, and so on. Some games, however, are specifically designed to deal with behavioral issues, both on content and process levels. *The Classroom Behavior Game* (The Center for Applied Psychology, Inc.) is a good example of how a game can be used both to teach behavioral principles and transfer those principles to the real world. Players earn points playing the game by answering questions about common classroom behavioral issues, for example: raising your hand to ask a question, waiting your turn, listening to directions, and so on. Also included in the game is a behavioral chart which can be affixed to the student's desk, who can then continue to win more points by demonstrating positive behaviors in the actual classroom.

The best games to teach behavior require a child to exhibit a new behavior as part of the game. Often when I am meeting with a child and parent for the first time and the child's behavior is the presenting issue, I like to demonstrate the power of games to help make children behave more appropriately at home. I say to the parent, "I'm going to teach you a game that will make your child behave *exactly* as you wish when you play it, without punishments or threats. Just tell me what you would like your child (let's call him Marty) to do, and I will show you how to get Marty to do it without fuss."

Usually the parent is puzzled by this invitation and the child is waiting in anticipation. I then repeat to the parent, "Just tell me something you want Marty to do, right now in this office, and I'll show you how he will do it and have fun too!" With this, I give Marty a collaborative wink, for I am winning him over to my side. He is going to do something which will surprise his mother, and I have told him already that it will be fun.

I then ask Marty if he has played the game "Simon Says."

> Marty: Sure, I guess so.
>
> Dr. S: Well, this is played the same way, except it is called Dr. Shapiro Says, or if your Mom plays it with you, it would

be called Mommy Says. Okay?

Marty: Okay.

Dr. S: Good! Now, Dr. Shapiro says, Put your hand on your head. (He does.) Now, put it down. (He doesn't.) Good! I can see that you are going to be good at this! Dr. Shapiro says stand on one foot. Now put that foot down. (He does not.) Good again! Now, put it down. (He doesn't.) Dr. Shapiro says, put your foot down. (He does.)

We typically go on like this for a few minutes, and almost invariably the child gets caught up in the game. Then I turn to the parent and say, "Now did you think of something you want Marty to do?"

Mom: Well, he doesn't clean up his room at home. I would like him to do that once in a while.

Dr. S: That's easy. Here, I'll mess up my office a little (I take a few toys and throw them around the room. This usually gets me a laugh or two). Now let's play some more. Marty, Dr. Shapiro says, touch your nose. (He does.) Touch your ear. (He doesn't). Hop! (He doesn't.) Dr. Shapiro says, would you pick up that ball next to you and hand it to me? (Marty does so without hesitation.) Thank you. Dr. Shapiro says would you pick up that checker over in the corner and hand it to me? (He does, stealing a glance back at his mother, who remains speechless). Very good!

And so on. Within a five-minute period, Marty will have picked up the mess that I made, and feel very pleased with himself for doing so. Very few children play this game incorrectly. It is my belief that most children *want* to be good, but we must frame opportunities in which being good is the easiest choice to make. Once they begin on this road, it is hard to stop, as I show my pleasure at their cooperation and their parents sit amazed at seeing this side of their difficult child.

The next step, of course, is to get Marty's mother to play the same game, but whether or not to attempt this yet takes clinical judgment. Most children will play as well with their parents as with me, but children who are very defiant will wait for this opportunity to show the parent and me who is really the boss. If I mistakenly ask a parent and child to play this game before the child is ready to cooperate, and the child starts to show off or be uncooperative, then I just stop, saying,

You know a game is only fun when the rules are followed. I

can see that you don't like the rules when your mother or
father play this game, so we will see if there is another game
at another time that you might like to play with your parents. In the meantime, since my office is a mess anyway,
and I made the mess, I will play Mommy Says with your
mother, and let her help me clean up the room.

Usually this salvages the session. The parent still has a chance to
exert his or her power, and it is clear that the child is making a choice
about being cooperative. Another game might now be played which
can give the child the *experience* of appropriate behavior. My next
choice of a game might be a treasure hunting game, where the child
has to search for treasure clues while cleaning a room. A clue can
only be given when a particular area has been cleaned and the treasure must be something that the child will value. The treasure can
only be won if the entire room is cleaned and all the clues are
answered correctly!

Token Economies and Response Cost Systems

There are many behavioral programs that are commonly used with
children, from positive reinforcement, to natural consequences, to
time-out. When matching a behavioral program to a particular child,
one must consider the current discipline style of the parents, the parents' ability to administer a new program consistently, the severity of
the behavioral problem, and of course the age level and cooperation of
the child.

In my own work, I find that a token economy combined with a
response cost system is the most widely applicable and effective
behavioral program. A token economy system involves winning
points or tokens for specific behaviors designated as important. The
behaviors must be very specific, observable, and the expectations for
change must be reasonable. It is unreasonable, for example, to expect
a child who didn't do his homework all semester to suddenly do 45
minutes of homework five nights a week. It would be more reasonable to expect this child to do 15 minutes of homework a night for all
five nights, building up the habit of doing homework in small incre-
ments.

While a token economy system which gives rewards for positive
behavior is often effective, it can be undermined if a child's misbehavior is extremely entrenched or has significant dysfunctional rewards
(e.g., stealing is valued by the child's peers). With this in mind, I typ-

ically use games of all types to help the child win chips which can be added to a token economy chart.

For example, suppose a child has five goals to work on as shown in Figure 4.A:

Figure 4.A
Token Economy Chart

	M	Tu	W	Th	F	Sa	Su	Total
Doing homework								
Being polite								
Doing chores on time								
Not teasing the baby								
Showing good table manners								
							Total	

Each night the program is reviewed, and the child gets 1 point for an attempt at each goal, 3 points for mostly completing the goal, and 5 points for completing the goal perfectly. It is possible for the child to earn 25 points a day for 7 days, or 175 points for the week of the program. If a child gets 175 points he or she wins a prize, perhaps a meal at a fast-food restaurant (I prefer activities as prizes, rather than physical objects. Ideally a reward menu should be presented to the child, and he or she can choose prizes each week). Needless to say, it is unlikely that the child will get a perfect score and win a prize, *but* if we add in tokens that can be won during a game, for example *The Good Behavior Game* (see *The Book of Psychotherapeutic Games*, Shapiro, 1993), then the child is very likely to win the needed points *because he or she can create positive experiences in order to win points.*

Usually after a week or two of using the token economy and game approach during which the child almost always wins a prize, I see whether or not the behaviors are changing fast enough. I look at the pattern of how each behavior is changing and the percentage of points won in the game versus the real-world behavioral program. If I think that the child is not cooperating enough, I then add a response cost element to the game. I say to the child with the parent present,

I am glad that you are winning points and getting your rewards, but of course the reason we are doing this is to improve your behavior. Improving your behavior is very important to your parents and that is why you are here with them and why they pay me to help you. So to do my job a little better, I am going to add another part to your token economy chart. You can still win points by meeting your goals and playing these games, but if you do negative behaviors, then we will take points away. For a small infraction of the rules, your parents will take away 1 point; for a more serious infraction of the rules, they will take away 3 points; and for a very serious infraction of the rules they will take away 5 points.

Certain types of children (for example ADHD children) seem to respond much better to a system that both punishes and rewards. In these cases, I introduce the response cost part of this behavioral program in the beginning, since I know that it is likely to work better.

Although it is difficult to put in place, one of the most effective token economy-response cost systems involves the use of TV and video games as rewards and punishment. Using this system, each point translates into five minutes of TV watching or video game playing time. In the previous example, the child can win 175 points a

Figure 4.B
Token Economy Plus Game Chart

	M	Tu	W	Th	F	Sa	Su	Total
Doing homework								
Being polite								
Doing chores on time								
Not teasing the baby								
Showing good table manners								
Points (chips) won at games								
Totals								

week, which translates into just over 14-1/2 hours of TV/video game time, about two hours a day. This may seem like a lot, but the average child sits in front of the TV 24 hours a week, which in my opinion is far too much. As simple as this program is, I often find that controlling TV habits in a family is very difficult. Who monitors the TV when the parents aren't around? What if the parents watch TV all the time, do they lock the child out of the room? I have found an excellent solution to this problem: the Homework Helper (made by Mindbenders, Inc.). Homework Helper is actually a TV manager which connects the TV and the electrical socket. It can be programmed by the parent and then locked so that the child must enter a passcode to watch TV or play a video game. Once the child's allowance of TV time is used up, the TV shuts itself off. As the child wins more points, more TV time can be added to allowance. This simple aid can help a family not only

Figure 4.C
Token Economy and Response Cost Chart

	M	Tu	W	Th	F	Sa	Su	Total
	+ -	+ -	+ -	+ -	+ -	+ -	+ -	
Doing homework								
Being polite								
Doing chores on time								
Not teasing the baby								
Showing good table manners								
Points Won at Games								
Totals								

implement an effective behavioral program, but prevent children from spending too much time in front of the TV as well, which in itself may be an important therapeutic intervention.

It may be helpful to use one of these three types of token economy systems with the entire family, rather than just an individual child. I generally prefer to use a token economy system with games with a family, because introducing the concept of response costs to a family can sometimes create more problems than it solves. In this case, family member has his or her own chart (see Figure 4.B). Each member can be working towards an individual reward and be simultaneously working towards a family reward.

For example, a child can be accumulating points to win a trip to a movie on Saturday with a friend. He or she gets the 150 points needed to win this reward and so goes to the movie. But these l50 points are also pooled with 100 points won by his mother, 125 points won by his little brother, and 75 points won by his father, all of whom are working on goals important to them. The family needs 500 points to take a day and go to the amusement park together, a reward that they mutually agreed upon.

MULTIPLE BEHAVIORAL PROGRAMMING WITH THE DEVELOPMENTALLY DISABLED

This section of this chapter is a discussion of two behavior programs I developed for developmentally disabled adolescents. When most people think of short-term therapy techniques, they think of the most common problems therapists see, rather than the problems which are chronic or which may be common to highly problematic populations. However, during my career, I have spent a significant amount of time working with complex cases of children with multiple behavioral problems and a variety of handicapping conditions as well. With these children and adolescents I have often implemented short-term programs which have had a profound effect on the quality of their lives. For many reasons, therapists do not tend to treat this population, and I think that this is an unfortunate circumstance.

The children and adolescents commonly found in self-contained classrooms, group homes, residential schools, and even state-run institutions, rarely respond to traditional play therapy techniques, but this certainly shouldn't eliminate them as candidates for therapy. Although these children and adolescents may have difficult or even bizarre behaviors which challenge the therapist's imagination, other positive factors make them very appropriate candidates for short-term therapeutic interventions. Most of the time, they live or go to school in a very controlled environment. There is usually a high staff-to-client ratio, and the staff is almost always very motivated to help with the therapeutic program, since any improvement in the client's behavior will make their lives that much easier.

Secondly, a little success means a lot. Helping a child behave more appropriately in public so that he or she can go out on community outings makes a world of difference. Once I worked with a moderately retarded young woman who had been confined to her bed for five years because of her weight problem and mild aggressiveness. The staff at this state-run hospital had lost her wheelchair and decided it was easier to just let her stay in bed. In three days, I had this woman wheeling herself the 100 yards to the activity room. A simple program, which took five hours of my time, changed this woman's life.

In writing about the clients in the rest of this chapter, it is my sincere hope that some therapists, particularly those in private practice, will consider the rewards of working with these forgotten children and teens. In presenting these programs, I will assume that the reader has a working knowledge of basic behavioral principles as well as some practical experience. Before I begin, however, I will review some basic tenets of working with severe behavioral problems.

Working with Severe Behavioral Problems

In working with children with severe behavioral problems, it is helpful to consider the following points:

Keep Accurate Data. Behavior modification was developed in accordance with the principles of empirical scientific investigation, and removed from this means of support it becomes a house without a foundation. Behavioral programs need to be based on objective data from beginning to end, and the data should be able to pass at least minimal criteria for reliability and validity. The most common errors in data collection include: no baseline data is taken before the program begins; the targeted behavior is not the one being measured; the behavior that is being measured is not operationally defined; the measurement of the behavior is so difficult or awkward that it is eventually given up; there is no postprogram measurement to see if the behavior is being maintained.

The Design of the Program Should Be Simple and Comprehensible. The person who designs the behavioral program for severe behavioral problems is rarely the one who carries it out. Usually programs are written by psychologists, but carried out by parents, teachers, and a variety of paraprofessionals. Unfortunately, this situation provides many opportunities for miscommunication which can undermine the entire program before it gets underway. To avoid this the written program should be brief and concise, and the concept behind the program should be clearly explained. If the person who designs the program neglects to consider the strengths and weaknesses of those who will implement it, he can find himself with a very pretty flying machine that won't get off the ground.

The Persons Who Design the Program and Implement It Must Work Together. The prototype for the relationship between the person who writes the behavioral program and those who carry it out is that of architect and builders. One cannot work without the other. In the best and most effective behavioral programs, there is a spirit of cooperation and camaraderie founded in a mutual commitment to help the child. There is no place in a successful program for elitism or competition.

The Behavioral Program Must Be Flexible and Yet Consistent. Even the most thoroughly planned program is still largely an experiment. Situations change rapidly, and there is always something new for the therapist to consider. But being flexible with a program is not synonymous with being inconsistent. Use of alternative techniques will invariably need to be considered in the course of implementing a behavioral program, but changes should only be made when they are consistent with the basic principles of the therapeutic program, when they reflect a logical interpretation of the data, and when they are consonant with the subjective experience of the people responsible for implementing the program.

Problems with the Program Should Be Anticipated. Sometimes behavioral programs don't work, or don't work to the extent anticipated. There are many reasons for this and finding them out may be the greatest challenge of the program. In designing the program, the therapist must consider all the variables that can help it succeed and all those that can impede it. He or she should use these variables to set the criteria for changes and for the eventual termination of the program. But if the criteria are not met in a specified amount of time, the therapist should be ready with previously discussed alternatives. Planning alternatives, however, is very different than planning for failure. As discussed later in this chapter in the case of Ronnie M., it involves careful consideration of the potential for change of both the client and his or her environment.

These reminders are true for all behavioral programs, but they are particularly important when working with the multi- and complexly handicapped child or adolescent. Although these clients represent a very small percentage of the number of children with psychological disorders, they have become a particular concern to psychologists over the last few years due to the nationwide trend toward deinstitutionalization and increasing fears about the adverse effects of psychotropic medications. As a result, public and private institutions, parents, advocacy groups, and even the judicial system are looking to psychologists for help.

As more severely handicapped youngsters and adults are placed in community settings, they naturally have a wide variety of adjustment problems. Some learn to live in small group homes and commute to a school or sheltered employment in just a few weeks. But others have severe behavioral problems which, although tolerated and manageable in an institutional environment, are unacceptable in a community setting. These problems include self-abuse, excessive self-stimulation, aggressiveness toward others, pica, bedwetting and soiling, and a wide variety of idiosyncratic habits and mannerisms that make these clients difficult to teach and to live with.

Particularly challenging to the therapist are the intricate psychological, social, and ethical issues that must be considered when working with the multi-handicapped client. Aside from having multiple behavioral problems, many are nonverbal and may perform below a three- or even a two-year-old level according to standardized intellectual tests. If their behavioral problems have been severe, they may have suffered from institutional neglect or outright abuse, and probably will have been exposed to a variety of medications designed to calm them down, some of which may have done more harm than good.

In addition, these clients are often referred to the therapist in a time of crisis as were two cases I will discuss in the following paragraphs. Their community placements, chances for education, and job training may be threatened, as in the case of Mary S., or they may present an immediate danger to themselves or others, as in the case of Ronnie M. In every example, there are compassionate adults who care deeply about the well-being of the client. But if they are the parents, they will be emotionally exhausted from a mixture of fear, guilt, anger, and frustration. And if they are the front-line workers, who care for and train the client, they will be underpaid, overworked, and feel unappreciated.

This is the typical situation in which the therapist is called upon to set things right, and to succeed, he or she must come up with an innovative approach. To be innovative, however, the treatment program will have to be more than just new. It must also be fresh and creative. It must be built on sound behavioral principles, but at the same time be responsive to the human needs of the client who is to be served. The truly innovative program is not bound by traditional thinking, but rather derives its ingenuity and originality from careful observation of the client's individual personality and style.

Innovative therapists do not settle for the obvious, nor are they complacent in regard to the needs and rights of the child beyond the immediate problem. They seek positive approaches to militate a change in the child's behavior, preferring to reward new behaviors rather than punish old ones, build self-esteem, and stimulate compassion and caring in the child's life.

The following two cases were selected for their complex and serious natures and to demonstrate the importance an innovative spirit as well as technique had on their resolutions.

Treating an Adolescent with Multi-Behavior Problems in a Crisis Situation

Mary S. was a moderately retarded adolescent who when I met her, had lived the most recent 10 years of her life in a state institution. At 17, she was part of a large group of children and adults placed in community settings under a court order. Although the motives behind the court-ordered deinstitutionalization were humane and correct, its implementation was short-sighted. The primary problem was that the court assumed that the same agency that had done an inadequate job educating and caring for these clients for so many years could now take up the more difficult task of finding community placements and handling the problems that were bound to occur. As a result, the deinstitutionalization process had become a disaster for many clients: Mary S. was a case in point.

When I met Mary, she was temporarily living with her parents, having spent less than four months in her assigned group home where they felt that they could no longer put up with her problem behaviors. After she was expelled from her community placement, the state agency responsible for her education and care wanted her to return to their facility, in spite of the deinstitutionalization order, deciding that she was not yet ready for normalization. Mary's parents, on the other hand, felt strongly that she should not be returned to a facility which had been continually accused of inadequate programming for its clients, and certainly there was no reason to think that they would prepare Mary any better for life outside the institution a second time around. The two major goals of Mary's treatment were to make her time at home productive for Mary and tolerable to her parents and to prepare her to move into a new group home as soon as one became available.

The most extraordinary thing that first struck me about Mary was the long laundry list of complaints about her. In the initial interview in her parents' living room, at which Mary was present, rocking and mumbling to herself, her mother listed her immediate problems as: echolalia; pacing; an inability to stay with a group of her peers (this was the primary cause of her dismissal from the group home); foraging for food; unrestrained eating habits (gobbling up foods almost to the point of choking, which in turn caused obesity); mild aggressiveness in the form of pushing and charging at people who were in her way; picking at her skin, particularly around the mouth and on the legs; verbal and nonverbal self-stimulation (i.e., yelling nonsense words, repeating phrases or single words in a sing-song voice, rocking back and forth and running in circles); a variety of ritualistic habits, such as making and unmaking the bed, or turning all the food on the shelf so that the labels pointed one way; getting up early in the morning and roaming around; and general obstinacy.

Mary's parents were gentle people in their late fifties. Although they had visited Mary every weekend while she was in the institution, they did not feel prepared to keep her at home except for a limited amount of time, and yet they could not bear the thought of her going back to the state institution. The question was more where to start than what to do, so I sat down with Mary's mother and we came up with a prioritized list of her problems. Her constant picking at her skin was problem number one.

Facial Picking

We began with a program to stop Mary picking at her skin because it was the most irritating behavior to Mary's parents, because it had health implications, and because it detracted so much from Mary's appearance. She picked at her face constantly, presumably out of boredom and habit, unless told to stop. She had large welts around her mouth, swollen lips, and frequently infected sores.

In deciding which symptom to treat first in such a complicated case, I had to choose one that was significant and a good chance for immediate success. This was not only to demonstrate that behavioral programs could work, in itself important, but also to give momentum to the complex job of improving the quality of life for Mary and her parents.

Considering all of Mary's behaviors, her skin picking seemed to be one of the easiest to change. The behavior itself was discrete, and its effects were clearly discernible. From the initial interview with Mary's mother, I knew that this particular behavior came and went, suggesting that it was not completely intractable (as compared to her echolalia, which was always present and remained at about the same level). In addition I observed that Mary already had developed some control over her picking. During our first interview Mary raised her hand to her mouth several times, and her mother was able to prevent her from picking by an admonishment or even just a raised eyebrow. This told me that Mary could interrupt the behavioral chain of the habit, and that she was willing to do so with only a minimal cue to please her mother.

The Program. The program we used was a modified form of habit control suggested by Azrin and Nunn in *Habit Control in a Day* (1977). The primary elements of the program were as follows. When Mary picked at her face, her mother or father were to say "No, Mary" in a loud voice and sit her down in a chair for five minutes time-out. During this time Mary was to put on plastic dishwashing gloves. At the end of five minutes, Mary was verbally praised for cooperating and for being patient, and was then given lotion to put on her hands and legs (which were also frequently scratched) and a medicated cream for her lips. Again Mary was praised for her good behavior, and for this appropriate way of taking care of her body) while deriving tactile stimulation). Finally, Mary was told to repeat the words "no picking," which, because of her perseverative echolalia, she did several times.

Principles. The principles of this technique worked because they were simple and straightforward. Breaking the process down, there were four behavioral tenets being applied:

> *Contingency Management.* The behavior of skin pick-ing was not reinforced as it had been in the past. Time-out was used as a neutral response to the behav-ior; putting on the gloves was a mildly aversive response.

> *Symptom Substitution.* Azrin and Nunn (1977) suggest that to break a habit you must substitute another habit that fulfills the same basic psychological and physio-logical needs, but in a more socially appropriate way. Using hand cream, facial cream, and lip balm is cer-tainly more appropriate than picking at one's skin, yet

involves essentially the same areas of the body and the same motions, and can be done frequently during the day without harm.

Positive Reinforcement.   Positive attention for new, appropriate behaviors can never be overdone. In this case, it focused Mary and her parents on her successful achievements and helped build her self-esteem.

Symptom Competition.   Telling Mary to repeat the words "no picking" was an experimental use of Mary's echolalia as a cognitive mediating technique (see Chapter 5). Echolalia and other common perseverative uses of language are common in moderate and severely handicapped individuals, and there are several theories about their origin and purpose. It has frequently been observed that echolalia can be a form of self-control and might serve some adaptive purpose.

In Mary's case I speculated that the repetition of the phrase "no picking" might have some inhibitory effect on the action itself. This use of one symptom or habit to counteract or compete with a more serious one can be extremely effective when used judiciously. The second symptom must be carefully selected as one that later will not become more maladaptive than the first, and must be a behavior which can be tolerated, even valued, as part of who the client is.

Data Collection. Measuring two variables in the primary behavioral program provides the therapist with the most information about the effectiveness of the program. One should show an increase in positive behaviors, and the other should reflect a decrease in the maladaptive ones.

The positive outcome in this case was Mary's clearer complexion. I asked her father to record this change by taking a Polaroid picture of his daughter's face every morning for 10 days and counting the number of discernible marks. This method of data collection took less than a minute a day and truly measured the effects of the program. In addition, it was a satisfying way for Mr. S. to interact with his daughter and to provide her with feedback on her appearance.

At the same time I measured the decrease in the targeted behavior by asking Mary's mother to mark on a 3 X 5" card the times of the day that the behavioral program was administered. This measure corresponded to the number of times that Mary was observed picking her skin and gave me a clearer picture of the relationship of the program to the actual improvement in Mary's appearance. It was expected that these two measures would be highly correlated: the less frequently the habit control program was administered, the fewer marks Mary would have on her face. These measures could have been related in other ways as well. If, for instance, the number of marks on Mary's face stayed high, yet the number of times that picking was observed began to diminish, then we would assume that the picking was being done at night or in private, and that the present program was ineffective. If, on the other hand, Mary's face began to clear, but the number of times she was seen picking stayed the same or even increased, then we might assume that while some aspect of the program was working, Mary was using this behavior largely to get attention.

The data supported the effectiveness and success of the program (see Figure 4.A). Within 10 days, Mary's complexion had almost completely cleared, and her mother said that "the problem was solved."

I stated things a little differently: "A good technique has been found." I cautioned Mrs. S. that the majority of behavioral problems of the multi-handicapped come and go; only a few stay away. What is important is that we know how to treat them when they appear, and can almost immediately diminish their quality and quantity.

Stubbornness

Mary liked to do things when and only when she was in the mood, and because of her size and slightly belligerent nature, few people were ready to argue with her. I wasn't sure just how her stubbornness had been dealt with in the state institution, but in putting together bits of information, I concluded that not too much had been expected of her, and if she were in an obstinate mood, then she was just left alone to brood, make perseverative noises, rock, pace, or perform one of her ritualistic behaviors.

In her former group home these behaviors isolated Mary from the other clients and antagonized the staff. In spite of their patient efforts, they could not get Mary to leave her bedroom and had to leave a much-needed staff member behind with her. It was this strain on their staff resources which finally made the situation intolerable. At home Mary was so willful that her parents were afraid to take her out of the house for fear that she would run away (which she had done on several occasions) or cause an embarrassing scene.

On the surface, Mary's stubborn and recalcitrant behaviors may not have appeared too bad. She was petulant and threw childish tantrums, but she really didn't hurt herself or anyone else. But if we

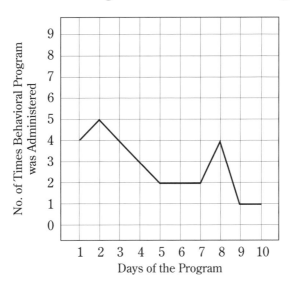

Figure 4.D
Data Showing Decrease in Face-Picking

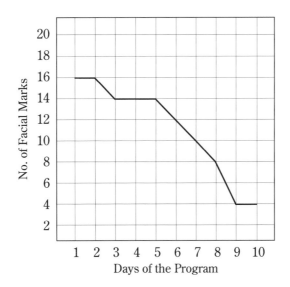

looked just below the surface we could see how her stubbornness had catapulted her into a crisis situation, where she couldn't move forward or backward. She was isolated and unstimulated: a prisoner in her own home. Decreasing her stubbornness became the focus of her treatment plan.

The Program. To decrease Mary's stubbornness and increase her cooperativeness, I used a simple contingency management technique, rewarding positive behaviors on a fixed schedule and taking away rewards when she refused to cooperate.

To begin, Mary was given a small notebook with an attractive cover. Each page was to be used for a half-hour interval, in which time Mary could earn three Happy Faces for cooperative behaviors. However, if she showed any uncooperative behaviors at all, then she would have the smile of one Happy Face turned into a frown, or if no Happy Face had been earned, she would get a Sad Face drawn into her notebook. The program was to run from nine in the morning to nine at night and was administered solely by her mother. Mary's rewards for good behavior were desserts at lunch and dinner. If she had earned nine out of a possible twelve Happy Faces before then, she was able to win a dessert, which she looked forward to with great relish.

When Mary was given a Happy Face, her mother was to say, "Good girl. You've been very cooperative doing (whatever the task was). I'm very proud of you." When Mary was given a Sad Face however, her mother was to raise her voice and say, "No, that (the name of the behavior) is not good behavior. I will count to 10 and if you do not stop by then, you will get a Sad Face, and if you get four Sad Faces, then you will not get dessert." If Mary did not stop her behavior by the count of 10, then her mother entered the Sad Face in the notebook, and took Mary by the arm and led her to a chair where she had to sit for three minutes of "time-out." If Mary were already sitting (usually on the stairs), she still had to get up and sit in a chair.

To administer this program only in Mary's home would probably have been the simplest strategy, but it would have confined the behavioral changes to an artificial situation. Mary didn't belong at a home with her parents any longer; her appropriate placement was in a community-based group home with four or five of her peers. Mary's behavior could only be judged in community settings, so twice a week when I visited Mary in her home, we went on community outings: to the drugstore, to restaurants, to the grocery store, and so on. I encouraged Mary's parents to take her on similar daily outings as well.

As we had anticipated, Mary's behavior was less than ideal, but with each experience I learned more about how to anticipate her reactions. The first time we went out, within moments of our leaving the car, Mary dove for a trash can and started rummaging through it. Her parents, confused and embarrassed, watched her until I took her by the hand and forcefully led her away. I immediately reminded her, "No! That is not good behavior. You must walk away right now or you will get a Sad Face" and I counted to 10. Since Mary would not walk away on her own, I entered a Sad Face in her book and reminded her that if she got three more Sad Faces, she would lose her dessert.

What was significant about this experience was her parents' reaction, or, rather, their hesitation to react. There was a span of five or ten seconds between the time that Mary spotted the trash can and moved toward it. This reaction time was critical. In subsequent outings, I learned that if Mary felt the strong presence of an adult, either physically or through a forceful verbal reminder of her Happy Face program, then she could control her impulses. However, if this time period passed, an attempt to get her to change her behavior was likely to result in a confrontation.

It is this type of information about the behavioral quirks and idiosyncrasies of the client that is most helpful in his or her habilitation: perhaps even more helpful than the program itself. My goal in working with Mary, as it is when working with most handicapped clients with multiple-behavior problems, is to make even the most outrageous behaviors more acceptable by making them more predictable. As we come to understand that every behavior of a client is an attempt to fulfill his or her basic human needs, then we come closer to accepting them as whole people.

Mary's formal treatment program ended when she was enrolled in a group home for the moderately retarded about a half hour's drive from her parents' home. Although many of her behaviors still needed to be addressed, Mary was able to weather this important transition period, and, because of the therapy, take a step forward in her life. In addition, the people who would now work with Mary had more information about her than anyone had before, giving her a much greater chance to succeed.

The Chronic Head Banging of a 13-Year-Old Boy

Ronnie M. was referred to me by a private special education school for his constant self-abuse. Diagnosed as severely retarded from birth, he began to bang his head and hit himself beginning at three years of age in response to not getting what he wanted. Although many behavioral programs were tried over the next ten years, the severity and frequency of Ronnie's self-injurious behavior kept increasing.

His parents noted that Ronnie would go through periods lasting one to three months when his head-banging and hitting would be more intense. During this time they would keep his helmet on day and night and would put pads on his hands, knees, and shins. These periods seemed to coincide with any change in Ronnie's schedule: a new teacher in the classroom, a brother going off to college, moving to another bedroom. As hard as his parents tried to keep Ronnie's life consistent and predictable, they never knew what might trigger these episodes.

Between periods of extreme self-abuse, Ronnie would be relatively quiet and easy to live with. Although he was severely handicapped with developmental skills in the two- to three-year-old range and a vocabulary of only three words (yes, no, and his name), Ronnie was also friendly, affectionate, and very popular with the staff at his school. His educational program consisted of learning self-help and prevocational skills such as the ones he might need in a sheltered workshop. Even though his potential was limited, it was thought that at some time he would be able to live in a group home and care for some of his needs.

At the time of the referral, Ronnie's self-abuse was so frequent that his school wasn't sure that they could keep him. Even when he was wearing all of his protective equipment, he was attempting to harm himself, wailing and thrashing out nearly 50 times a day. They had assigned a teacher's assistant to spend all of her time with Ronnie to try and reduce this behavior, but it was all she could do to keep him in the classroom. She couldn't control his self-abuse, and in spite of his padding Ronnie had bruises on his legs and arms and large welts on his face. If Ronnie's hands were free for a moment—to go to the toilet, to eat, to put on his clothes—he would abuse himself. Since the beginning of this intense period of self-abuse, virtually no training or education had been done, and the school staff was on the edge of despair.

At home there were fewer things that Ronnie enjoyed more than following his older brother or his parents around the house. He liked to watch them and to have them talk about what they were doing. In quiet periods Ronnie would reluctantly stay by himself and watch TV or flip through magazines. But when he was agitated and self-abusive, he thrashed about in violent tantrums when left alone, knocking over tables and chairs, hitting his helmet against the wall, and trying to remove his protective padding.

In considering programs for clients who are self-abusive, I always assume the worst: someday they will irreparably damage or even kill themselves. For this reason I believe in leaving no stone unturned when considering ways to extinguish these behaviors, and will often try approaches I find too controversial for other situations.

In cases like Ronnie's, where self-abuse has been going on for years, there is relatively little hope of eradicating this behavior completely. It is more realistic to see it as a cyclical problem, to train the people who live and work with the client to recognize the early signs of increasing self-abuse and agitation, and to be prepared with a full range of resources and alternatives that will immediately diminish the behaviors. To do this, I use the following as guidelines:

- What conditions in the environment will generally keep the internal and external stress of the client at the lowest level possible?

- In times of severe stress, what are the maximum resources that can be applied to reduce the self-abuse to an acceptable level and protect the client?

- How can the client be trained and educated in spite of the severity and disruptiveness of this behavior? How can he or she be kept in a community placement?

Mary S. had problems that could be weighed against one another and treated one at a time, but we did not have this luxury with Ronnie. There was only one important behavior to reduce, the number of times that he hurt himself. In accordance with the multi-method approach, we used seven interventions simultaneously to produce the quickest effects possible. Rather than presenting these in order of importance (before we began we really had no idea which interventions would be effective and which ones wouldn't), they are presented in the order in which they were implemented.

The Use of a Vibrator to Decrease Self-Abusive Behavior

A few studies suggest that self-abusive behavior can be reduced by replacing painful stimulation with pleasant tactile stimulation in the form of vibration. The studies hypothesized that these children and adolescents suffer from a lack of tactile and kinesthetic stimulation which they crave most acutely in times of boredom and distress (the same times that many of us also seek additional stimulation in the forms of eating, smoking, drinking, etc.). Although we don't know just why these clients choose such a primitive form of stimulation, it is assumed that they cannot conceive how to get the intense level of excitation that they need by any other means than striking their heads and limbs.

But what if another form of stimulation can be provided, one that is equally intense and point-specific? If this type of stimulation reduces the client's level of physiological distress rather than raises it, then won't the need for self-abusive behavior also be reduced? In Ronnie's case, we attempted to see if an intermittent reinforcement with a hand-held adjustable vibrator would reduce his self-abuse.

The vibrator was first presented to him in his schoolroom, as he sat in his chair, clearly agitated, trying to hit one knee against the other in spite of his teacher's protests. I took the vibrator turned to full strength and with a mirror placed in front of him so that he could see what I was doing, slowly stroked his upper back and shoulders.

His response was almost immediate. He leaned back in his chair, and let his shoulders and back drop to a relaxed position. His whole body began to lose its tension. For 15 minutes he sat there, nearly motionless, while I moved the vibrator over his arms and legs, watching for spots that might be more pleasurable or more irritating. Like most people, Ronnie seemed to enjoy being massaged most on his shoulders. He disliked having the vibrator on his arms and legs, possibly because it irritated his many bruises. We decided to give Ronnie three five-minute periods of stimulation with the vibrator, at random intervals, every half an hour.

A Time-Out Room

Although federal and state laws have discouraged and sharply restricted the use of time-out or isolation rooms as a form of behavioral treatment, they are still used in many parts of the country, primarily with aggressive patients. Ronnie's records had revealed that a time-out room had been used with him several times in the past, as a consequence of his self-abusive behavior, with very dramatic results. At a group conference attended by his parents and the school staff, we decided to give it a try.

Replicating the treatment strategy that had worked in the past, Ronnie was led to the time-out room every time he hit himself, no matter how hard; he was to remain in isolation for two minutes. If Ronnie hit himself during his two-minute period, he was led out of the room, admonished, led back in, and had to remain in isolation for another two minutes.

When I first heard of this program, I didn't think it made much sense. I knew that Ronnie loved to be with people, but I didn't see how two minutes of removal from them would be a very significant aversive consequence. I also didn't understand why Ronnie wouldn't use the time in isolation to try to hit himself, and even though the rooms were well padded with no hard or sharp surfaces, I saw this whole procedure as a potential revolving door with Ronnie and the counselor going in and out of his small room all day. I expressed my misgivings, but bowed to the decision of the principal of the school who had known Ronnie when the time-out room had been used in another school. She said it worked, and so I went along with her judgment.

Within three days, the combination of using the vibrator and the time-out room had reduced Ronnie's self-abuse from nearly 50 times a day to two times a day. A second time-out room was built the following week in Ronnie's home, and the same procedures were implemented.

A Change in Medication

During the 10 years that Ronnie had been self-abusive, at least five medications had been tried in attempts to reduce this behavior. When I began the case, Ronnie was on a high dose of a major tranquilizer, which he was given regularly even though it was not having the desired effect and may have been making Ronnie more irritable. When I called up the neurologist that Ronnie was seeing, he frankly admitted to being confused about the whole case. The next day I advised Ronnie's mother to seek another medical opinion.

The second physician, a pediatrician who specialized in working with the handicapped, decided to take Ronnie slowly off the medication he had been using. Before prescribing anything else, he wanted Ronnie to have a drug holiday, completely free of medication, to see what his baseline behavior would be.

A Change in Protective Equipment

In an initial conference with Ronnie's family and the staff at his school, the question of his protective equipment came up. There was a controversy over when Ronnie should wear it, what it should consist of, and by what criteria it should be removed. The school personnel felt that Ronnie should wear his equipment as little as possible, because they felt that it inhibited his range of motion and kept him from working at tasks that he otherwise might be able to do. His parents, on the other hand, felt that the equipment itself helped quiet Ronnie down, and that with it on he felt safe from himself. They mentioned that on several nights he had gone to bed very agitated without his protective equipment on, but that putting it on had an immediate calming effect and he was able to sleep through the night.

We finally compromised by having a member of the school staff find out about obtaining lighter and less bulky equipment from an occupational therapy specialist. However, since we knew that the old equipment did seem to calm Ronnie down, and since his bumps and bruises suggested that he still needed it, we decided to have him continue wearing it on a full-time basis.

Relaxation Training

One of Ronnie's teachers had read about the effects of relaxation training on the severely handicapped and tried this several times with Ronnie. At the beginning of the day, when Ronnie arrived, she had him sit very quietly with his feet up and eyes shut while he listened to soft music. After about 15 minutes she approached him gently and guided him toward his first work task. I agreed with the teacher that this technique could have an effect in reducing Ronnie's agitation, and certainly couldn't hurt.

We decided on a program where Ronnie would relax for 15-minute periods three times a day: in the morning, just before lunch, and in the early evening. I cautioned, however, that relaxation training should not be contingent on Ronnie's abusive behavior; that is, she should not try to calm him down by relaxation techniques when he was abusive. To do this would be to reward a negative behavior with a pleasurable response, and would certainly contribute to the maintenance if not an increase in Ronnie's self-abuse.

Positive Reinforcement and Choosing Appropriate Tasks

When I first met Ronnie, the staff at his school was using a single positive-reinforcement program to try and decrease Ronnie's self-abuse. The program consisted of giving Ronnie raisins at three-minute intervals if he did not hit himself. If he did hit himself, he was admonished and did not get raisins.

Unfortunately, there were several flaws in this program. Although we knew that Ronnie liked raisins, we had no indication that this reward was strong enough to extinguish such a long-standing habit as his self-abuse. In fact, data from this program showed that it had very little effect, and certainly not enough to justify the time of one staff member to give Ronnie raisins every five minutes. In addition, it was not clear whether admonishing Ronnie, and so giving him attention for hitting himself, was reinforcing his self-abuse or not.

My suggestion was to make positive reinforcement contingent on completion of a task, rather than on abuse-free time periods. It was necessary, in any case, for Ronnie to learn self-help and work skills. His teacher agreed to set up a hierarchy of tasks, from simple ones which Ronnie could do easily to slightly more difficult ones requiring more time and concentration. Ronnie got a reward whenever he finished a task in the allotted time period, whether or not he hit himself during that period. In this way we set up a second dependent variable to measure Ronnie's progress, and did not pin all our hopes on changing one behavior. I emphasized that although the tasks should gradually increase in complexity, they should be designed to ensure getting a reward at least 80 percent of the time.

As I mentioned, by the third day of our program Ronnie had reduced his self-abusive behavior by 96 percent just by using the vibrator and the time-out techniques. So why did we keep on experimenting with other techniques? Because we needed to find a formula that would maintain this low level of his abuse with minimally intrusive techniques over the longest time period possible. Clearly we did not want to use time-out rooms indefinitely if some other technique would work just as well. Nor did we want to remove Ronnie's protective equipment if there was even a remote chance that he could hurt himself seriously. By combining all techniques at once, we wished to diminish the behavior to its lowest level possible for at least a month. Then we would try eliminating the most intrusive and time-consuming techniques to see if Ronnie's abusive behavior began to increase again.

A strict behaviorist would probably do things the opposite way: consider one variable at a time rather than confound results with a potpourri of techniques. This might be appropriate in some cases, but not when a child is in danger. Although we did not use the most rigorous methodology with Ronnie, I believe we used the most compassionate. Innovative behavior programs begin and end with people caring about people. When we add our imagination and creativity to this simple formula, I believe that there are very few children who cannot be helped.

On-Site Therapy

I use the phrase "on-site" therapy to refer to any technique which occurs at the physical location where the child or adolescent is having difficulty. Parts of the treatment programs mentioned earlier in this chapter with developmentally disabled clients were instituted on-site, but there are many other situations where on-site therapy is the treatment of choice. More and more I hear about therapy which is done in the child's home or a residential setting. Some of these therapies use family therapy techniques and some even use client-centered play therapy techniques. In the majority of cases, however, on-site therapy is done for children with predominantly behavioral problems, and it is assumed that the behavioral solution must be learned where the problem is actually occurring.

Since the on-site technique requires a commitment of concentrated blocks of time by the therapist, it is generally done in a short amount of time, usually not more than a month. Problems that can require treatment over an extended period of time may be better handled in milieu therapy. For example, a toddler needing more than a month's worth of concentrated home visits by a therapist may benefit more from the treatment available in specialized therapeutic day care centers.

On-site therapy, where the treatment is done in the client's home, community, workplace, or school, can be effective when everything else has failed. It can keep handicapped clients from being institutionalized or from losing their jobs. It can help parents more effectively meet the needs of their atypical infants, preventing the development of much more serious problems. It seems to be the treatment of choice for nearly all severely phobic children. It may have even wider applications as it becomes more accepted as an alternative to traditional approaches.

Of course, practicing psychotherapy outside the office is really not new at all. Even Freud was known to invite his patients to be his house guests, and he took at least one patient on vacation with him so that analysis could continue uninterrupted. Many therapists make school visits to observe children, and any therapist working in an institution or hospital setting will be constantly using his or her skills in the child's living environment. However, what is different about the on-site technique of psychotherapy is the systematic treatment of the child exclusively in the place and at the time where the problems most frequently exist.[1]

Although on-site therapeutic techniques can be extremely effective and are sometimes the only effective treatment for specific disorders, there are good reasons why therapists are reluctant to venture out of their offices into the cold, unpredictable world. Practical problems like time management and cost figuring; ethical problems revolving around the artificiality of having a therapist in the day-to-day life of a client; and, problems of technique when a therapist steps out of his or her office, many of the traditional rules and techniques of therapy are changed. For example, what would a therapist do in the following situations?

- You are working with a mildly handicapped child who is having extreme behavioral problems both at

---

1 On-site therapy is also referred to as contextual therapy, a phrase coined by Dr. Manuel Zane in his work with phobics.

home and in his school. As you enter the house on your third on-site session, the child's mother indicates that she would like to talk to you more about how she sees the problem when you are done working with the child.

• You are working with a child who is phobic toward escalators. While doing treatment in a department store, you are addressed by a friend of the family who has recognized the child and is wondering what you are doing with her.

• When you arrive for an appointment at the child's home, he is throwing a tantrum in his bedroom and refusing to come out.

• You are working with a mother to help her learn how to stimulate her blind infant. The treatment is proceeding very smoothly when one day the mother brings up her suspicions that her husband is having an affair and wants your advice on what to do.

Practical Issues

On-site therapy is usually performed in concentrated blocks of time, sometimes as much as four or five hours a day, five days a week. When properly used, the on-site therapy technique is definitely cost-effective for the client. Therapy is usually accomplished in a fraction of the time that it would take to address the same problem through conventional therapy and usually at significantly less cost. But scheduling on-site treatments is a constant juggling act for a busy therapist. The therapy must take place at the time and place that the client's problems occur, rather than at the therapist's convenience. Since the treatment is both rapid and intense, it is virtually impossible for a therapist to have more than one on-site client and still maintain an office practice. This problem can be overcome, however, by the use of therapy assistants.

While I have usually worked with MA-level psychologists as therapy assistants, graduate students and even trained volunteers can be used to implement many types of programs. Obviously the degree of skill and training required of the therapeutic assistant will vary according to the type of problem being treated. The primary advantage of using therapy assistants is that they have more flexible schedules and can accommodate themselves to be with the client at the times when they are most needed. They also usually work at a lower hourly rate than the primary therapist, reducing the cost of therapy for the client's family. Even when therapy assistants are used however, it is still the responsibility of the primary therapist to know the children, their environments, and their problems, as well as if the primary therapist were actually providing the treatment. This means doing assessments, writing the treatment plans, observing the therapy as it progresses, and closely supervising the therapy assistant.

The other major practical problem using this technique of psychotherapy is dealing with the geographic distance of the clients from the therapist's office. While this problem is sometimes cumbersome, it is not insurmountable. In most cases I feel that if clients live close enough to me to come for an office visit, then they are close enough for the primary or assistant therapist to go to them. In many cases the location of the client will be a factor in selecting an assistant. I was once able to treat a client who lived 40 miles from my office by using an assistant who lived in the same community and who only had to travel to see me once a week for supervision. Typically, the on-site technique is carried out in two to three hour blocks of time and sometimes more, to avoid the need for unnecessary travel.

There are many other practical issues that have to be considered as a therapist begins to provide on-site treatment programs. If assistants are hired, they will have to be supervised closely. Since they will be working for you, under your license, you will have to consider whether or not they are covered under your liability insurance, how they will be paid, and how you can best monitor their work without making them feel that you are restricting their own therapeutic knowledge and creativity.

While these and other practical problems must be taken into account, I view them as minor hurdles in this type of treatment: a treatment that can have a profound effect on a client's life. Thorough planning before the treatment begins is always the best insurance against unwelcome surprises.

Ethical Considerations

Stepping into a patient's daily life in order to provide the best method of treatment takes daring and courage on the part of the therapist. It is outside the normal realm of our training and experience and puts our theories right on the line. But is also an artificial intrusion on our clients and their families and should not be undertaken lightly. For this reason, therapy should not proceed without a written contract outlining just what can be expected from the therapy and what cannot.

A related ethical concern in on-site therapy is the issue of confidentiality. As in all forms of psychotherapy, clients have a right to privacy regarding their treatment, and the therapist has the responsibility to protect that right in all circumstances. But what happens if relatives drop in while the therapist is in the home, or a neighbor inquires who the woman is accompanying the child to and from school? The privacy of the therapy is suddenly public. Each circumstance will be handled differently, but it is the therapist's job at the onset of therapy to make sure that the family understands the issue of confidentiality and has anticipated the situations that might come up. Excessive concern about what others may think may indicate to the therapist that this therapeutic technique is contraindicated.

Another more subtle ethical consideration has to do with the role of the therapist working with a family in the home or community. All our cultural mores will push the therapist and his or her clients to personalize the therapeutic relationship. There are no social rules for having a therapist come into a client's home; each may, quite naturally, turn to the common rules of social etiquette. But the therapist must never lose sight of his or her role as a professional.

When I am using on-site techniques, I follow the same formal social etiquette that I use in the office. As one experienced therapist puts it, when it comes to social etiquette, the therapist should treat the client as a formal guest. I believe that the same rule holds true for therapy done outside the confines of the office. A therapist who is overly solicitous and responds to the client as to a neighbor or a friend loses objectivity and with the loss of objectivity goes the therapist's professional standing. Stepping out of the formal role as therapist, even just a little bit, implies promises to the client or his family that the therapist will not be able to keep.

Issues of Technique

Another reason that the therapist must remain formal and objective when working on-site is to anticipate and therapeutically deal with family dynamics. Each individual should be considered part of a larger family system, as if he or she were in the office.

Complex and powerful family dynamics are always operating. Some members will try to get the therapist to ally with them, some will reject help, and others will become dependent on the therapist and think that he or she can do no wrong. The therapist's specific approach to the family will vary according to his or her particular orientation, as well as to the stated objectives of the therapy plan. On entering into the lives of any family, the therapist will see many conflicts and problems.

While it is the therapist's ethical responsibility to identify these problems and suggest potential remedies, the therapist should not directly intervene unless it has been designated in the therapy contract that he or she should do so. Of course, if the problem of another family member is impeding the progress of the client, then the therapist must meet with the family and rewrite the contract to reflect this new knowledge. An extreme example of this type of situation might involve an alcoholic father who verbally abused other family members including the phobic child the therapist was hired to work with. In this situation, continuing to treat the child without first restructuring the family dynamics would be fruitless.

On the other end of the continuum are family members who seek out the therapist for problems and concerns that are not related to the problem of the client. Again, while these problems may be real, it would be no more appropriate to treat the problems in the context of doing on-site therapy then it would be to treat problems brought to the attention of the therapist at a dinner party. If approached by a family member (or anyone else in the client's life), the therapist should try to clarify his or her role in implementing the treatment plan for the identified client. The therapist should then invite the family member to schedule an appointment at some convenient time.

On a day-to-day basis, the ethical problems, practical concerns, and questions of therapy technique tend to blend together, and although there are many guidelines, each therapist will have to develop his or her own style in handling these issues. To return to the hypothetical scenarios that I presented at the beginning of this section: I have noted my reactions based on my experience in similar circumstances and my training in analytically-oriented therapy and a systems approach to families. Your reactions may be different; however they should be consonant with your theories, your experiences of doing psychotherapy, and the specific techniques that you have chosen to use on-site with your client.

> *Problem:* You are working with a mildly handicapped child who is having extreme behavioral problems both at home and in his school. As you enter the house on your third on-site session, the child's mother indicates that she would like to talk to you more about how she sees the problem when you are done working with the child.

> *Response:* I would explain to her that although I'm sure what she has to say is important, I plan each ses-

sion out carefully and need to leave exactly when it is over. I would invite her to schedule an appointment with me at the office by calling me later that day. If I think that this is an attempt of the mother to try and develop a special relationship with me as a way of acting out some dynamic of the family system, then I would explain when she called that I would prefer to discuss these issues with all the family members present, and ask if she and the rest of the family could come in for an appointment.

Problem: You are working with a child who is phobic towards escalators. While doing treatment in a department store, you are addressed by a friend of the family who has recognized the child and is wondering what you are doing with her.

Response: If possible, I would avoid identifying myself as a therapist out of respect for the family's right to confidentiality. If the friend was worried about the child being with a stranger, I would reassure him or her as needed. Fortunately, this is rarely a problem. Anyone who might know the child and also might see you with him or her in public would also see that you had a special caring relationship and that there was no need for worry. If you work in a community where this is likely to happen often, then this possibility should be discussed thoroughly with the family beforehand, and you should help each family member come to terms with his or her own feelings. Typically, you will be working in on-site situations where the client's problems will have already become public to some degree, and each family member may have some feelings of guilt, shame, and anger.

Problem: When you arrive for an appointment at a child's home, he is throwing a tantrum in his bedroom and refuses to come out.

Response: This can be an extremely awkward situation, with each person thinking, "Just who is in the authority here?" The parents might feel that since it is their home, they must handle the situation. But then again, they see the therapist as the identified expert, so they may want to see what you do. You can ease this situation by being very clear about what *you* think is appropriate for the stated therapeutic goals.

Perhaps one of the therapeutic goals is to help the parents learn to handle their child's tantrums. In this case you are fortunate to have an example of the behavior to work with (although you probably won't feel quite so lucky at the time). Then, whether you model how to handle the child or whether you want one or both parents to intervene will depend on where you are in the treatment program. If, on the other hand, this is unusual behavior for the child, it may be an expression of his or her anxiety at having you in his or her home or a more general conflict having to do with the nature of treating his particular problem. In this case you must bring the same intuitive empathy and therapeutic skills that you would have with any child who is hurting, and with patience and understanding the therapeutic bond between you and the child will be strengthened.

Problem: You are working with a mother to help her learn how to stimulate her blind infant. The treatment is proceeding very smoothly when the one day the mother brings up her suspicions that her husband is having an affair and wants your advice on what to do.

Response: As in the first example, I would stick to the therapy plan for that session, taking note of the mother's concern and anxiety only insofar as it relates to the care of her infant. The therapist's role in on-site therapy is not one of counselor or confidante. He or she should stick to the therapeutic task at hand and handle other problems in their own time and place.

Phobias: A Five-Year-Old Who Wouldn't Go to School

If I hadn't been standing at her doorstep when the large yellow bus wheeled to a stop in front of her house, I might have thought, like the school psychologist who diagnosed her, that Tina had a school phobia. But she wasn't afraid of going to school. She was afraid of the school bus. I watched as she turned pale at the sight of the bus, frozen in terror until it pulled away. This, her mother had explained, had happened every day for two weeks since the beginning of kindergarten.

That day, I rode with Tina and her mother in the car to the elementary school about two miles away, and I was struck by how calm and relaxed she looked making up songs in the back seat. But as we pulled into the parking lot, Tina stiffened again, holding her stomach and complaining that she felt she was going to be sick. I noticed that she wasn't looking at the school, as I would have anticipated: she was staring at the parked lot full of school buses.

Tina entered her classroom stiffly, like a robot. Since she was having such a hard time adjusting to school, her teacher suggested that she only stay for an hour each morning until she was more used to it, and directed her mother to the teacher's lounge. As her mother turned to go, I was again surprised at Tina's reaction. She hardly seemed to notice her mother leaving. She went into the block corner, said "Hello" to another little girl, and started to play.

The assessment is just one area of treating a phobic child in which the therapist who is working on-site is at an advantage. The irrational nature of phobias in adults as well as in children often belies understanding, and treating the patient away from the actual phobic experience obscures the problem even more. In Tina's case no one had ever noticed that she was afraid of buses. As far as could be recalled, she had never been on a bus before. Nobody could remember any particular event that might have led to such a fear. Tina was always timid and withdrawn, an only child who was kept at home rather than sent to nursery school because her mother reported: "She just doesn't seem to like other kids that much." She had nightmares since the age of two, but these seemed to have diminished in their frequency and intensity in the six months before she began school.

The entire treatment for Tina's fear of buses lasted two weeks, after which time she was riding in the school bus to and from school and remaining there for the full four hours of the kindergarten program. The parents were seen for biweekly sessions for three months more so that they could learn ways to foster their daughter's newly-found independence. A six-month follow-up showed that Tina had made an excellent adjustment to school and was considered to be one of the more outgoing children in the class.

To understand why on-site therapy is so much more expedient and precise than an office approach in working with phobic children, it might be worthwhile to do a comparison between the therapy done with Tina, and the therapy I might have used in the office.

On-Site Therapy

Assessment: The assessment of the phobia took three hours one morning with the client and her mother in observation and interview.

Treatment: The treatment began the next day, a technique of systematic desensitization toward buses, done in nine two-hour sessions.

Session 1
Tina was taught how to relax and breathe deeply when she was upset. She practiced this technique while looking at pictures of buses and standing on her front porch pretending the school bus was coming. Tina spent one hour in her class afterwards.

Session 2
We talked about buses and why they were scary to Tina. We read a story about school buses and practiced progressive relaxation. Tina spent one hour and 10 minutes in her class afterwards.

Session 3
We walked around the neighborhood looking for buses and counting them. We went back to the house and drew pictures of the buses we saw. Tina spent 1-1/2 hours in her class later that morning.

Session 4
Tina and I waited for the school bus to arrive in the morning, and then as we had prearranged, walked half-way to the bus door, waved to the driver, and watched the bus pull away. All this time Tina practiced her deep breathing and muscle relaxation. We then drove to school and Tina had a friendly talk with the school bus driver 10 feet away from the bus.

Session 5
A repeat of Session 4, but when the bus arrived, we walked up to the open door to say hello to the driver; later when we met the driver at school, she asked Tina if she would like to see the inside of the bus. We all went in and the bus driver told us funny anecdotes

about driving a bus. We stayed in the bus for 15 minutes. Tina went to her class for the remaining two hours, staying through lunch.

Session 6
Tina and I greeted the bus in the morning, went in and sat near the driver. We rode for one block and then got out and walked the rest of the way to school. It was pretty tiring. We repeated the same procedure when her class was over at 1:00 p.m.

Session 7
Same as Session 6, but we rode for four blocks on the bus to and from school.

Session 8
We rode the entire way to and from school. I sat next to Tina on the way over, but about half-way through, I changed seats with one of her friends in the class. On the way back Tina sat next to her friend, and I sat near the driver.

Session 9
Tina rode to and from school by herself. I saw her off and was there when she returned after school to say good-bye. We had ice cream and cake to celebrate Tina's graduation.

Office Therapy
Assessment: The assessment would take two to five hours, probably scheduled in two or more separate visits. It would consist of an interview with the mother, a fear rating scale, one or more projective tests, and observation of the child's play. All the information about fear would be *inferred*.

Treatment:
Sessions 1 to 4: The initial session would be devoted to finding out more about the exact nature of the fear, and would include exposing various stimuli to the child in the form of pictures, sounds, toys, videotaped sequences, and so forth. The child's reaction to each stimulus would be recorded and rated according to

the degree of anxiety that was manifested. The stimuli would then be organized into a hierarchy from
least- to most-anxiety-provoking stimuli. With 50-
minute sessions, twice a week, this would take about
two weeks.

Sessions 5 to 27: The principles of systematic and progressive relation would also be used in the office,
beginning with the stimulus that was least-anxiety-pro-
voking in the hierarchy. As each stimulus or set of
stimuli was presented, the child would be instructed to
relax until a minimum of anxiety was present. This
procedure, continuing on through the hierarchy,
could take two months, meeting twice a week. In addition, the parents would have to be trained to use the
same technique with their child at home; this might
take another four sessions. (This would not, however,
be the same as family therapy that would work on the
causes of the problem. If indicated, family therapy
would take four to 10 more sessions.)

Comparing these two types of therapy, done by the same therapist,
for the same problem, we can see that the office therapy would take
27 or more hours over two to three months, while the on-site therapy
would be accomplished in 22 hours of work with the child, in nine sessions over a period of two weeks. Even if the two techniques were
equally effective, the on-site technique would have the child in school
and past an important developmental hurdle in less than one-tenth of
the time.

Work Adjustment Training

I have seen many job training programs for the mild to moderately
intellectually handicapped that train clients for work in electronic
assembly, messenger services, janitorial work, kitchen work, beauti-
cian services, clerical work, and so forth. But even the best of these
programs can't anticipate the kinds of programs that might come up
on an actual job.

Carl B. had been in a special education school since the age of five;
at the age of 15 he had been enrolled in a prevocational training program emphasizing kitchen skills. He could do salad preparation,
bussing, general cleanup, and dishwashing, but what he enjoyed was
making the sandwiches for the school lunch program. When he grad-
uated from school and found a job, however, it was in a small diner.

They didn't need salad preparation, because their salads were bought ready-made. They used paper plates at a single counter so there was no dishwashing or tables to clean up. What they primarily needed Carl to do was to slice the meats for their submarine sandwiches and to do the janitorial work. Neither of these were problems for Carl. They also needed him to go through a checklist twice daily to see what kinds of supplies needed to be ordered, what frozen meats needed to be defrosted, and what ingredients needed to be put out for the pizza chef. The mechanics of these tasks were easy enough for Carl, but his academic skills were only at a second grade level, and he couldn't read the checklist.

Having known Carl for some time, I offered to supervise an on-site training program to prepare him for the job. I promised his employer that within a week Carl would be able to do every aspect of the job as well as if not better than the previous employee. A few days later I reported for work with Carl and listened while the manager explained Carl's various duties. Except for the supplies checklist, Carl was familiar with all the other job requirements and seemed to catch on immediately to the routine. The diner had a very informal atmosphere, but since Carl was used to working on a strict schedule in his vocational training program, I made up a time schedule for him as he performed each of his required job functions. Since he could tell time only to the half hour, we used the half hour as the basic time unit and made up a time chart for his duties in picture form.

It was clear that the manager of the diner and the other employees had never seen anything quite like us: Carl, with his spotless overalls, and me, with a clipboard and stopwatch, looking like an efficiency expert for a large corporation. But no one seemed to mind, and when Carl did all the work in one morning that had taken the last employee all day to accomplish, the manager was delighted. He immediately thought of several more maintenance jobs that he had put off for years that Carl could begin in the afternoon.

That left only the supplies checklist to be tackled. The manager showed us around the storeroom and the walk-in refrigerator and pointed out all the supplies that had to be monitored daily. I drew a schematic drawing of the room, indicating what the manager had explained were the maximum and minimum of each type of stock that he wanted to have on hand. There were 25 items in all. The manager then took us over to where the pizza chef was cooking, and showed us how his ingredients were laid out on the counter. Each ingredient had its own container that Carl had to refill twice a day from the supply room.

That evening, I redrew the illustration I had made of the supply room, indicating the subtraction that Carl would have to do in order to determine what had to be reordered. The next day I met Carl after lunch at the diner to train him to use his checklist. Although Carl couldn't read, I thought that he could match the words from the schematic checklist with the label on each product, but this proved to be too slow and cumbersome. So, to aid in matching the products to the checklist, we numbered each of the items and put a corresponding two-inch high plastic stick-on number on the location of each of the supplies in the storeroom. We practiced finding each of the products in the storeroom and matching it to the corresponding place on the checklist.

Carl then practiced counting each item and entered each total on the appropriate box in the checklist. When the 25 items were checked, Carl then sat down with a calculator to determine how much of each item needed to be reordered. Although he could do a simple subtraction, Carl often made mistakes and said that math gave him a headache. Using a calculator, however, appealed to Carl's newfound sophistication.

It took just under 2-1/2 hours to teach Carl how to use the supplies checklist and another half hour to teach him how to use the calculator and to transfer the numbers on the checklist to a standard reordering form for the manager. While it took Carl longer to check the supplies than it might take someone without a handicap, Carl more than made up for this loss of time in his diligence in other tasks. After a few weeks when Carl was thoroughly familiar with the stockroom, we were able to do away with the schematic drawing and the calculator and use a checklist that Carl could handwrite for the manager. Carl had made a step into community employment that might not have been possible without the aid of on-site training. The total treatment time: six hours, in 1-1/2 days.

CHAPTER 5

THE COGNITIVE MODALITY

Cognitive Therapy assumes that if children or adolescents can change the way they think, these new thoughts will in turn affect the way that they *act* and *feel*. Because Cognitive techniques can be taught, they are particularly appropriate for use in short-term therapy plans. Cognitive techniques are by definition nonintrusive because they primarily involve therapeutic interactions combining conventional counseling and teaching.

Cognitive techniques are designed to teach children to think differently. On one hand, this seems like a formidable task. Watching an impulsive child in the classroom or on the playground, flitting from one thing to the next, talking out of turn, poking and pinching other children...How we can get this child to act differently by thinking differently when very little thought seems to be going on? On the other hand, we sometimes forget that children learn to think differently every day as they mature cognitively, and how much easier it is for them to learn and change than adults.

Consider, for example, the way that we learn a foreign language. We learn vocabulary and to conjugate verbs, but until we become fairly proficient at the language, we have not truly changed the way we think. As students speaking a foreign language, we tend to think in English and then try to translate our thoughts into the new language according to the basic syntax and structure of the language. But something changes when we become fluent. There is no longer a translation process; we are actually thinking in the new language. When this happens we haven't just learned the language, we have changed our Cognitive pattern, the way that we think.

To most Americans, who tend to be foreign-language phobic, changing our Cognitive patterns *still* sounds like a formidable task. But consider the fact that children in many European countries learn to speak at least one additional language fluently, if not two or three! I remember being at a dinner party once in Paris and everyone there seemed to speak four or five languages, except me, who spoke English and a little French (poorly). That same week I read that Harvard University was considering implementing a policy to excuse students from their foreign language requirement for *psychological reasons*. The Harvard students claimed that they had a psychological block against learning a foreign language.

There are several points to this story. To begin with, children show a tremendous capacity for changing their basic thinking patterns, as demonstrated by the ease with which they learn a second language when exposed to it at an early age. Adults rarely appreciate that the Cognitive capacity of children goes far beyond our definition of intelligence. If we compare foreign language acquisition to changing in Cognitive patterns, we can see that young children have a greater capacity for change than adults. This capacity can be retained by the child through adulthood. We must also consider that our culture may have expectations of children that are too low. Children probably have a much greater capacity for Cognitive change than we give them credit for.

Of course the Cognitive change that is a component of Cognitive therapy is different from the Cognitive change involved in learning a new language. In most cases, we are asking children not just to change the way that they think, but the way that they behave as well. Research has suggested that Cognitive training alone is rarely effective in changing real-world problems. Children can learn to think and act differently in the context of the office where the training is taking place, but the effects of the training do not generalize to the child's actual environment. Cognitive training *is* however effective when combined with behavioral contingency programs, experiential learning in the child's natural environment, and when the Cognitive training occurs in the context of a dynamic therapeutic relationship.

Cognitive Therapy Techniques take many forms. All forms of Cognitive Therapy assume that there is an interactional relationship between thoughts, feelings, and behaviors. Our behaviors certainly influence our thoughts and feelings. If a child steals something and is caught, he or she will feel guilty and act remorseful. Our feelings similarly affect our behaviors and thoughts. If a child is happy, he or she will be likely to behave more pleasantly and to think more positively. Cognitive Therapy assumes that if behaviors and feelings can affect our thoughts, why then can't our thoughts affect our behaviors and our feelings?

This chapter describes techniques which fall into two basic categories of Cognitive Therapy. One category, Cognitive Mediating Techniques, assumes that thoughts first influence our behaviors which then influence our feelings. Another category, Cognitive Restructuring Techniques, assumes that thoughts first influence our feelings which then influence our behaviors. Theoretically, the difference is in the direction of the link between thoughts, behaviors, and feelings; in actual practice, this paradigm is less important.

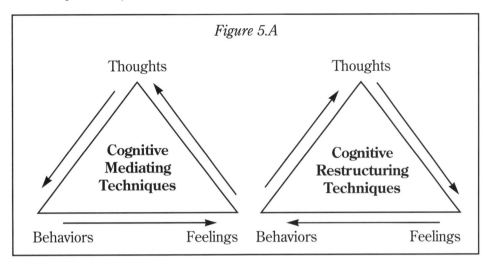

Figure 5.A

Cognitive Mediating Techniques

Cognitive Mediating Techniques, also referred to as Cognitive Behavior Modification, emphasize the link between cognition and behavior. These techniques have been most widely applied with children with problems in impulse control and are based on a deficit model. The deficit model assumes that children who act impulsively or inappropriately do not have the Cognitive skills to control their behavior or find better alternatives to their dysfunctional behavior. Cognitive Therapy Techniques that fall into this category include:

Self-Guided Thinking: Getting children to use new thoughts to change their behavioral patterns (the new thought becomes a mediating factor, or new link, in a chain of behavioral events).

Self-Monitoring: Children learn to monitor their attending behaviors.

Self-Instruction: Children learn a new procedure for starting, attending to, and finishing tasks.

Learning a New Skill: Children learn to break down a new or unfamiliar skill or task into small sequential tasks. This can include social tasks or skills, such as making new friends, being cooperative, and so on.

Problem-Solving: Children learn a process for making decisions and solving social problems by considering consequences, weighing alternatives, and generating and testing new solutions.

These Cognitive techniques have considerable overlap and are frequently combined in Cognitive Therapy.

Self-Guided Thinking

Teaching children self-guiding thoughts helps children think before they act. Various researchers have taught children to first think aloud as they do various mazes, puzzles, or act out social scenarios. They then whisper these self-guiding thoughts to themselves, and finally just think the words.

Consider how a novice tennis player learns to play. The player can begin by taking a ball and a racquet out to the court, finding a willing partner, and swinging away. The main objective, she knows, is to hit the ball with the racquet, and this she does in an enjoyable but fairly haphazard way. But she soon begins to notice that she doesn't play like the more advanced players she sees on the courts. She doesn't hit the ball as hard, as low to the net, or nearly as often. She looks and feels clumsy, so she decides to take a few lessons. What she will most likely learn from her teacher will be *Cognitive self-guiding thoughts;* thoughts that she can say to herself to help modify her behavior: thoughts to mediate her actions.

After a few lessons, she will go out to the court, and now before swinging, will say to herself, "Keep your eye on the ball. Keep your knees slightly bent. Position yourself before the ball bounces. Step into the ball with your left foot for a forehand, with your right foot for a backhand. Follow through with your racquet." Our player will practice until these new movements become automatic. When her game is poor, she will know that her form is probably off, and will begin to talk to herself again. "Keep your eyes on the ball. Keep your knees slightly bent..." and so on.

The Cognitive Mediating Technique was first introduced by Donald Meichenbaum and his colleagues, and has been most frequently applied to overactive children who have a difficult time in school. In numerous studies, children who were labeled hyperactive were shown to be characteristically impulsive in the way that they solved problems. In solving mazes, for instance, these children would charge ahead as soon as they were given a pencil, entering blind alleys, cutting corners, and adding extraneous marks to the paper. Other children, who were not reported to have problems in the classroom, approached the mazes with a more reflective style, examining alternative routes before choosing which way to go.

On closer examination, it appeared that the major difference between the trial-and-error style of the impulsive children and the more analytic style of their reflective counterparts was that the impulsive children were not thinking about what they were doing: they just acted and tried to finish as quickly as possible. Basing his model on the work of the Russian psychologists Vygotsky and Luria, Meichenbaum hypothesized that hyperactive children, with their uncontrolled and frequently aggressive behaviors, had not developed the ability to use internalized speech the way that most children do by the time that they are five years of age. While reflective children use an internal dialogue to solve a new problem or understand a new situation, impulsive children, like the proverbial frog, leap before they look. In further studies it was found that children identified as having behavioral problems in class were universally less sophisticated than their peers in decision-making skills, in seeing alternatives, in generating hypotheses, in word attack skills in reading, and in computational skills in math.

In developing a therapy for these children, Meichenbaum surmised that since these children were not less intelligent than their peers (all the studies compared groups that were matched by IQ), they must have a developmental delay in the specific use of their internalized speech to mediate and regulate their behavior. He patterned his technique on the way that children normally develop internalized speech, designing a four-stage process to teach children to think about problems before they act. Using a wide variety of visual and verbal puzzles and games, the therapist demonstrates the problem first, saying his or her thoughts out loud. The children then try the same problem, but rather than resorting to the usual trial-and-error tactics, try to imitate the therapist's words exactly, and to do just what he or she had done. In putting together a puzzle, for instance, a child might begin by saying, "Now I have to examine the pieces before I put them together. I'll lay them out in a row and look for two pieces that have the same color in them. If I see something on a piece of the puzzle that looks familiar, I'll make sure that the piece is right side up..."

After imitating the therapist's thoughts at each stage of the problem, the children then go through it again, rehearsing the same thoughts out loud as they work. Then they do the same or a similar puzzle again, but this time the children whisper the self-guiding statements to themselves. Finally, the children do the puzzle one last time, but this time saying the words, which are now internal thoughts, to themselves.

Although this treatment is based on a developmental pattern, its principles are rooted in Behavioral theory. The children learn to use self-directing thoughts just as if they are new behaviors. They model the use of the thoughts from a therapist whom they value and who reinforces them each time they use this new way of solving problems. Like any behavior it is rehearsed over and over again, matched to specific environmental cues or antecedents, and slowly transferred as a new behavior to the place where the problem originally existed, the classroom.

Since Meichenbaum's early work, many programs have been developed to teach children self-guiding thoughts. I personally prefer programs which teach these skills in the context of the environment in which they are most needed, usually the classroom. Dr. Kenneth Dodge, a professor at Vanderbilt University in Nashville (see Chapter 5, *Child Therapy Today*, 1994) is involved in a program researching children with conduct disorders called FAST Track. This program uses a very concrete metaphor of a traffic light to help children stop and think about their behavior.

When children misbehave they are immediately directed towards a red light. This can be a literal red light, a red circle on the floor to stand in, or a red spot on their desks that they touch. When they are at the red light, they must count to 120, taking deep breaths in order to relax. Then the children go to a yellow light to think about what to do next. Younger children may generate only one solution, but older children may be directed to imagine different solutions and the consequences that might occur with each alternative. Finally the children go to a green light and try out a solution to see if it works. If they hit someone, they will certainly have to apologize. If they take something, then they will have to make reparations, and so on.

What makes this technique so appealing?

1. It uses an effective and yet flexible psychological principle.

2. It is concrete and can be applied effectively in the counselor's office, the home, or the school.

3. It has both Cognitive and physical aspects. Children's emotional reactions are much more physical than adults, and this technique allows children to "deal" with their emotions in a physical as well as a cognitive way.

4. It is fun. It is particularly fun if you use real red, yellow and green lights, for the child to go to. Going to the different lights and standing near them reminds me of running to a base in tag or softball, which children of course enjoy.

5. This technique works on the metaphorical as well as the concrete level. The stop light is something that all children can relate to as a symbol of adult traffic rules. The three types of lights represent stages and as the child moves from one to another he or she makes progress towards a higher stage of functioning. The base represents a safe zone to children in most games: a place where they can catch their breath and take a moment's time out from the game.

Although the majority of research on teaching self-guiding thoughts has been done with hyperactive children, studies have also been done with other populations who do not appear to use logical thinking to guide their behavior. In particular, this technique seems to hold promise for thought disorders associated with schizophrenia, children with state-specific anxiety (such as test anxiety), aggressive children, and children with impulse control disorders. The following examples show how this technique can be integrated into widely varying treatment plans.

A Mildly Retarded Adolescent Learns to Control Her Sexual Impulses

Like other teenagers, many intellectually handicapped adolescents experiment with alcohol, drugs, and sex, but their lack of judgment and caution in the form of internalized self-guiding speech make them particularly vulnerable to the social and psychological problems associated with their adventures.

Alice B., for example, was a 17-year-old girl with a full scale IQ of 73 and a level of academic achievement at about the fourth grade. Although her parents had several complaints about Alice's impulsive behavior, including her excessive drinking, her use of obscenity, and her truancy from school, Alice felt that these were not problems at all. She agreed with her parents, however, that she had a problem regarding sex. She couldn't say no to any boy who wanted to have intercourse with her, even though she felt that she was often taken advantage of by boys. She had contracted venereal diseases several times and was teased unmercifully at school.

Alice's parents accepted the fact that she would continue to have sexual relations, but they wanted her to adopt better standards in selecting partners and where the acts took place. Naturally the parents didn't want to see Alice hurt. I was particularly concerned about the inherent dangers in Alice's lack of judgment and her inability to control her impulses. She would get into a car with nearly any man who pulled up and asked her to get in. She would have sex in abandoned buildings in dangerous parts of town without concern for her own safety. She had already at least once become involved with a man who threatened her with violence.

For such a serious problem, I initiated a variety of crisis-oriented interventions, including family therapy and weekly consultations with Alice's school where she was receiving group therapy and counseling. The following paragraphs discuss only the cognitive mediating techniques which were used to help Alice improve her judgment.

The first task was to find out just what Alice was thinking when she was approached by a man. I took 10 pictures from magazines and asked Alice to tell a story about each one, following the format of Murray's Thematic Apperception Test. The pictures showed young men and women in various stages of romantic encounters. Some pictures were clearly suggestive, but others were fairly neutral (e.g., a man and a woman sitting next to each other on the bus but looking in opposite directions.) I asked Alice to tell me what each person was thinking, and tape recorded her responses. The following response, which was given to a card showing a close-up of a man and woman looking at each other, was typical.

Alice: The man and the woman are about to get it together.

Therapist: Do you mean have sex?

Alice: That's right. He's thinking, 'I wonder where I can lay this chick? In the stairwell? No, somebody will find us there. In the classroom? Yeah, we can find an empty classroom and do it on a desk.' And that's just what they did!

Therapist: What was the woman thinking?

Alice: Oh, she wasn't thinking about much. She kind of liked his wavy brown hair and eyes, and thought he was a pretty good-looking stud.

Therapist: What happened?

Alice: Well, they went into an empty classroom and did it, just like the guy said.

Therapist: And then what did they each think and feel?

Alice: Well, the guy felt good and proud of himself, and said

to himself, 'That is some good lookin' chick.' But the girl
didn't feel so good about herself. She thought, 'Maybe I'll
get the clap again. This guy probably doesn't even like me
very much. I'll bet I'll never even see him again, and he'll
go around bad mouthin' me and such.'

Card after card suggested Alice was totally preoccupied with the
seductive words and behaviors of men and she seemed almost
unaware that she could have anything to say about whether or not the
encounter was going to turn into a sexual experience. While there
was no doubt that Alice was flirtatious with men in general, and probably more so when they showed some interest in her, she did not see
that her coquettish behavior had anything to do with her problem.

The purpose of using a Cognitive Mediating Technique with Alice
was to get her to identify situations that might be potentially dangerous to her, and then learn to say no and walk away as a matter of
choice. We began by making a list of situations where Alice had sexual experiences that she later regretted. These included:

1. A boy came up to me in the hallway and wanted me to have sex with
him on the stairs.
2. A neighborhood boy wanted me to have sex in his garage.
3. A man pulled his car over, told me to get in, took me to a parking
lot, and we had sex in the car.

We then made a list of appropriate self-statements that Alice could
have made in each situation. For example, if a car pulled up to her and
a man began to flirt with her, she would say to herself: "Any stranger
who tries to pick me up in a car is up to no good. I won't talk to him.
I'll just keep walking and look straight ahead. If he keeps on talking,
I'll turn around and walk somewhere the car can't go and there are
other people." In a shortened form these statements became: "Look
ahead—walk away."

Because I wanted Alice to practice these self-statements until they
became automatic responses, I asked Alice's female counselor at
school to come to her therapy sessions and act as a model. First, I
role-played each situation with the counselor, who said the self-statements out loud. Then I role-played the same scenarios with Alice
three times: first, she repeated the self-statements out loud; then she
whispered them; and then she kept silent, but thought them to herself.
We videotaped each situation and also looked for the nonverbal cues
that Alice might be giving that will encourage someone to continue
pursuing her. If any of the videotapes were not perfect, we role-played

again until they were.

Over several weeks, we watched these tapes 10 times. The object of this repetition was to strengthen the self-statements as conditioned responses, but it also helped heighten Alice's awareness of the problem and her responsibility to find a different solution to her former pattern of passivity, blaming her problems on everyone else, and suppressing all her thoughts and feelings about painful incidents.[1]

Reducing Anxiety and Aggressiveness with the Cognitive Mediating Technique

Arthur was a bright child who consistently performed poorly on tests because of his unorganized and erratic approach. He had a hard time following directions, frequently guessed at answers, and did not try to solve problems for which he did not have an immediate answer. The anxiety he experienced taking tests made matters worse, inhibiting the skills he showed in less stressful situations. Since spelling was Arthur's worst subject and was also the subject in which he was most frequently tested, we began the therapy with it.

An analysis of Arthur's prior tests showed that of 25 words, he only attempted to spell an average of 18, but of those 18, 16 (88 percent) were correct. To begin, I gave Arthur a spelling quiz in my office that exactly simulated the classroom tests. An analysis of a videotape of his performance revealed:

> Word 1: Arthur takes 10 seconds to think about the word before he begins to write. He writes out the complete word slowly. He is still forming the last letters of the first word when the second word is read.

> Word 2: Arthur hesitates 30 seconds before beginning to write the word. He appears to be trying to remember just what the word was, since he was not paying full attention to the examiner when it was read. He writes very slowly, and appears to be anxious. Arthur is only halfway through writing the second word when the third word is read.

> Word 3: He is still working on the second word. He

---

1 For a comprehensive treatment using Cognitive/Behavioral strategies to learn assertive behavior, see *Responsible Assertive Behavior,* Lange and Jakubowski, 1976.

> writes the end of the second word even more slowly, as if denying the fact that another word has been presented. He does not attempt the third word at all. He appears lethargic and looks up at the examiner, sheepishly, in readiness for the fourth word.

This general pattern repeated itself for the remainder of the 25-word test, with Arthur leaving six words out, but correctly spelling 80 percent of the words he attempted.

The therapy program for Arthur was aimed at trying to get him to write his words faster; to leave a word unfinished if the examiner was going on to a new one, and come back to the unfinished word later; and to stress the importance of attempting every word. The following self-statements were taught:

> Before the test: "Work quickly. Write quickly. Listen carefully."

> On hearing a new word being presented: "STOP! Listen to the new word. Write it quickly."

> On having a few moments pause after an easier word: "Quick. Go back to the last incomplete word. Say that word to yourself. Finish it quickly."

Once these statements were learned by imitating the therapist, Arthur was shown the original videotape and asked to identify the places where these new thoughts should occur. When he did so, the tape was rerun in slow motion, and he first had to repeat the correct self-statement out loud, then whisper it, and then think it to himself. This process was then repeated for a new list of spelling words, delivered in groups of five. On the first set of words, the therapist identified where the self-statements should go and said them out loud. On the second set of words, Arthur said them out loud. On the third set he whispered them to himself. On the list of words he had written, 18 out of the 20 words presented to him; all were correct. The two he missed were started, but incomplete. His score was 90 percent.

While anxious children are typically over-reactive to their internal cues, the reverse is true for aggressive children who are so attuned to their environment that their responses appear to be reflexive. Aggressive children are often in a high state of readiness: one hint of an angry feeling or even just a word about fighting and their dander is up. For this reason, role-playing or presenting other stimuli that can evoke aggressive responses should be avoided in favor of approaches that desensitize the child.

Eddie S. arrived in a rural school in Colorado after having been raised for nine years on the streets of Chicago. To establish himself in the pecking order of his fourth grade class and also to draw attention away from his problems in reading, Eddie fought at least once a day. After having been suspended from school three times in one month, he was referred for psychological help.

The ultimate goal of Eddie's treatment program was to help him establish an identity for himself that did not focus on such a limited view of what he was and could be. But my immediate concern was to get him to stop fighting. I explained to Eddie that his fighting would eventually cause serious harm to himself or someone else, that he was in danger of being expelled from school (which might mean that he would be sent away to a boarding school), and that he was even beginning to get a reputation with the local police. As a positive incentive to change, Eddie won a chip for every day that he didn't fight. He could cash in the chips with his father at the end of the week, and either save his money or take it to town to spend.

The therapy program was carried out at Eddie's school in 30-minute sessions twice a week. In the small room that also doubled as the infirmary, I had Eddie recline in a cushioned chair, asking him first to relax the small muscles in his feet, then the muscles moving up his legs, the muscles in his fingers, forearms, upper arms, and shoulders, and finally the muscles in his chest, head, and face. This relaxation process took about seven to eight minutes.

Then I asked Eddie to imagine himself in various scenes as if he were looking at a movie in his mind. The scenes were adaptations of his fights, described to me in lurid detail by his teacher. At the point in the scene where Eddie would usually fight, however, I had him say, "I'm not going to fight. My muscles can relax. I can win this one by walking away." Eddie was then to visualize himself walking away from the fight and to see a crowd of proud faces (including his friends, his father, and myself) cheering him on his victory. As in the other examples of the Cognitive Mediating Technique, Eddie repeated the scene and the new self-guiding thoughts three times: first out loud, then in a whisper, and finally as a thought.

We usually ended each session by reading short vignettes that I had brought in about heroes who showed their bravery by walking away. As part of Eddie's program, I had his parents strictly limit his TV watching, completely eliminating all violent shows.

Self-Instruction and Self-Monitoring

Self-instruction and self-monitoring should be a part of a treatment plan for most children with ADHD. These children are particularly difficult for teachers and parents to handle because they need so much supervision.

Self-instruction teaches children a procedure for doing a particular task. This procedure emphasizes a concrete way for children to start the task, the specific stages of the task, and ways to stay ontask until it is completed. An example might be doing nightly homework. The procedure would be:

1. Be at your desk at exactly 5:00 p.m.
2. Clear your desk of everything but the homework that you are doing.
3. Make sure that there are no distractions.
4. Set your timer for 30 minutes.
5. Work until your timer goes off.
6. Set your timer again for five minutes and take a break (stretching or relaxing, but no reading, TV or phone calls).
7. Set your timer again for 20 minutes.
8. Work until the timer goes off.
9. Set your timer for 5 minutes. Use this time to check your work.[2]

This sequence can be written out and placed in clear view of the children as they work. The children can be required to read it aloud several times before beginning the homework and then several more times, saying it to themselves. It is hoped that this systematic procedure will eventually be internalized in the child's thoughts, and will then generalize to similar situations like classroom work. Even if the internalization doesn't take place, however, the child will be experiencing a systematic way of organizing time. An alternative for very impulsive children is to make a 55-minute tape recording, with the instructions occurring at the appropriate time on the tape. Then the tape will guide the child through the homework session.

The self-monitoring technique is similar to self-instruction, but is not task-specific. For example, suppose the child needs to learn to stop talking to his classmates during independent study time. He is told to remember the rule: "I will not talk to other children during study time." He is then given a tape recorder (with earphones), and he plays a tape during study time which beeps or gives him another reminder at random intervals. At his seat, he has a chart where he marks a "+" if he was *not* talking to anyone when the beep goes off and

---

2 From *The ADD Tool Kit,* Gauchman and Wong, 1994.

a "-" if he was talking. At the end of the session, the teacher tallies his points and gives him an appropriate reward.

Learning New Skills

Cognitive Mediating Techniques have also been used successfully in teaching children new skills. First the task is broken down into small steps in a logical order. Then the adult demonstrates how the task would be done, talking out loud, and he or she models statements which show planning, evaluating, and persevering, for example:

> Now, let me see the next step.
> If this doesn't work I'll try another way.
> Just three more steps and I'm done.

Then the child tries the problem, also thinking out loud as he works, encouraging herself through the steps until the task is done. This technique has been applied to academic as well as physical tasks (e.g., chores), but also works well in learning social skills. For example, suppose the child has very few friends and the therapist is trying to her find a new friend from her class. The child is shy, and doesn't know how to strike up a conversation. The therapist might break down this task into the following steps.

1. Try and find a time when the child is doing something that you would like to join in (the therapist might identify likely activities).

2. Say hello.

3. Say, "I'm Mary, and I know that you are Sarah."

4. Say, "That looks like fun. Can I do it with you?"

5. Ask Sarah questions about herself (the therapist might identify specific questions).

6. Thank Sarah for letting you join her.

Ideally the therapist and the child first practice these steps by reading them aloud and then role-playing them. A videotape of the role play can be made and shown to the child several times, which would give the child additional reinforcement in this cognitive rehearsal (see The Video-Self Modeling Technique in Chapter 7).

Problem-Solving

All cognitive techniques must take into consideration the cognitive abilities of the child. Children's ability to solve problems naturally follows their age and cognitive development, and while children as young as three can solve rudimentary problems through both deductive and inductive reasoning, more formal problem solving does not really appear until between the ages of eight and 10 (or the cognitive equivalent). I use a simple rule of thumb to determine if children are ready for problem-solving training: when children are comfortable with the multiplication tables and can understand the mathematical logic behind them (as opposed to rote memorization), then they are probably ready for the cognitive technique of problem-solving training.

Again, using a deficit model, we assume that the child is capable of solving problems independently, but for some reason he or she does not use these abilities at the appropriate time or place. For example, Tom is being teased daily on the playground by an older boy. Daily Tom breaks into tears and the other children his own age avoid him more. Every day he is more isolated and depressed. Tom does not see any alternative to his situation so he becomes more withdrawn, starts having stomachaches at home, and begs his mother not to make him go to school.

Problem-solving training is aimed at helping Tom see and act on more appropriate ways to handle his problem. All problem-solving programs teach a sequence of steps, such as:

1. Identifying the problem.
2. Brainstorming for possible solutions.
3. Considering the outcome or consequences of each solution.
4. Choosing the best alternative.
5. Acting on that alternative.
6. Evaluating the success of the solution.

Like other cognitive techniques, problem-solving training involves modeling by the therapist and then practice by the child in relevant and interesting scenarios. It is worth noting that most children (particularly those with problems in impulse control) have the most difficulty with the first step, identifying the problem. These children have difficulty in identifying and interpreting external as well as internal signals, including facial expressions, body posture, and the social meaning of different behaviors.

The other point at which this technique often fails is the fifth step, acting on the solution. Typically, children with this type of cognitive deficit also have behavioral deficits as well; that is, their behavioral and social skills are less sophisticated and appropriate than that of their peers. In implementing a problem-solving program the therapist must take the time to identify and help the child practice specific behaviors related to the problem at hand, including: ignoring, cooperating, reacting to failure, resisting peer pressure, controlling anger, taking turns, and so on.

In presenting the technique of problem-solving training to children, it is important for them to understand that you are teaching a *way* to solve problems, not necessarily a solution to the problem at hand. The children may not, in fact, be able to solve the problem at hand, due to their own difficulties or factors beyond their control, and the therapist does not want to set up a situation where the child will fail. Presumably the therapist will be using a multi-modal approach which will bring many techniques and resources to the presenting problem, and the cognitive technique of problem-solving will only be a part of the answer. I try and explain to the child that:

> Someday you will be able to solve your own problems. Everyone learns to do this as they become responsible adults. I am going to teach you how to solve problems, but you may not be ready to apply these skills just yet. You will know when you are ready. It is a little like learning the piano. First you have to learn the notes, and you have to practice, and then you can play a song. But I don't believe in forcing children to play a song in front of others before they are ready. Do you? When you are ready to perform, and really use these problem-solving skills, you will know. And I will be very proud of you when you do this!

Cognitive Restructuring Techniques

The second major school of cognitive therapy links cognitive changes to the child's feelings or affective state. These strategies assume that children and adolescents can make themselves *feel* more positive about themselves and/or what they are doing, and this improved affect will in turn lead to improved behaviors which will reinforce those feelings. cognitive restructuring is not really a deficit model. It assumes that the child, adolescent, or adult, has mediating internal thought processes, but that these thoughts are essentially dysfunctional. Rather than making the client feel better, they make the client feel worse. The treatment then focuses on replacing irrational, dysfunctional, or incorrect thoughts with ones which help the client feel better and behave more appropriately.

Consider our novice tennis player who used cognitive mediating techniques to learn the game. By now, she is really becoming expert, and has decided to start entering local tournaments. In many cases she is a much more polished player than her opponent, but she always loses. She loses because of a set of statements that she repeats to herself which do not have anything to do with how she learned to play the game, but are the result of things she learned to think about herself when she was very young. Before a match, she automatically says to herself, "I know I'm going to lose again. I'm just not a winner. I *want* to win, but I'm so anxious that I choke." She begins to play, but even when she is playing well, she is thinking: "This can't last long. I'm beginning to get nervous. This is where my game begins to fall apart every time." And sure enough she becomes more tense, her anxiety level rises and she begins to swat the ball right into the net.

Our player has fallen victim to self-defeating thoughts. They have very little to do with the reality of how well she plays the game; they certainly don't help her play better. She says to herself before the game, "I know I am going to lose again," but how can she know this? She has never seen her opponent play and has no idea whatsoever how either of them will be able to exhibit their particular skills that day. This is an example of faulty thinking: specifically, overgeneralization. Previous negative events have been abstracted into a "rule" of self-defeat. Our player begins her match on a note of self-pity and depression. She becomes doubting, insecure, and anxious, rather than enjoying the game and the benefits of the competition that she has chosen to enter.

The cognitive restructuring technique would have her learn to change her irrational self-statements into rational ones. A rational replacement for "I know I'm going to lose again" would be: "Well, I lost last week's tournament because I choked. But I don't have to do that again. I know I will play best if I just relax and concentrate. And if I don't win, it's no big deal. I'm really out here to get exercise and have fun."

Cognitive restructuring techniques have different historical roots from cognitive mediating techniques. They are primarily based on the work of Aaron Beck (see Beck et al, *Cognitive Theory of Depression,* Guilford Press, 1979) and Albert Ellis, the developer of Rational Emotive Therapy (R.E.T.). Although these two theories use different language and terms, they are very similar, helping clients change self-defeating thoughts into ones which will help them become more active and productive in dealing with their conflicts.

For children, the most common form of cognitive restructuring is teaching positive self-talk or self-encouragement. A more formal method of cognitive restructuring, for adolescents and adults will be presented following this discussion.

Self-Encouragement

Do you remember the story of *The Little Engine That Could?* He told himself, "I think I can. I think I can. I think I can. *I know I can!"* Self-encouragement really works. It seems to help us concentrate on a task and try harder. It helps us *feel* better about ourselves: more positive and self-confident.

Self-help groups particularly endorse encouraging oneself through affirmation. Affirmations are designed to build a basis for positive self-esteem. Douglas Bloch (see *Positive Self-Talk for Children: Teaching Self-Esteem Through Affirmations,* Bantam Books, 1993) notes that self-talk fosters independence, autonomy, and responsibility. In addition, he explains that positive self-talk can shift a child's self-confidence from being externally based to internally based; it can provide an antidote to unhealthy shame, and help children resist negative peer pressure, and develop positive attitudes and enthusiasm about the future.

Affirmations, or positive self-talk, can be modeled by the therapist by helping the child see positive characteristics of themselves, and it can be directly taught as well. Bloch gives an example of how a nine-year old whose mother was dying of cancer said, "It's just so hard for me, especially in the afternoon when I think of how sick she is." Her school counselor replied, "It must be hard to see your mom in pain and not be able to do anything about it. One of the ways to help you feel better is to replace the worries with some other thoughts about you and your mom. Would you like to think up some different thoughts with me?" Together they came up with affirmations like: "My sadness is okay. Nice people are helping my mom. I can find people to talk to when I am upset."

Learning to Argue with Yourself

Cognitive restructuring techniques, unlike the cognitive mediating techniques described previously, assume that clients are constantly thinking about themselves and what they do. These thoughts, which include perceptions, attitudes and beliefs, determine many of the moods clients have, and these affective states motivate specific behaviors.

The thoughts of adolescents and adults with intrapsychic conflicts, however, are invariably based on faulty logic. For example, depressed clients, for whom cognitive restructuring has been most successful, formerly used their thoughts or self-statements to keep themselves depressed and inhibit behaviors that would improve their sense of self-worth. Common thought distortions of depressed patients include:

- Overgeneralization
- Absolute thinking
- Focusing on negative details
- Disqualifying positive occurrences
- Minimizing or maximizing the importance of events
- Overpersonalizing the reactions of others

Dr. Aaron Beck and his team at the Center for Cognitive Therapy at the University of Pennsylvania School of Medicine developed a method of cognitive therapy which restructures the distorted *automatic thoughts* of depressed patients so that their moods and behaviors become more aligned with the realities of their experience.

The techniques developed by Dr. Beck et al have been used primarily for the treatment of depression, the "common cold" of psychiatric disorders. Usually lasting only three months, Beck's procedures for treating depression consist primarily of a series of paper-and-pencil exercises which are first done with the therapist and are then practiced at home. Although the depressed patient characteristically wants to withdraw and become inactive, the therapy requires diligent and constant work that is entirely the patient's responsibility to accomplish.

To change the thought distortions of his patients, Beck teaches them to identify automatic negative self-statements and to talk back to them. One method for doing this is the triple-column technique, which requires the patient to write down his or her self-critical thoughts and to label the type of distortions these thoughts are examples of, rebutting them.

Figure 5.B was done by Stacy C., a depressed and withdrawn adolescent who felt that he was not wanted by his family and rejected by his peer group at high school. In the Cognitive Restructuring Technique, it is the therapist's job to represent an undistorted view of the world and the way it works, but adolescents like Stacy may find this hard to accept. As part of their struggle to form their own separate identities, teenagers characteristically reject the viewpoints of

Figure 5.B
The Triple Column Technique

Automatic Thought	Cognitive Distortion	Rational Response
1. I'm all alone in the world.	This is the way I feel, but it is not really true.	I feel lonely, but there are many people I care about, and who care about me. But I still feel I want more. There are things I can do about this.
2. I'm doing lousy in school. There is no reason to try and study harder and go to college.	I am maximizing my failures.	I'm doing poor in some subjects, but well in others. Everyone has strengths and weak-nesses.

adults. This is an issue in every type of adolescent psychotherapy, but it is particularly critical in a directive psychotherapy such as Beck's in which the therapist appears to be telling the client how to think.

Adolescents must be helped to understand that the therapist's job is not to tell the adolescent what to think, but how to think and to point out a rational way of thinking which is free of distortion. Rational thoughts are based on fact, not on opinion. They should reflect the way that things are, not the way that the therapist wants them to be. Rational statements are objective, and, at least in principle, can be proven.

For instance, consider Stacy's automatic thought, "I'm all alone in the world. Nobody cares." I interpreted this distortion as an example of disqualifying positive events. In fact there were many people who cared about him and showed it in various ways. Even his family, who criticized him harshly, did many things to express their love and understanding. To prove this, I directed Stacy to list for three days all the positive things people did which showed that they cared. I explained that this could include anything from a friendly smile and a hello to the unsolicited gift of a solid gold Cadillac. I told Stacy that there was no need, yet, to change the way that he responded to other people if he didn't want to, but that he did need to be completely honest and diligent in recording every positive incident that occurred.

At the end of three days, Stacy brought in a list of 132 positive things that had happened to him. Just a few examples were:

"The doorman said hello five times."

"Mom fixed my favorite supper, because she said I looked frail."

"Joan asked me to eat lunch with her and Peter and Sam."

"Mr. Thomas (English teacher) said he liked my composition, and that I was 'an original wit.' Ha ha."

This exercise, like many others in the cognitive restructuring technique, was designed to replace automatic self put-downs with new, rational self-statements grounded in verifiable facts. In Stacy's case, thinking, "I am all alone in the world. Nobody cares," stimulated a mood of self-pity and depression that in turn led to more social isolation, lethargy, and passivity. But after the exercise the behavioral chain was different. When he felt alone and uncared for, he would think of the rational response he had learned in therapy and remember the exercise where he realized that this was an unrealistic attitude. Rather than initiating a cycle of depression and withdrawal, he would instead ask himself, "What made me think that? What triggered this automatic thought?"

At this stage of therapy, the client can be directed toward a more sophisticated form of self-analysis that uses the Daily Record of Dysfunctional Thought developed by Beck. This form is an analysis of the inertia that depressed or other clients with significant symptomatology frequently experience. It directs clients to consider what triggered their self-critical thoughts, what specific emotions the thoughts are associated with, and to what extent rebutting the self-criticism with rational self-statements will help reduce the negative emotions associated with the depression.

As an example of this expanded form, we can look at another set of Stacy's automatic self put-downs as recorded on his Daily Record of Dysfunctional Thought.

While Beck's therapy is designed to alter the way patients think about themselves, there are also other behavioral techniques involved in this method, giving it added power. The Daily Record of Dysfunctional Thought form serves to focus the patient on the antecedents as well as the consequences of the behavior (i.e., the automatic thoughts) to be changed. The emphasis is on what can be observed and what can be quantified (the rating of the patient's emotions).

The underlying principle of Beck's rating scales is his hypothesis that depressed people need to act in order to start feeling better about themselves. Apathy and lethargy are common symptoms of depression which contribute heavily to the patient's cycle of self-defeat. While a traditional psychoanalytic approach would emphasize understanding the unconscious conflicts causing the depression before entering any new endeavors, the cognitive restructuring technique recommends action as a way of breaking the reciprocal negative relationship between a patient's thoughts, feelings, and behaviors. The apathy of depressed patients is related to their cognitive distortions. They devalue their positive experiences, overgeneralize negative ones, and require perfection of themselves and everyone around them. Their inactivity and social withdrawal feeds the cognitive distortions that they are worthless and deserve no better than what they have. To break this spiral of defeat, patients must force themselves to be active, by planning every hour of the day if necessary.

Stacy couldn't imagine that he could do anything else but sit in his room and watch TV or listen to his stereo. But I impressed on him the importance of keeping busy, even if it seemed to him that he was just marking time. Our dialogue went something like this:

> Therapist: You're basing this attitude on more distorted thoughts, aren't you? Watch the word "nothing." How can "nothing" be fun? There are half a million people who are playing tennis right now. Thousands are playing chess. How many are at movies, swimming, at the library, walking, sailing, practicing an instrument...?
>
> Stacy: Please stop. I get your point.
>
> Therapist: You are also using some faulty information about the nature of emotions. You seem to think, "because I feel it, it must be true." But as we have seen, your emotions, while they are certainly important, are not the same as facts.
>
> Stacy: (Smiling) Right again, Doc. But what would you do if you were me? You probably have a million girlfriends and a private plane waiting for you at the airport to take you to your yacht in the Bahamas. But what about me? I can't even drive.

Figure 5.C
Excerpt from Stacy's Daily Record of Dysfunctional Thought

Date & Time	Dec. 10, 7 p.m.
Situation that precipitated the emotion	Studying for physics exam. Material is very hard. Can't concentrate.
Emotions: Specify exact emotion and rate degree of emotion 1-100%	Discouragement. Apathy. Depression. *Blah.* 90%.
Automatic thoughts	I'm stupid. I'll never amount to anything.
Cognitive distortions	Magnification.
Rational response	So I'm not so hot in physics. I'm getting an A in English and maybe in French. But if I don't hack away at this crap, I'll flunk.
Outcome: Specify and rate emotions 1-100%	Discouragement 40%. Impatient 10%.

Therapist: Your teasing me is revealing. You know that exaggeration makes for good humor. Your jokes tell me that you can tell the differences between distorted thinking and reality. Perhaps comedy is an interest of yours. I've noticed that you like to crack a lot of jokes, and I've seen you in the halls of the school with a crowd of people around you while you dropped one-liners.

Stacy: Yeah, I like to crack a few. I'd like to write jokes for David Letterman someday.
Therapist: It sounds like we may be getting close to finding an activity that you would enjoy. Reading on the history of humor? Writing down gags? You might even be able to sell them. There are plenty of good movies around. How about going to the new Woody Allen movie with a friend...?

Stacy: Okay, Doc, you got me, just please stop talking. I'll
do something. I swear it!

By the time this playful session was over, we had filled an activity
schedule for the upcoming weekend with several fun things for Stacy
to try, and of course many mundane tasks as well. After a few weeks
of this, Stacy settled into a more active schedule and rarely complained of being bored or feeling all alone. I pointed out that it is perfectly normal to feel this way some of the time.

Another one of the many behavioral principles that Beck et al
(1979) have built into their therapy is data keeping to keep track of the
severity of the depression. The Beck Depression Inventory (BDI) is
a 21-question rating scale that can be filled out in a matter of minutes,
and yet research suggests that it gives an accurate reading of the
client's level of depression. Used for a minimum of once a week and
as often as once a day, the BDI gives the therapist and client a clear
indication of whether the therapy works. In Stacy's case, his BDI
score changed from a 23 at the beginning of treatment (in the range
of moderate depression) to an 8 by the end of our time together (in the
range of normal mood ups and downs).

Although the majority of research on cognitive restructuring techniques has been done with depressed patients, this technique also
holds promise for other disorders characterized by extreme mood
states and maladaptive behaviors. Similar treatment methodologies to
the ones I have described have also been used with eating disorders
and with several types of phobias, and an even wider application of
these techniques may be on the horizon.

Transactional Analysis (TA)

Many therapists think that using cognitive therapy techniques with
children is too unexciting. Cognitive techniques involve a systematic
look at the way children think, and thinking about thinking is not something that most of us choose to have fun. However, there are ways to
make cognitive change more interesting to adolescents and children.
Transactional Analysis is a theory and system of techniques that can
appeal to children, adolescents, and adults. Although proponents of TA
may not classify it as a cognitive technique, my use of this technique
has focused on its concept of how we internalize three voices that guide
our feelings and behaviors: a child, a parent, and an adult. These voices can sometimes be at conflict with each other causing us needless
emotional pain. Changing these voices is a cognitive task.

TA is a humanistically-oriented therapy, emphasizing the right and ability of each individual to develop his or her potential to be fulfilled, loving, and loved. The key phrase, popularized in the title of a book by Thomas Harris (*I'm OK, You're OK,* 1969), is that everyone is OK. Being OK translates as having self-worth and an acceptance of one's strengths and weaknesses, values, and feelings. TA asserts that we are all born OK, but early in life, we learn that certain things we do, think, and feel do not please the people who are most important to us, and their reactions make us feel not OK: childish, stupid, inferior. The conflicting messages we get from our parents and other people important in our growing years cause us to develop three distinct ego-states or voices inside us: a child, a parent and an adult.

The child is the part of us that wants immediate gratification. It is the part of us that is selfish, demanding, inconsiderate, and irrational, but it is also the part that can have fun and be creative. The parent voice includes our beliefs, values, and prejudices. The parental voice often makes us feel badly about ourselves, telling us that we have mis-behaved or not accomplished what we should have. It also keeps tabs on our ethics and moral code and limits some of our excesses. The adult egostate is the voice of rationality. It deals with the present by seeing the world as it is, not the way it should be. TA also recognizes subdivisions of these three ego states (such as the critical parent and the nurturing parent) and various ways that they can overlap.

Transactions in this schema occur in the form of strokes which can be physical or verbal or gestural. Positive strokes (called "warm fuzzies") are naturally what we all seek and like, but in their absence, negative strokes ("cold pricklies") will sometimes have to do. Anything is better than the absence of strokes, of human interaction.

There are many more interesting and useful concepts in TA, but these are the basics. If TA is new to you, you may be interested in *The TA Primer* by Adelaid Bry (1973), which presents these concepts with simple prose and illustrations. If you work with adolescents, and I think using TA is particularly helpful with them, I would highly rec-ommend the book *T.A. for Teens* by Alvyn M. Freed (1976). Dr. Freed has also written books for younger children (*T.A. for Kids* and *T.A. for Tots)* and has developed records and audiovisual packages as well.

My successful use of TA occurred some years ago when I was treat-ing Janet, a 17-year-old girl with a severe behavioral problem at home. In the office Janet was shy and diffident, as well as slightly coquettish, and it was difficult to imagine her as the defiant shrew described by both of her parents. The therapy plan written for Janet included fam-ily therapy sessions to address her rebelliousness at home, but I also contracted with her and her parents to see Janet for 10 individual sessions to help her with her social problems at school.

Janet was extremely unhappy because she didn't have a boyfriend. She dated frequently, largely as a result of her seductive behavior with boys whom she had just met. But once they went out with her, the young men she flirted with wouldn't see her again. Often they responded to her forthright physical advances with immediate sexual overtures, and then when she then became coy and romantic, they would quickly lose interest. With each new experience, Janet found herself hopelessly in love, and pined unhappily until the next prospective boyfriend came along.

The idea of using TA with Janet first occurred to me when I saw her doodling in the waiting room before one of our appointments. Her drawings, which were original and very creative, were a concretization of her romantic daydreams and dating experiences. They were drawn in a comic-book style, each one telling a similar story of unrequited love and frustrated passion. The dialogue was extremely melodramatic:

> José: "My darling, I will never see you again. I go off to fight a battle I could never win. I will probably die, but I shall have your name on my last whisper.
>
> Edwina: Oh, José, my darling. I will never forget you. Give me your ring and I will wear it next to my heart until they bury me."

In the next session I began to talk to Janet about the principles of TA, using illustrations to talk about the three different voices in all of us, how to give strokes, and so on. My illustrations were laughable compared to Janet's, and for her homework, I had Janet draw me her own examples of what she had learned. As I had hoped, her examples were about dating. She drew a cartoon story about a boy who ran after girls because the child inside him kept seeking positive strokes by getting attention from girls. But when it came to having a deeper relationship with a girl, the parent voice inside him gave out only prohibitions: "If you get involved you'll only get hurt. You'll get someone pregnant. You'll get a disease."

We then began to role-play Janet's own dating experiences from her initial encounters with a new boy to her depression about being rejected. After each scene we drew cartoons of how a conversation might look if her adult voice was talking to the adult voice of her date. Five sessions later, Janet was fixed up with a boy from out of town. It was the first date that she could remember where she had not first thrown herself at the boy to get him to ask her out. Using TA diagrams, we conjured up what the transactions might be if Janet acted the way she usually did on dates, and then how they might look if she treated this new young man as one adult to another (see Figure 5.D). The date went smoothly, and Janet continued to correspond with this young man until the end of our sessions together.

In our remaining sessions Janet began to apply her new TA skills to other kinds of social relationships with her friends, parents, teachers, and, of course, with me. She read several books on TA and soon began to know much more about this method of self-analysis than I did. In a letter that I received from her after a six-month followup request, Janet told me she was still dating the same boy from out of town, and two other local boys as well. She was graduating from high school that spring, and wrote that she was thinking of majoring in psychiatry or biochemistry. She made it very clear that she saw her life as full of choices. And that she was feeling very OK.

Using Games in Cognitive Therapy

Cognitive therapy can be made more fun through the use of games. Games are particularly relevant to cognitive therapy because they employ such a wide variety of cognitive and language elements; memory, planning, strategy, thinking out loud, and so on. Nearly every game has certain cognitive elements which can be manipulated towards a therapeutic purpose. Published board games use both cognitive mediating and cognitive restructuring techniques. For example, *The Anger Control Game* developed by Dr. Berthold Berg (see *The Book of Psychotherapeutic Games,* Shapiro, 1993), addresses six cognitive-behavioral deficits identified in the research literature: the ability to empathize; the ability to distinguish between aggressive and nonaggressive acts; the ability to use self-statements to diffuse anger; the ability to generate and evaluate alternatives to aggression; the ability to identify feelings underlying anger; and the ability to evaluate the opinions of others on aggression. *The Anger Control Game* contains cards in each of these deficit areas, encouraging children to analyze the points of view of others and change their internal dialogue. For example:

> Zach started talking to a classmate who was working on his homework. When his classmate didn't answer him, Zach thought, "Bad timing. I'll have to catch him

Figure 5.D
"Old Voices"/"New Voices"

"OLD VOICES"

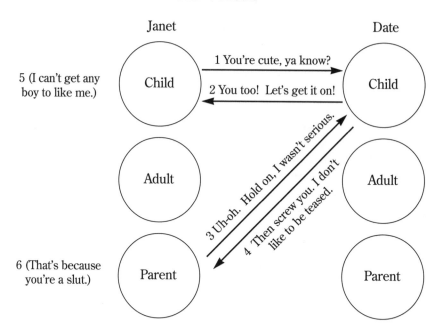

"NEW VOICES"

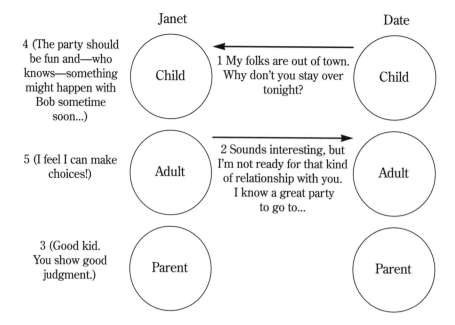

when he's not busy trying to finish an assignment."

What did Zach say to himself?

What else could Zach say to himself?

Other games deal with helping children restructure dysfunctional thinking. For example, *My Two Homes* (see *The Book of Psychotherapeutic Games,* Shapiro, 1993) deals with the cognitive distortions that children frequently acquire when their parents divorce. This game helps dispel common childhood myths (such as *children* are responsible for their parents' divorce); gives children the facts about divorce (e.g., they are not alone in this experience; over 40% of the children in the US are affected by divorce); and gives children the vocabulary that they need to understand what is happening (e.g., defining such words as alimony, child custody, visitation). This game, like many others, helps children get a new perspective and attitude about their problems, which in turns affects their feelings and behaviors.

Games are a particularly relevant medium for cognitive techniques because they add the elements of fun, reinforcement, and repetition. Following is a pencil-and-paper game that I developed in response to my own childhood memories (a great source for making up *your* own games; see Chapter 6, the *Make-a-Game Technique*). When I was in the fifth grade, I played a game in which I held a pencil about six inches above my desk and then dropped it like a bomb, trying to hit tanks and planes that I had drawn on a piece of paper. I don't remember why I liked doing this so much, but I did. Thirty years later, I devised the following game, which I call, "The Battle Against Negative Thinking" (from *The Building Blocks of Self-Esteem,* Shapiro, 1992).

Figure 5.E
The Battle Against Negative Thinking

People who are successful usually have a positive attitude. They are aware of problems or difficulties, but they don't let negative thoughts keep them from trying to do their best.

Keeping negative thoughts away can be a battle for some people, and that is just what this game is about. You can help Gerald get rid of his negative thoughts.

To Play:
1. Make copies of the opposite page. You will need one copy for each time you play.

2. Get a pencil and hold it about one foot above the battleground on the page.

3. You have 20 tries to "bomb" the negative tanks below by dropping the pencil on the tanks.

4. When your pencil hits the tank and makes a mark you can cross that tank off.

5. To win, you must hit all 10 tanks in 20 tries, protecting Gerald from negative thoughts. If you hit Gerald, you automatically lose.

(For non-readers: The adult should read the directions and the sayings on the tanks to the child and explain why negative thoughts are harmful).

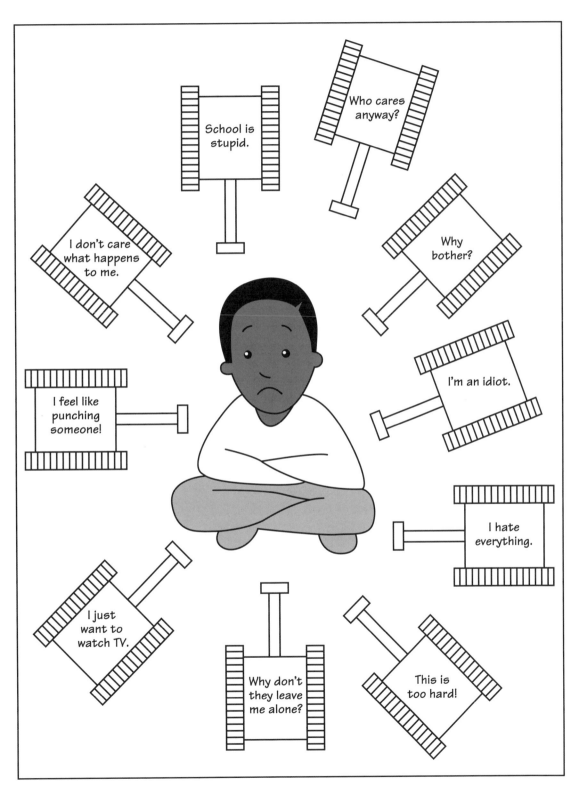

CHAPTER 6

THE DEVELOPMENTAL MODALITY

The Developmental modality may be perhaps the most difficult modality to address in terms of interventions, but it is also one of the most significant in terms of being able to predict long-term therapeutic success. Every child therapist and counselor realizes the importance of understanding the various developmental theories as they pertain to understanding the uniqueness of each child. Sigmund Freud theorized about how children learn to tame basic drives; Jean Piaget investigated the way children develop their cognitive abilities; Erik Erikson defined personality development in terms of specific conflicts occurring at various ages throughout the life cycle; and Anna Freud described various developmental issues including a child's level of mastery and social attachments.

Familiarity with these theories is essential. Hundreds of other researchers have detailed the development of perception, empathy, identity, and other psychological constructs. But to date this research and theory has not been translated into an understanding of how the normative developmental issues of childhood relate to the treatment of specific psychological disorders.

Equally important is understanding the *atypical* developmental stages that children experience as a result of specific life circumstances. For example, we know that latency-age children can go through predictable stages of grief, much like adults, as the result of a significant loss. Children may experience stages of denial, anger, depression, and acceptance in reaction to the death of a parent, grandparent, or even a beloved pet. Unlike adults, however, these stages are influenced by other aspects of the child's development which can make these stages more or less difficult to work through.

Similarly, children of divorce go through predictable reactions depending on their chronological age, and they also have predictable developmentally-related problems. Figure 6.A shows a developmental table of children's experience of divorce compiled from a variety of sources (*Child Therapy Today,* Volume 1, Chapter 2, 1994), as well as common problems, prevention strategies, and recommendations for custody and visitation.

In a multimodal approach to therapy, the therapist must consider both the typical and the atypical developmental issues that coincide with the child's presenting problem. Unlike the other five modalities

Figure 6.A
Developmental Table of Children's Experience of Divorce

AGE	REACTIONS	COMMON PROBLEMS	PREVENTION	RECOMMENDED CUSTODY/ VISITATION
0-2	Aware of loss of parent	Regression; developmental delays; withdrawal; heightened stranger anxiety	Maintain routines; support caregiver; supplement care-giver	Frequent, short visits with noncustodial parent
2-3	Fears abandonment; misses absent parent	Regression; developmental delays; withdrawal; heightened stranger anxiety; toileting and sleeping problems; sex role confusion	Simple explanation to child; maintain routines/discipline	Overnight visits with noncustodial parent
3-5	Fears abandonment; misses parent; feels unloved	Regression; developmental delays; withdrawal; heightened stranger anxiety; toileting/sleeping problems; sex role confusion; clinging, whining or "perfect" behavior; sadness	Simple explanation to child; maintain routines/discipline; assure that child did not cause divorce; separate bed from parents	Overnight or longer visits no more than ten days apart
6-8	Fears abandonment; misses parent; feels unloved; fears for future; feels guilty; feels betrayed	Anger, behavior/academic problems; withdrawal; depression; dependency	Simple explanation to child; maintain routines/discipline; assure that child did not cause divorce; separate bed from parents; help child to stay out of parents' conflicts; keep as consistent an environment as possible	Longer visits; contact during week; some flexibility around child's school/social activities; involvement of noncustodial parent in school activities
9-12	Fears abandonment; misses parent; feels unloved; fears for future; feels guilty; feels betrayed; may feel rejected; needs someone to blame for divorce	Worries about custody; hostile toward one or both parents; academic/behavior problems; may be parentified	Maintain adult supports for parents; maintain/improve parenting skills; help child process anger	May need to decrease frequency if had high frequency before; regular, flexible visits; involvement in school activities
12-18	Feels grief for loss of family life; fears about own future; feels responsible for family members; feels angry	Withdrawn from family or clinging; decreased self-esteem; academic/behavioral problems; concern about relationships with opposite sex; difficulty with career plans	Maintain discipline; keep low-profile of parental sexual activity; help child cope with ambivalent feelings; support career goals, higher education	Flexible visitation schedule; possible trial living with noncustodial parent
Young adults whose parents divorced earlier		Sleeper effect for girls—in general, difficulty in establishing relationships with opposite sex; confusion about career plans; difficulty with higher education	Therapy; re-involve parents	

discussed in this book, developmental goals may not always bear directly upon the therapeutic goal. Consider, for example, the child with Attention Deficit Disorder with Hyperactivity as a predominant feature (ADHD). The presenting problem will typically be a behavioral one, and the therapist's role will be to help the child act more appropriately both at home and at school. Learning to listen, to follow directions, and respect rules will undoubtedly have a profound effect on the child's personality, as he or she gets more parental acceptance and approval and becomes a less difficult student at school.

But developmental problems will also exist. We know that children with ADHD have difficulty with peer relationships. In many cases, ADHD children are isolated and avoided by other children, or develop only short-term relationships with children with similar social problems. Their impulsivity, tendency to be overly aggressive (in about 40% of ADHD children), and lack of ability to read social cues, makes it difficult for them to pass through normal stages of developing friendships and other peer relationships. These children typically lack important social experiences and are not able to resolve important development tasks related to their ability to form attachments to others. Specifically, they may not be able to find a best friend or a significant group to identify with, such as a club, team, or other peer group based on common interests and a sense of belonging. Theorists have suggested that when children miss out on these important age-specific developmental tasks, they may have social problems throughout their adolescence and into adulthood.

The Developmental Task Approach

In addressing the Developmental modality in short-term therapy, therapists must ascertain and define developmental goals that are important for the child's overall development, although they may not bear directly on the child's presenting problem. Once identified, we must break down these goals into incremental steps, and guide the child (and parents and teachers) towards achieving them.

With the ADHD child who is socially isolated, the ideal would be to help this child find an appropriate best friend, but we will settle for having the child develop some of the skills necessary to find and maintain friendships. Begin by defining the steps necessary to find a friend:

1. Make a list of all the children your age whom you know.
2. Put a check by each child who you like.
3. Put another check by each child with whom you have played before.

4. Put a third check by each child with whom you have something in common.
5. Make another list of the things that you have in common with each child who you have checked, including: interests, hobbies, favorite TV shows, neighborhood, church, etc.
6. Choose the two children whom you have listed with the most check marks.
7. Role-play asking them to do an activity that you both like.
8. Call them at home.
9. Schedule a time and place to do the activity for no more than a two-hour period (the activity should be highly-structured if possible).
10. Plan a second activity with the first child, or with another child on your list.

Once the steps or subtasks have been defined, the therapist or parent will lead the child through each step, remembering the basic principles of behavioral learning:

• Look for small amounts of progress.
• Don't be discouraged by setbacks (they are common when learning a new behavior).
• Reinforce positive change.
• Use other techniques to reinforce the child's change (e.g., cognitive mediating techniques and token reinforcement).

The importance of addressing developmental tasks in the child's treatment plan cannot be overemphasized. Hopefully, by persisting with these tasks, the child's natural resources and inclinations will take over and the developmental process will move ahead.

The Make-a-Game Technique

Another way to help a child achieve a particular developmental task is to make a therapeutic game specifically for the child addressing the task to be accomplished. When I began writing about the use of therapeutic games more than 15 years ago, I advocated that therapists make up their own games to use with children (*Games To Grow On*, Shapiro, 1981). The power of a therapeutic game is enhanced by making up a game that exactly fits the developmental level of a child as well as his or her interests and life circumstances. Unfortunately, therapists as a group seem reluctant to take the time to make up games; as more and more published therapeutic games become available, therapists naturally prefer to just open a box, read the instructions, and play the game. Although making up your own therapeutic game can seem time-consuming and outside the training of most therapists, I still believe that the most effective therapeutic game you can play is one you have made for a particular child.

When you make up your own game, it can mirror the child's circumstances in a way that no published game possibly can. Frequently, I am asked questions like, "Do you know of a game for a girl who sucks her thumb, has a slight learning disability, whose parents just got separated, and whose sister has cerebral palsy?" I always pause for a minute at this type of question, wondering if this person wants to hear that there is a "Don't-Suck-Your-Thumb-Or-Worry-About-Your-Sister-Or-Parents-But-Try-Hard-In-School Game." I reply, "No, I don't know of a game that can address *all* those problems, but *you can make a game that does!*"

Making a game is really not difficult. Figure 6.B shows a template for designing a game that can be adapted for use with almost any child. Dice and pawns can be borrowed from existing games, and cards can be made out of colored index cards. Once the game is created, it can be easily mounted onto foamcore (a Styrofoam-type board available at most stationery stores). That's all there is to making a game!

The important therapeutic elements of making your own game for a specific child actually occur in two stages: during the making of the game and then during the playing of it. In most cases I ask the child, adolescent, or even the whole family to join me in making the game. I begin by showing them a few published therapeutic board games, and explain how effective this technique can be. Most children love the idea of having a game made just for them and eagerly join in the game-making process.

First the therapeutic goal is defined. In my own mind I have a specific developmental task that I want the game to focus on, but I have to present the game so that it defines a goal to which the child can relate. For example, Carl, an eight-year-old boy whose parents had just separated, was exhibiting a variety of defiant behaviors. Carl's father was moving several hundred miles away, and both parents agreed that Carl was now the "man of the house." Instead of acting like an adult, as his parents suggested, Carl seemed determined to tease his younger sister Sharon unmercifully, even though he knew that this was wrong and he was frequently punished for it.

Having chosen to make a game as a treatment approach, I now had to decide exactly what I wanted the therapeutic game to do. From a developmental perspective, and considering the parents' recent sepa-

Figure 6.B
Template for Designing a Game

ration, I assumed that the increase in Carl's teasing was a result of his anger about his parent's decision to separate, and a regressive reaction to their desire that he be the man of the house. Teasing his sister provided both an outlet for his aggression and a defiant message to his parents: "I *won't* be the man of the house. Why should I act grown-up when you don't?!" A more appropriate developmental reaction towards his younger sister would have been to become a "big brother" to her and help her with her reaction to the divorce (note that being a big brother is very different than being the man of the house).

Two developmental tasks were associated with this game: to help develop age-appropriate coping skills to the parent's divorce and to reinforce Carl's identity as a big brother. In introducing the Make-a-Game technique, I said to Carl,

> We both know that you are unhappy about your parent's separation. And I don't blame you for being angry! When parents separate, they think that they are doing the right thing, but it can still be very painful for children. We can invent a game that can help you find a better way to let people know how you feel and to keep you from getting punished all the time.

As we began to make up the game, I explained my goals to Carl. I talked about how divorce is difficult for most children, particularly boys, but that it is something that children learn to deal with. I talked about how the divorce was affecting Sharon, and how important it was for *her* to deal with the divorce. The overt intention of the game was for Carl to play the game with his sister, helping her understand ways to cope with her parents' divorce, but the game was primarily intended for Carl as a vehicle for him to reframe his relationship with his sister, so I suggested that the game we were making could be played with Sharon to teach her the things that Carl learned in therapy. Even before we began to play the game we were addressing the developmental task: encouraging Carl to do something that would put him in the role of teaching and helping Sharon.

As we designed the board and wrote the cards, I talked to Carl about the reactions that most children have towards a divorce. We made one pile of cards entitled "Things You Can Tell Yourself When You Are Feeling Bad," and another pile of cards entitled "Things You Can Do When You Are Feeling Bad." As we made the game, I reminded Carl of the most important element of any game: it has to be fun! So we designated certain squares on the game board as "Silly Squares," and we wrote down things that would have to be done if a player landed on those squares. I directed Carl to select stunts that were silly, but also emphasized his role as an older brother and that would lead to an improved relationship with his sister. For example:

> The largest player must lift the smallest player off the ground.

> All players must say things that they like about each other. You get a point for each thing you can think of.

I also wrote down the rules. As discussed in Chapter 2, rules are the driving force of games and they must be both clear and simple. After spending about two and a half sessions developing and making the game, I told Carl that I would finish it up, because in using this technique over the years, I generally find that while making the game is very therapeutic, there is a point (after about two sessions) when it becomes tedious. At this point, I complete the physical aspects of the game myself: writing the rest of the cards, coloring and mounting the board, and so on. I asked Carl to bring in his sister to our next session and we would all play together.

A Neglected, Learning-Disabled Boy Stops Running Away

Jay was an eight-year-old boy who had been tragically misplaced in institutions since the age of three. According to his social service record, he had been placed in state custody shortly after his parents' separation. He was described as a discipline problem with moderate mental retardation (a misdiagnosis) and sent to a large public institution with a reputation for poor care. No one there paid attention to the fact that this child did not function like a retarded child, but rather like a child suffering from neglect and specific developmental delays in several cognitive areas.

I saw Jay for the first time at the age of eight in an intermediate care facility where he had been placed as a step toward deinstitutionalization. When admitted, Jay appeared to be a sweet-natured boy, clearly suffering from his twin misfortunes of parental rejection and institutionalization. The staff was naturally shocked at the discrepancy between the child's appearance and his past history. There was a general feeling that Jay's stay at this facility would be short and that he would soon be placed for adoption.

Hardly more than a week had passed before Jay began to exhibit a host of behavioral problems. He was belligerent to the staff and other children. He stole money, toys, food, almost anything that was of value to anyone. For a small boy, he had an incredible vocabulary of obscenities; he used them to punctuate nearly every sentence. He was particularly troublesome in school where his difficulty in learning pre-academic skills was masked by these disruptive behaviors.

The most troubling problem of all was Jay's propensity for running away. Many children run away between the ages of seven and twelve. While they usually set out to express their anger and discontent, they also use this behavior as a metaphor for their growing sense of autonomy and their ambivalence about it. Running away from home, no matter how feeble the attempt, demonstrates the desire of children to test their limits for survival in the world. The proverbial peanut butter sandwich and bag of marbles wrapped up in a bandanna are a symbolic gesture. Children are saying, "See, I don't need you! I can survive on my own," but at the same time, they have an equally strong wish to be proven wrong and yanked back into the nest. At this age children test themselves to see how far they can go, and their family to see that they don't allow them to go too far, into danger.

However, running away in Jay's case appeared to be a different metaphor entirely. Jay's compulsive need to try and run away was not the gesture of a latency age child testing his independence, but rather was the gesture of a toddler being left out in the cold. Jay wasn't testing his inner resources; he wasn't aware that he had any. He wasn't seeing just how nurturing his environment could be; his experience told him he wasn't stretching the limits of familial love—he would hardly be missed. In considering the meaning of his behavior, we must also recognize that Jay generally functioned at a level two or three years below the eight years consistent his appearance. Jay's concept of home meant only one thing to him: a place where he did not belong.

The therapeutic game designed for Jay was called "Find Your Way Back Home." It consisted of a three-dimensional game board (see Figure 6.C) that used small toys to recreate the neighborhood around the facility where Jay was living. At the center of the game, was a drawing of Jay's home at the facility with a small photo of Jay and his counselor inside. The game also included a small family of dolls (a mother, father, little boy, and little girl) to be used as markers and a spinner with numbers 1 through 7 (as high as Jay could count).

The rules of the game were designed to create situations in which Jay would have to use a variety of new emotional, cognitive, and behavioral skills. These skills are discussed below.

Figure 6.C
Plan for "Find Your Way Back Home" Game

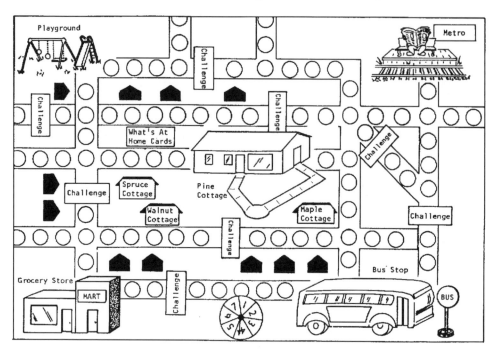

Rules for "Find Your Way Back Home" Game

1. Each player chooses one of the dolls to represent himself or herself in the game. A family of dolls was chosen so that Jay would have opportunities to express feelings about his family of origin. A "loaded" stimulus such as this will often stimulate important play outside the game.

2. Each player spins the spinner; the highest number goes first. Even the most basic rules can teach new skills. This rule introduces elementary concepts of cooperation, taking turns, and the fairness of chance.

3. The players can begin play from any of the corners: the metro station, the bus stop, the grocery store, or the playground. The game begins with a metaphorically important choice. In all choice situations, the therapist has an opportunity to model his or her thought processes and values (see the Cognitive-

Mediating technique described in Chapter 5).

4. Each player spins the spinner and advances in the direction of his or her choice in turn, but each route eventually leads through the center (home) of the board. Unlike most board games there is no specified end point; the players can wander around the board indefinitely. The game ends when the players mutually decide that it will end. In spite of the implications of the title, the object of the game is to explore the neighborhood and to learn new skills while doing so.

5. Throughout the neighborhood, various squares direct the player to take a Challenge card. Each card describes a problem that the player must solve in order to win points:

How much money does it take to ride the bus?
What do you do when you see a mean-looking dog in someone's backyard?
What is the phone number of Mr. A (the counselor) if you get lost?

6. The game is over when the players mutually decide they want to stop. At this time, each player may choose to "go home" and pick from a second set of What's At Home cards. On one side of each card is a description of something that is at home; the other side is the answer:

Something good's for dinner. It used to go gobble, gobble, but now it just lies there in gravy.
Who's thinking of you when it's past dinnertime and your seat is empty?
What's the largest picture you have in your room?

If the correct answer is given, that player receives a 10-point bonus. It is taken for granted that the players go home after their adventures in the neighborhood, although this is not part of the rules, but a choice for each player. Since bonus points can be won by going home, this is an added incentive to continue the metaphor.

Each time Jay played the game, he had the opportunity to win points towards field trips with his therapist or his primary counselor. Although the game had no specific end point, that is, no one won or lost, it was recommended that the playing time be not be more than 20 minutes, for this was about the limit of Jay's attention span. During this time, it was anticipated that Jay would win between 30 and 50 points by solving the Challenge and What's At Home cards.

Jay played the game every other day, either with his therapist who saw him twice a week, or with his counselor who was with him every day. Thus Jay had the opportunity to win 100 to 200 points a week. Since Jay did not have advanced number concepts, a pie with 10-point slices that were colored in after every session was used to keep the cumulative score. When Jay won a specified number of points, he could trade them in for a trip to get a hamburger or ice cream, a movie, or another outing of his choice.

It is important to note that these trips were in no way contingent on improved behavior. Even if Jay ran away every day, he would still get his trip when he won enough points. Because Jay could not control his running away, to withhold trips would have made him a prisoner in his own home and fueled his need to escape. Instead, contingencies for his running away were included in a separate behavioral program, which rewarded him with increased privileges in his cottage and punished him by removal of these privileges.

The Find Your Way Back Home game was played over a period of two months, and it was continually revised to meet Jay's changing needs and interests. With Jay's help, new Challenge cards, as well as new What's at Home cards, were made. The board was extended to include a downtown metro line that Jay wished to explore on the board as well as on his outings. Each change in the game gave the therapist a chance to learn more about Jay's way of thinking and interacting with the world, and this knowledge was then applied to the milieu treatment he received throughout the facility.

For example, everyone who worked with Jay was given a 5 x 8" card with Jay's picture mounted on it. The cards briefly and simply explained the nature of Jay's learning difficulty and suggested optimum ways to communicate with him:

> Speak slowly in simple sentences. Note if Jay is watching you and showing his understanding through his interest. Reinforce what you say with your own gestures. If it is important, ask Jay to repeat what you say. Be patient.

Jay sharply curtailed his running away within the first two weeks of the program, but it is impossible to say whether this was due to added precautionary measures or to the treatment program. Because Jay's roaming around in the winter was so dangerous, the staff decided that they couldn't wait to see if the behavioral program would be effective, and an alarm system was installed in Jay's bedroom: a loud siren would go off if the windows or doors were jarred. When Jay needed time alone, he spent it in his bedroom; at all other times he was part of a buddy system, where he was required remain in sight of a counselor, teacher, or older resident. Running away or hiding was used as the measure of the behavior we wished to extinguish; this decreased from an average of twice a day to twice a month by the end of the official treatment program.

Helping an ADHD Child Be at the Right Place at the Right Time

From our first session together, it was clear that Ralph didn't like coming to psychotherapy. He much preferred playing ball with his friends or watching cartoons on TV than going to see a doctor about his problems. Fortunately Ralph did like to play games. Games could make him laugh, dance, reveal his thoughts and feelings, and even sit down and work: quite an accomplishment for a boy whose special education teacher had described him as the most overactive child she had ever worked with in 10 years of working with problem children.

Although Ralph had been calmer since taking medication prescribed by a pediatric neurologist for his attention span disorder and hyperactivity, he still had significant learning and behavioral problems. He was suspended from school at least once a month for infractions ranging from tardiness to provoking fistfights on the playground and stealing gum from his teacher's purse. His parents described him at home as a happy-go-lucky kid, but completely irresponsible. He would leave his chores after a few minutes, come home late for dinner, and play mischievous pranks that bordered on serious delinquent behaviors.

Ralph's parents and teachers agreed to participate in a token economy system to get Ralph to be more responsible at home and in school, but they all complained to me of one obstacle: Ralph was never where you wanted him to be. "How can we use a token economy system," they said, "when Ralph is always late and doing something that he is not supposed to?" Naturally, being on time was one of the objectives on his token economy chart, but I was still faced with the dilemma of increasing Ralph's sense of punctuality and responsibility so that he could win points for improvement. To address this problem, I invented a game.

The Time On Your Hands Game

I asked Ralph's parents to purchase a digital watch, since digital watches are easier for most learning disabled children to read. To Ralph's delight, they chose a Batman watch. To make sure Ralph wouldn't lose it, I advised them to pin it each day to his shirt cuff or belt loop. After reviewing basic time facts and making sure Ralph could read his new watch, we were ready to play.

The game began by drawing three pictures of the face of Ralph's watch and writing in the three times that it was most important for him to be punctual. The times selected by his parents were 9 AM, the time he had to be at his desk in school; 6 PM, the time he had to be at home for dinner; and 9 PM, the time he had to be in bed. Each of these pictures was then taped to an object near where Ralph had to be at that particular time: his desk in school (9 AM), the back of his chair at the dining room table (6 PM), and his bed post (9 PM). To win points, Ralph had to be at the right place at the exact time when the face on his watch matched the time shown on the drawing. Being early didn't count, since Ralph could then wander away and end up being late. Naturally an adult had to be at each point to check his punctuality, give him his points, and to give Ralph encouragement for his new-found sense of punctuality.

As the people in Ralph's life began to play with him rather than criticize him and despair over his behavior, a subtle change began to appear in the way they talked about him and treated him. Where once his mother had greeted him after his therapy sessions with complaints and hard looks, she now began to greet him with smiles and hugs. His teacher reported that Ralph still had difficulties in class, but was a happier child and made friends more easily. A month after Ralph had started therapy, his school suspensions ceased. He finished the year without any other further disciplinary action from the principal.

CHAPTER 7

THE EDUCATIONAL MODALITY

The model that I have developed for short-term therapy promotes techniques that move the treatment along the most direct route to helping children. It acknowledges that changes must occur simultaneously within as well as outside the child in his or her social system, in the context in which the problem exists. In order to ensure these changes occur in the briefest amount of time, we must not overlook the importance of simply educating the child and the adults in the child's system towards change. After all, learning is what children do best. With both children and adults, the motivation to learn is enhanced when there are clear benefits to acquiring new knowledge and when the means of learning is fun.

But therapists do not typically see themselves in the teaching business. Mental health workers tend to ally themselves in the professional pecking order more with the medical profession than with the teaching profession. Teaching, some mental health professionals seem to think, is something that anyone can do, but therapy is something else; only highly trained professionals can do it. But all this is really beside the point. Therapists have always used educational principles in their work, just as teachers have always used psychological principles in theirs. As Chapter 2 suggests, in a multi-modal treatment plan, effective techniques of any kind can be used to help children; the compatibility of the theories associated with those techniques is inconsequential.

This chapter introduces techniques which to some extent put the therapist in the role of an educator. These techniques are enhanced by incorporating the power of specific psychological principles and strategies.

Bibliotherapy with Parents

Bibliotherapy is exactly what the name implies: therapy through books. Since Dr. Spock's first book on child-rearing influenced the care of a generation of children, thousands of books have been written to help parents. There is virtually no subject on child-rearing that has not been written about, and many bookstores see this category as one of their "hottest" areas.

There is no question that books and other information to help children are there for the asking, but how do you get parents to use them?
Obviously if it was simply a matter of going to a bookstore, finding a
book, and reading it, then parents would rarely need the advice of a
therapist. But this isn't the case. Parents can have difficulty finding
the right books. And even when they find them, and despite their
good intentions, the books may never be read. Sometimes, even if the
books are read, what they suggest may not fit the parents' lifestyles or
abilities or may not be implemented properly.

In other words, a book is only a book. But in the hands of a therapist, a book can be a *technique.* There are certain principles that can
be followed to enhance the use of books as a psychological technique;
that can make reading a book a process of real change.

Choosing the Right Book

As with any change, the initial steps are frequently the hardest.
There are thousands of books in print to help parents, but which ones
are right for any given parent? This is a question that the therapist
should be able to answer, and it should go without saying that the therapist should have a thorough knowledge of the books available on a
certain subject, as well as know how to find more obscure or specialized books. A therapist who tells a parent, "Oh, just go to a bookstore
or a library and get a good book about discipline" is not doing his or
her job. If it was that simple, the motivated parent would certainly
have already done it. The unmotivated parent would probably not
have made the trip to a bookstore or library, but the therapist's casual
suggestion will not be enough to get him or her there either.

The therapist using Bibliotherapy as a technique must have an
appropriate collection of books to give to or recommend to parents.
Some therapists put together a lending library. They put a card in the
book showing when it is due back, have the parent sign it out, and may
even require the replacement cost of the book as a security deposit.
Some therapists find this awkward at first, but dealing with a problem
in a realistic way is always therapeutic, and the reality is that parents
often don't return books or other materials even though it is their
responsibility to do so. Usually when I recommend a specific book to
parents, I ask them,

> Do you want to sign out my copy, like you would at a library,
> or do you want your own copy? I want you to read this book
> (or parts of it) and it is very important to your child's thera-
> py that you do so. But I also understand that you are busy,
> and that you have a lot of things on your mind, and it may

be hard for you to find the time to get the book or to read it. I want to make it as easy as possible for you. The book I am recommending really is a good book and I think it will help. So tell me what I can do to help you? How can you find the quiet time to read it? How long do you think it will take you?

These questions are designed to consider every possibility of how the parent might try to avoid or unconsciously undermine his or her task. My intent is to identify with the parents and to ally myself with them in getting them to do as I ask. If they elect to buy the book rather than borrow it from me, I make sure that this task will be easy to get done. I know many therapists who have asked their local bookstores to carry a certain selection of books that they frequently recommend to parents, and the bookstores are more than happy to do this. Similarly, neighborhood libraries will often stock a selection of books on a therapist's request. Don't be surprised at how cooperative bookstores and libraries will be; it is *their job* to get people to buy or borrow books!

A therapist should also know the appropriate resources to find and acquire books. Libraries and larger bookstores have copies of *Books in Print*, which is an encyclopedia-size reference of all the books currently in print, indexed by topic, author, and publisher. This is the resource that bookstores use to order books, and most bookstores will help order the books that you want, once you have identified the title, author, and publisher. The Center for Applied Psychology, Inc.'s Childswork Book Club lists hundreds of books specifically selected for Bibliotherapy purposes.[1]

The point of all this is to emphasize the need for the therapist to make book selection easy for parents. Like any technique, the book will work most effectively if it is matched to the parent's style, interest, and reading ability. When evaluating a book to recommend to a parent I look for books that are well-organized and to the point, that describe practical strategies, and that make the principles that they are teaching clear and concise. I rarely recommend books that are overly theoretical or long. Parents should be able to extract the information they need from a book in one or two 45-minute sittings. Asking a parent to do more than this is simply unrealistic.

The therapist should also not overlook recommending children's books to parents. Children's therapeutic books, which are discussed in following paragraphs, can be read very quickly, but often have a profound effect on parents. They are typically simple and poignant, and I know many parents who have been moved to action or to confront a

---

1 For information about the Childswork Book Club write P.O. Box 61587, King of Prussia, PA 19406 or call 1-800-962-1141.

decision as a result of reading these stories.

Using Books to Define a Menu of Techniques

Once a book has been chosen, acquired, and read, it is up to the therapist to help the parent utilize the information from the book. The book will undoubtedly have suggested a variety of techniques to deal with the problem at hand, and the parent must now decide which ones to implement. I usually ask parents to write down the techniques that they read about and bring them into the office. I try and explain to them that many techniques can help their child, and that they should select the one that best fits their style of parenting, much like they would select from a menu at a restaurant. I explain to them that there is seldom a perfect solution to any problem, but since I am the one who will have to find the solution, I should make this decision. I, of course, will act as the expert in helping them decide and then understand and practice the technique that they have chosen.

Encouraging Accountability and Making the Technique Work

Bibliotherapy emphasizes that parents (or other caretakers) are accountable for their child's change. As a tool for teaching parenting skills, it is most effective when used with other modalities in a short-term treatment plan. The following are examples of books that fit into the multi-modal scheme which is the basis for my model of short-term therapy:

Affective Modality: Many parents need to learn to express their feelings more openly, and at the same time they need to help their children express themselves. I might suggest the popular book *How to Talk So Kids Will Listen and Listen So Kids Will Talk* (Faber and Mazlish, 1980).

Behavior Modality: Perhaps parents need to learn new discipline techniques. There are many books on the market, but I like *SOS! Help for Parents* by Dr. Lynn Clark (1985) or *Assertive Discipline for Parents* by Lee and Marlene Canter (1982).

Cognitive Modality: Affirmations are a great way to help parents feel good about their parenting skills. One of my favorite books is *Daily Affirmations for Parents* by Tian Dayton (1992).

Developmental Modality: Developmental books help parents understand the typical or atypical developmental problems that their children might be experiencing. One of the better books on helping parents with common developmentally-based behavior problems is *Good Behavior Made Easy* by S. Garber, M. Garber and R. Spizman (1993).

Educational Modality: A book selected for this modality will probably be aimed at helping parents understand a particular issue or theme in their children's lives or in their own lives. As discussed, I prefer giving parents books that are easy to read in just a few sittings and that emphasize practical advice. Sometimes I will give parents books which help them explore their own feelings as children, such as *A Journey Through Your Childhood* by Christopher Biffle (1989), an interactive workbook that helps parents remember what it was like to be young.

Social System Modality: When parents seek the help of a therapist or counselor, they explicitly or tacitly admit that they don't have the answers they need to help their children. This is an unfortunate occurrence in the life of the family, for it disrupts the natural order of things. Parents *should* have the answers that they need to feel that they are "good enough" parents. The concept of being a good enough parent is an important one to explain. Parents don't need to be perfect. They only have to be good enough to raise children who can be independent, self-reliant, and responsible members of society.

When working with a parent, I sometimes ask, "What do you need to know to be good enough? What do you need to know that will make you feel good about your parenting skills?" At this point, I will probably choose a book that will address the issue that they feel that they cannot handle at home. Perhaps it will be *You Can Say NO to Your Teenager* by Jeanette Shalov (1990), or something very practical like *Pick Up Your Socks* by Elizabeth Crary (1990). Most likely it will be a book that I can integrate into a broader parent training program to help the parent function as a cotherapist in addressing the short-term therapy goal(s).

Therapeutic Books For Children

In the past five years, more authors have discovered the rewards of writing directly to an audience of children for therapeutic purposes. While there have been many case histories of children who have been profoundly influenced by their reading, we still know relatively little about how to use this technique so that it can be maximally effective for a particular child with a specific problem. What books give the right message to the child? How can you know how the message will be interpreted? And even if the message is meaningful to the child, will it be translated into a new behavior, belief, attitude, or feeling?

As is the case with many therapeutic techniques, it is easier to identify children for whom Bibliotherapy is not an effective form of treatment than children for whom it should be recommended. Children with reading difficulties or poor attitudes toward school are less likely to derive therapeutic benefits from a book. Children with poor abstract reasoning abilities or a highly egocentric point of view can have difficulty in applying the information or message from a book to their own lives.

To determine which children are more likely to derive benefit from the Bibliotherapy technique, we should consider the four major types of books used in Bibliotherapy with children.

Metaphoric Books: These are fables or stories about people or animals that have higher-level messages or morals for children. We have only to look at Aesop's fables or Grimm's fairy tales to find stories that are so profound that they have had meaning for generations upon generations of children. A more recent trend has been to write politically-correct or psychologically-correct fairy tales, based on the originals: Cinderella takes more responsibility for her social life and joins a dating service rather than wait for Prince Charming; Goldilocks uses her wits to outfox the Big Bad Wolf, rather than just run away. Children seem to enjoy seeing problems faced and resolved in fantasy-world settings with real-world outcomes.

Realistic Stories: These are stories about real children facing real problems. In each instance, a child faces a real-life situation, finding ways to cope with or solve the problems that he or she faces. These books also stress that emotions are a normal part of life, presenting story lines in which the common conflicts of childhood are successfully overcome by the main characters: a boy who gets glasses learns to deal with being teased; a girl who has to go to the hospital learns that many of her fears are unfounded; a boy whose parents are paying more attention to his baby sister discovers appropriate ways to get attention for himself. It is assumed that by reading these books, children will see alternatives to their maladaptive behaviors and will model the successful coping strategies of the characters in the book.

Informational Books: Some books just give children very important information: about ADD (*Putting on the Brakes,* 1991); about death (*Lifetimes,* 1983); about stress control (*Take A Deep Breath*, Slap-Shelton and Shapiro, 1992); or divorce (*The Boys and Girls Book About Divorce*, Gardner, 1970). There are hundreds of books that provide children with important facts that can dispel myths they may associate with a particular situation, or to help them cope better.

Workbooks: Workbooks form a category of their own, because they create an experience for the child above and beyond reading. Workbooks such as *The Building Blocks of Self-Esteem* (Shapiro, 1992) or *Jumpin' Jake Settles Down* (Shapiro, 1993) provide activities which combine a variety of cognitive, affective, and even behavioral elements. And, most importantly, children love them!

The importance of Bibliotherapy can be seen with Mary C., a depressed child whose parents were going through a divorce. Mary's parents' divorce was for the most part worked out in friendship, although both parents suffered from recurring periods of guilt, remorse, and depression. But they didn't discuss any of this with Mary until the week before her father moved out. Finally, when a court date was set for the divorce decree, both parents sat down with Mary and asked her if she knew what "divorce" meant. Mary replied that she had friends at school whose parents were divorced and divorce meant that their mommies and daddies weren't going to be married anymore and that they weren't going to live together. Mary's parents agreed that this was exactly what they were doing. They told her that they were still going to be friends with each other, that they both loved her very much, and that she would still have two parents who just wouldn't be married. Afterwards, they congratulated each other on having raised such a sensible child.

Mary's parents didn't realize, as many parents don't, that her lack of questions and apparent acceptance of their separation was based on fear and unrealistic wishes rather than on an accurate assessment of reality. After about seven weeks of seeing Mary in treatment for sadness and increasing social isolation, we began to focus on her feelings about her parents' divorce, but they were very difficult for her to articulate. I didn't want to put myself in the role of a lecturer or educator, since she was just beginning to accept me as someone who could relate to her on her own level, so I asked her if she would like to read a book by Dr. Richard Gardner (*The Boys and Girls Book About Divorce,* 1970), who was someone who talked to children about their problems as I did, and who had written a book just for children whose parents had gotten a divorce.

She was immediately interested in the illustrations and seemed pleased to think that someone had written a book for children who were like her. I told her that I would be glad to give her a copy of the book and said that she could read any part of it that interested her by looking at the Table of Contents and turning to that section (this is how Dr. Gardner suggests that the book be used in his Foreword). Some of the sections that caught her attention were: "How to Get Along Better with Your Divorced Father" and the "Fear of Being Left Alone." I also told Mary that I had a book to give to her mother, also by Dr. Gardner, called *The Parents Book About Divorce* (1977), which might answer some of the questions that I thought her mother had.

Mary agreed that it would be nice for her mother to have such a book, sympathetically explaining, "she still seems awfully sad to me." I encouraged both the mother and daughter to talk about what they read with each other and with Mary's father if they wished. I also mentioned that I would like to hear their reactions to the book next week, if they chose to share them with me. As I hoped, Mary reported in the following weeks that she had read most of the book I had given her, and that she had talked about what she read with her mother and father. Mary's father also borrowed both books and scheduled a separate session with me to talk about his feelings and reactions.

Learning to deal with reality while maintaining a sense of self-worth is one of the most important benefits of psychotherapy. If books can dispel myths, provide useful information, and stimulate shared feelings, then they can be an effective element in many therapeutic programs.

Writing Books About Children's Therapeutic Progress

There are many excellent books available for Bibliotherapy, but nothing can replace books written for an individual child. Robert Ziegler, M.D. (*Homemade Books To Help Kids Cope*, Magination Press, 1992), discusses how books that parents can make help children face various life issues from the age of two through adolescence. But making books is an equally exciting and effective technique for therapists. A therapist-made book can not only serve as an effective technique to communicate with a child during an individual session, but it can serve as a way to tie an entire short-term therapy plan together. It can be used to create a gestalt of the various techniques used in therapy, creating a whole which is greater than the sum of its parts.

I have used this technique with children between the ages of five and 12. I introduce it by the second or third session with the child. I tell the child:

> You know we are going to do a lot of different things together. Everything that we do will help you work on your problems and feel better about things. But sometimes we may talk about something important or do something that is very special in our session, and then we might forget about it later! I don't want this to happen, so I'd like to take 10 minutes at the end of each session to write down, with you, what happened during this session.
>
> I like to write down what you learned or what was important to you. And to make this more interesting, we can make it into a book! So at the end of each session, we will have a chapter in our story about what you learned in therapy. And when we are done with our work together, I will make it into a book for you and you can take it home and keep it with your other books. Maybe you will read it with your parents, or with a grandparent. Or maybe you will read it five years from now, or even ten years! That is entirely up to you.

Making a book about the child's therapy serves a variety of purposes. First, it helps the child and the therapist review what has happened on a session-to-session basis and record it. This provides structure as well as a written history of the therapy. At the end of each session I first write down what happened during that session, emphasizing what the child's feelings were, and how what he or she has learned can be applied to his or her day-to-day situation. I prefer to write this down in a story line. The story is about that child, although it can be about a fictional child with similar problems, or even about an animal. Usually the more conflict and anxiety that the child is experiencing with the problem, the more they prefer that the characters in the story be someone or something else. For example, a child who has been sexually abused might prefer writing about a kitten or a puppy who has had that experience. The kitten or puppy then goes to the cat or dog counselor to get help.

Whether the child is writing about himself or herself, another child with a similar problem, or an animal, or extra-terrestrial, the procedure is the same. The main character will go for help to an adult, learn new ways to handle and cope with problems, and change. The actual production of the book can take three forms: drawing, collage, or computer-generated. Drawing is of course the simplest way to make

Figure 7.A

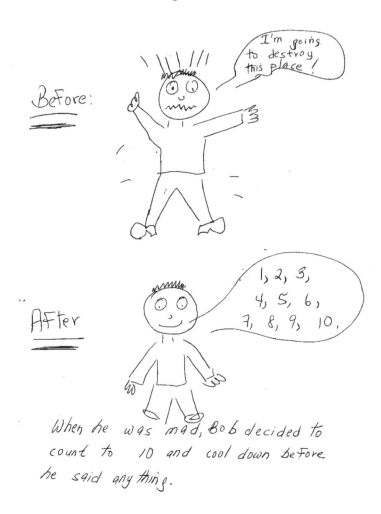

a book. The child can draw the pictures, the therapist can draw them, or they can draw them together. The drawings and text can use a standard storybook format or be done cartoon-style (see Figure 7.A).

Polaroid pictures combined with magazine photographs can also be used to make a collage book. The child can take a variety of poses which can be photographed with an instant camera and placed on a page, and magazine photos can be pasted in for background and props. The text can be entered on a separate page, at the bottom of the page, or as cartoon balloons.

My own preference is to make stories on computer. This gives the book a more professional look and books can be made very quickly as well. A variety of children's drawing programs are available which allow the child to draw on the computer screen, add text, and print out immediately. I prefer using clip art electronic images, which can be imported into graphics and drawing programs. There are literally hundreds of clip art image programs available for computers, including cartoon images and images of common objects, images for special celebrations and so on.

Recently I devised a set of psychologically-oriented clip art images called *Psych-Pix* (The Center for Applied Psychology, Inc., 1994) for the express purpose of creating therapist-made stories. *Psych-Pix* consists of five disks of images, showing kids with 50 different feelings, psychologically-suggestive people and objects, backdrops, self-control images, and images related to sexual abuse. As with any clip art, these images can be imported into pages on the computer, made smaller or larger, fatter or thinner, moved around and added to other images, and then text can be added (Figure 7.B).

Figure 7.B
A Page From a Storybook Made with Psych-Pix Clip Art

| "I have no friends. Nobody likes me!" | "I am always getting into trouble!" | "My parents and teachers are always telling me to calm down!" |

Whatever medium you use, the story should follow the course of the therapy from the introduction of the problem, to the various techniques tried, to specific conclusions in the form of changes in the child's life. Naturally the therapist directs the child into having a positive outcome by the end of the story. Even if the child doesn't experience the outcome as positive (for example, oppositional/defiant children will not necessarily define any particular session as a positive experience), the therapist can write the story as how things *can* be.

In many cases, I like to make a copy of the "chapter" from each session to send home with the child. This can serve as a way for the child to communicate with his or her parents or other caretakers as well as a way that I can send messages home about what is happening in therapy. Usually I leave it up to the child as to whether or not he or she wants to show the "book in progress" to his parents. Before we begin, I make it clear to the child that the parents will see the finished product anyway, since books (unlike diaries) are meant to be read by others. Making this clear from the start makes it less likely that the book will reveal any thoughts or feelings that the child does not want known.

As we approach the end of treatment, we naturally have to consider the conclusion of the story. Again, this helps us imagine a positive outcome of the therapy, even though the problem may not be completely resolved. The final "chapters" address the post-treatment issues that will confront the child and force us to consider ways that the progress made in therapy will continue.

We usually leave the titling of the book for when it is complete. If possible, I like the title to reflect a general theme of the therapy, something important that has been learned, or a goal that has been accomplished, for example: *Arnold's Book About Making Friends* by Arnold M.; *The Don't Tell Lies Book* by Mary C.; *The Happy Graduation Day* by Michael B.

The making of the book can serve many purposes: framing the therapy as a positive experience for the child, chronicling the sessions for the therapist, and communicating with parents. But even these attributes are not as important as what happens when the book is complete. At the last session I present a copy of the book to the child, bound with a heavy cover by a local copying store. I present the book like a diploma or a certificate of achievement, and urge the child to show it off to his or her parents, grandparents, or friends. The therapist-made book now serves as a physical/cognitive reminder of what happened in therapy.

Some children read these books over and over again for weeks after therapy has ended. Other children read them on occasion, but sometimes not for years. Sometimes it is the parent who asks to read the book again with the child. The book then serves as a stimulus to remember techniques, thoughts, and feelings revealed in therapy.

The Video Self-Modeling Technique

It is 7:00 p.m. and time for therapy to begin. Alex S. is sitting in his living room, alone. The lights are dim. Relaxed and yet eager, he turns on the TV and therapy starts. Loud rock music fills the room and Alex starts tapping his foot. His shoulders begin swaying to the beat and his hands pick it up. The title of the show comes on, as the beat gets even faster and louder—IT'S "THE ALEX S. VARIETY SHOW"— STARRING ALEX S. AND A CAST OF SEVERAL...the letters wander and flash across the screen, then fade...WRITTEN AND PRODUCED BY ALEX S....in large red letters set against a blue background (Alex's favorite colors). Now the music begins to fade...WITH THE VOICE OF DR. L. SHAPIRO. The music continues to fade and a scene comes on the screen. It's Alex in a bar with two other teenagers. The other two teenagers appear to be chain-smoking cigarettes. Alex is not. His friends have several empty beer bottles and dirty glasses lined up on their side of the table. Alex is munching loudly on a hot dog, drinking a Coke...

Therapist-made books are an effective way to tie a short-term therapy plan for younger children together, but adolescents will most likely find this technique childish. On the other hand, the Video Self-Modeling Technique is readily embraced by adolescents and can be an even more powerful psychotherapeutic tool. The Video Self-Modeling Technique created by Michael Greelis and Betsy Haarmann (see *ABC's of Video-Therapy,* 1980) is an imaginative blending of the latest video technology and basic principles of behavior modification. Although the video camera and monitor have become more and more commonplace in the treatment of a wide variety of psychological disorders, editing equipment and production equipment have not. Fortunately this equipment becomes simpler to operate and relatively less expensive each year.

This technique is based on one of the classic studies in behavioral psychology by R. Bandura, who demonstrated that children left alone in a room will imitate the aggressive actions of other children that they see in a home-made movie. Since the Bandura research, hundreds of studies have suggested that watching TV can have profoundly disturbing effects on the attitudes and behaviors of children, and yet there has been relatively little attention paid to the potentially positive therapeutic effects of this symbol of modern technology. Now that video recorders and cameras have become affordable, we must consider that the same principles that have been selling cereals, sneakers, and jeans, can be used to help change habits, teach reading, and even help a child or adolescent acquire new social skills.

The basic format of the Video Self-Modeling Technique is to present the child or adolescent with a corrected image of himself or herself performing a new learning objective or therapeutic goal. Imagine a girl who cannot pay attention in a group watching herself on TV. The image on the screen shows her sitting attentively in her classroom, making constant eye contact with the teacher or whoever is talking. She doesn't fiddle with her papers or rest her head on her desk. For the entire 10 minutes of the videotape she sits with rapt attention, eager to listen and participate. But how can this be, when this same child was observed just this morning with the same teacher in the same small group, looking as if her thoughts were on another planet? Enter the technology of videotape editing.

It is surprisingly simple to produce a videotape that can serve as a self-model for a child. First the client is taught some new way to behave or to cope with a problem and then he or she is videotaped. The original videotape is reviewed by the therapist and the desired performance is edited onto a new tape; undesired behaviors are left out. When the editing process is completed, the child will have a powerful image of what he or she will look like when the therapeutic goal is achieved.

Seeing your own image is in itself highly rewarding, but the effect is amplified when you see yourself doing and saying the kinds of things that meet the expectations of the important people around you. Imagine the pride of an aggressive eight-year-old boy who has never been able to walk away from a fight and now sees himself able to do it. Or the girl with a learning disability who was ashamed to read her compositions in front of the class, and now is able to show the class a videotape of herself, edited and overdubbed to emphasize her confidence and the self-assurance of her posture. Even more exciting is the opportunity to build reinforcers into the edited tape itself, reinforcers that accompany each new corrected behavior. The reinforcers can range from simple praise from the therapist, recorded while the tape is being made, to subtle techniques that would make a Hollywood producer salivate.

"The Alex S. Variety Show" videotape was made by a 17-year-old learning disabled boy who wanted to be able to resist the temptations of his peer group to smoke, drink, and take drugs. The tapes showed a series of vignettes of Alex and other members of his therapy group acting out situations in which he had previously been enticed into these unwanted habits and had been unable to say, "No." In individual and group therapy, Alex had opportunities to learn new techniques to increase his assertiveness and to get consistent support for finding his own identity and being accepted for himself (which included his learning handicap).

Every aspect of the videotape production converged to help Alex not only change the behaviors he disliked, but to give him the opportunity to express and affirm the characteristics that made him unique.

Alex had a hand in each stage of the video production. He wrote the scripts, directed and rehearsed the other actors, selected the music and the titles, and even helped in the editing. He selected parts of the filmed tape which he thought demonstrated his self-reliance and his ability to stick to his views, and edited out aspects of his behavior— slips of the tongue, hesitations, nonverbal gestures—that he felt were indicative of his "pasty old self."

The final product, which was very creative, consisted of five 10-minute scenes. One scene showed Alex walking down the street approaching a gang he knew; to demonstrate his swagger and new-found cockiness, Alex edited in a clip from a Humphrey Bogart movie which showed Bogart walking down the street in a strikingly similar scene. In another scene, the voice of a girl in Alex's therapy group was dubbed in, repeating a comment that she had made in the group: "You're gettin' your stuff together, kid."

While the preceding example demonstrates some of the more sophisticated uses of the Video Self-Modeling Technique, the mechanical and technological knowledge required to produce these tapes is surprisingly small. The use of a videotape camcorder can be learned in less than an hour, and good quality tapes can be made almost immediately with the basic equipment. Audio dubbing consists of simply plugging in a microphone to the videotape recorder and talking or playing music while the tape is running on "record."

Editing is more complicated, but can still be mastered in two or three hours. Unlike film editing, there is no splicing and mending involved. Segments as short as a single image can be recorded on a second VCR in whatever order the editor wishes, with the original tape remaining intact (see Figure 7.C).

Figure 7.C
Equipment for Videotape Editing

Raw Tape Image		Edited Image
VIDEO TAPE RECORDER 1 OR CAMERA	EDIT CONTROLLER	VIDEO TAPE RECORDER 1 OR CAMERA
Raw Tape Image		Edited Tape

The editing process involves three basic steps:

1. Select the material that you wish to use on the final tape by viewing the original and marking down the position of each sequence on the tape, indicating the counter number and the first and last words of the dialog of the sequence (see Figure 7.D).

2. Then record the designated sequences in a new order onto a second tape. An edit controller will make the transition smoother, but is not really necessary. In this stage you are looking at two TV screens, the first showing what you have on your original and the second showing the rearranged sequences that will be your final tape.

3. During the assembly of the final tape, you can add a variety of special effects. For instance, titles can be added by filming homemade sign boards, that are edited onto the final tape. If a character generator is available, it can give titles an even more professional look, allowing the editor to superimpose words onto any part of the final tape in a variety of type styles and colors. New scenes and images can be added by simply filming a few seconds' worth of faces, photographs, special objects, rooms, and so forth, and these shots are then edited onto the finished tape. Clips from films or TV shows must first be recorded off the air by the videotape recorder, and can then be added to the final tape like any other sequence. (It should be noted however, that at the time of this writing the practice of recording copyrighted TV shows off the air may be illegal in some or all states.)

Repetition is another principle behind the Video Self-Modeling Technique: repetition that usually does not include the presence of the therapist. Depending on the nature and purpose of the therapeutic program, the therapy tape may be shown from five to 10 times.

Figure 7.D
Log Sheet for the "Alex S. Variety Show"

Sequence No.	Counter Start	Counter End	Audio or Video Reference Begin	Audio or Video Reference End
12	618	810	Alex walks in restaurant, says, "Hello, Guys"	Alex sits at table: cut when he rests chin on hands
13	1003	1115	Pete says, "Whadda ya know, Buddy?"	Cut after close-up of Alex's smile
14	1301	1450	Alex says, "No, thanks."	Alex sips his ginger ale. Add reinforcement here (dub in therapist's voice)

After this, even the best made tape becomes a little boring. Tapes can be viewed on consecutive days, once a week, or on whatever schedule fits with the learning style of the client and the intent of the program. Parents, brothers, sisters, and friends can also view the finished tape (assuming, of course, that this is deemed to be appropriate by both the client and the therapist), adding still another dimension of reinforcement for the child.

An Aphasic Teenager Who Was Socially Isolated

The treatment of Ben S., a mildly retarded, aphasic adolescent, illustrates the multiple use of the Video Self-Modeling Technique. We used this technique to help Ben with his communication, for socialization and assertiveness training, to improve his hygiene, and even to help him with his reading.

When 19-year-old Ben was first referred to me, he was a small, wiry, unkempt young man whose speech was almost completely unintelligible. He was referred because his parents said that he had no friends, showed no interest in making any, and seemed to be becoming more and more depressed. Everything about Ben seemed to be a study in contradictions. Although he was referred for withdrawal and mild depression, he was smiling and affable in the office. It was nearly impossible to understand what he said, but he talked all the time. His mother made sure that Ben always dressed in clean, well-pressed clothes, but he wore them awkwardly, and he always appeared to be in need of a shave and a shampoo. Ben's intelligence was assessed to be in the mild range of mental retardation and he had demonstrated an above-average interest and talent for electronics. He had even learned to drive a car and had passed the state licensing examination. But his academic achievements in reading, spelling, and math were only at the second grade level.

It was clear from the onset that this wasn't going to be a "talking" therapy, and yet I didn't see how Ben and I could accomplish very much without having some means of communication. After interviewing his mother and his former speech therapist, we decided that Ben should learn to use an alternative communication system to be combined with the communication skills that he already had. There are many types of alternative communication systems for aphasics, and each one has to be matched to the client's communication needs and learning style. Ben's new speech therapist wanted him to learn manual sign language because he already used many gestures in his speech, and since the American Sign Language method is a complete language, he would have unlimited potential to express himself.

I, however, wanted Ben to learn to use a deck of communication cards. Communication cards consist of symbols, words, and letters which are mounted on cards. The client must choose a card or sequence of cards to get his or her meaning across. I argued that although sign language has unlimited potential for expression, because of Ben's intellectual deficits and poor performance in learning academic skills, we could not expect him to learn much more than 100 or possibly 200 signs, and even this might take years. In contrast, combining communication cards with iconic symbols with words could give Ben the same 200-word vocabulary with just a few hours of training. However, there were also good arguments against using a communication card deck. It was awkward to carry around and use. Its uncommoness would draw attention to a handicap that Ben preferred to try and hide. (It later became clear that one of the main reasons for Ben's withdrawal was that he would rather be alone than have people see him as abnormal.)

Finally, we decided on a compromise. We decided to try and teach Ben both alternative communication systems, to be combined with his intelligible spoken language and the 50 or so words that he could write. We reasoned that rather than choosing for Ben how we thought he would best communicate, we should give him the tools and let him make the choices.

Personal Adjustment Training

The Personal Adjustment Training Program (Zisfein and Rosen, 1971) was developed to teach developmentally disabled clients social skills that are important to their integration into the community, including how to get along with other people, how to make decisions and solve problems in a self-reliant way, and how to be assertive rather than acquiescent and compliant. These new behaviors are best learned in situations that are highly meaningful for the client, and for Ben this meant doing what made him feel most like the nonhandicapped people around him, driving a car.

In fact, a situation had occurred early in the therapy that underscored Ben's need for better communication and social skills. He had been in a minor automobile accident in a parking lot, scraping a car as he left, but instead of stopping to talk to the other driver, he drove away. The police tracked him down later that day; fortunately, he was not charged with leaving the scene of the accident and was let go with a warning. Still, it was clear that this could easily happen again and that Ben would be in danger of losing his license.

With the aid of the cotherapist who did most of the training with Ben, we staged a scene in which Ben would have an accident on the street outside my office. Prior to the filming, Ms. B. (the cotherapist) worked with Ben on using his communication card deck, and taught him a half-dozen easily understood gestures for communicating with the other driver. He was to explain that he had difficulty speaking, was sorry about the accident, and would provide his name, address, license number, and the insurance company's telephone number. Ben and Ms. B. role-played this scene until Ben could react with complete ease, even when Ms. B. (playing the other driver) varied her questions and responses.

On the day of the shooting, I hadn't seen Ben for several weeks and I was surprised at how confident and excited he seemed. He inspected the camera thoroughly, testing every feature. He was delighted when I asked him to work the camera and film Ms. B. and myself in the office. When it was time to go outside, I asked Ben how he liked the idea of being a star of his own show, and he flashed me a huge smile, and the gesture for "A-OK."

The actual shooting took only about 20 minutes. We recorded the tamest car accident in cinematic history, followed by a discussion between Ben and Mrs. B., the two drivers. We didn't even need a retake. In fact, the scene was so good that relatively little editing was needed. After taking out a few extraneous words and motions, we had a perfect 10-minute scene of Ben coping with a very difficult social situation. We had Ben select background music from his record collection, juicing up the scene considerably. During the one-half hour of editing, I dubbed in comments that reinforced each of his new skills.

Since Ben lived close to my office, he came over to view his video debut three times during the next week. On the third time, he brought a friend. This was the first social outing he had initiated in years.

Increasing Sight Word Vocabulary

Since Ben had responded so well to the first video self-modeling tape, we thought using this same technique would enhance other areas of learning such as the acquisition of sign language. Ben was learning about five signs per week with his speech therapist Mr. J., and we wondered if he couldn't double or triple this rate. I arranged to tape a speech therapy session with Mr. J. and Ben, where he would be introduced to 15 new sign words rather than the usual five.

Rather than teach Ben the American Sign Language system designed for the deaf (we thought it would be too difficult for him to master), we instructed him in sign language culled from several tribes of American Indians. This system of gestures is reported to be 90% recognizable by the general public because of familiarity or because the gestures imitate the actions they describe. To teach Ben this sign language, Mr. J. would introduce the new words for the week, he and Ben would practice them for 20 minutes in his office, and then they would stroll around the vocational training center trying to use both the old and new words in context. Reviewing the tape of the session that evening, I thought of how a TV commercial might sell the same material. I thought about "Sesame Street" (at the time, my daughter's favorite show) and the quick-paced segments that repeat the same material in seemingly endless variety.

For the final tape I attempted to use the best of commercial TV, rather than try to duplicate it. On TV that night was a movie aimed at a teenage audience that I was sure Ben would find interesting. I called Ben and asked him not to watch it, because he would see it at my office in a few days. Then at the editing lab I combined the tape from Ben's therapy session with the TV movie, substituting scenes from Ben's language therapy as if they were commercials. At each point where a commercial had been, I introduced a new sign language word and reviewed the previous ones as well. By the 15th "commercial" all 15 words were being reviewed; this continued for another 10 commercials. At the end of each new commercial, a 50-second blank space appeared, and my voice came on asking Ben to repeat the signs. He was then directed to check his memory by referring to a sheet (drawn up by Mr. J.) that showed pictures of hands as they formed each of the 15 signs. Ben watched the movie in four segments at my office after school. By the end of the week Ben was able to demonstrate all 15 signs without error.

This method tripled the rate of Ben's learning, but the time-conscious reader who had been counting the number of hours it took to make the tape might wonder if it was really cost-effective. In this case, I'd say that we broke even. In the traditional way of instruction, Ben would have met with Mr. J. for three one-hour sessions to learn the same material. For the tape, Mr. J. worked only one hour, but I worked two (an hour taping and another editing). For the second and third tapes, which used a similar method, however, I wasn't needed at all, and the time that Mr. J. and Ben spent in their regular sessions was spent considerably more efficiently.

Because Mr. J. set up the video camera on a tripod, no cameraperson was needed, and rather than spending the normal 60 minutes teaching and reviewing signs, Mr. J. was able to demonstrate and film new signs in 10 minutes. Ben wasn't required to try and learn the signs at this time; this would happen when he viewed the tape. The other 50 minutes of therapy were spent editing the signs into a new TV movie that had been taped previously at Ben's request. Each commercial consisted of not only the 10 new sign-language words, but a review of the previous 15 signs, editing in from the original tape (unlike film, the original videotape is never cut up or used up and can be used over and over again). The second tape took just over an hour to produce, but had the teaching equivalent of at least four hours (and of course we can't estimate how much more fun this way of learning was for Ben).

A third tape was made with the help of Ben's brother James to improve Ben's sight-word vocabulary (words that are read entirely by recognition rather than by any system of word analysis). James, who was two years older than his brother, was invited to my office, and I gave both young men a short demonstration on how to use this portable video camera. Their assignment was to re-create a typical day for Ben, starting in the morning when he got up to wash and brush his teeth, and ending with the 11:00 PM news. In between was the car ride to Ben's vocational training center, lunch at McDonald's, a drive around the neighborhood, an errand at the drugstore, and then the ride home again for dinner (see Figure 7.E). For the tape they were to shoot five- to 10-minute segments for each scene. Ben was to film the background shots, and James was to film Ben doing the action.

Figure 7.E
Directions for Filming the "Drugstore Scene"

Scene 1:   Ben entering the drugstore. Type of shot: Wide-angle, zoom into Ben entering door.

Scene 2:   Shots of the signs above the aisles. Shoot each sign for about 20 seconds. Pan from one sign to the next if they are close. If they are far away, press the pause button until you aim the camera at the next sign. Shoot other signs as well: "Sale," "Do Not Enter," "Exit" and the like.

Scene 3:   Ben going down the aisles, looking at the signs, examining various products until he finds the sign for toothpaste. Close-up of this sign. He picks up two tubes of toothpaste and examines them. The camera zooms in for a close-up of the price of each tube. Ben decides on the cheaper one, and he puts the other one back.

Scene 4:   Ben pays for the toothpaste. The camera follows Ben
                  to the cash register. Close-ups of any signs near the
                  cash register.

In each scene, I asked them to make sure to take closeups of any
printed words that it might be important for Ben to read. At home
these could be labels on a vial of medicine or directions on the laundry detergent. On the road there would be street signs and directions
to follow. At the restaurant there would be the menu to read, and at
the drugstore there would be more signs to tell the customers where
to find what they wanted, which items were on sale, and so on. I gave
them written scenarios to remind them of what scenes to shoot and
what kinds of things to look for (see Figure 7.E), and I reminded them
that they only had two hours' worth of tape that would be edited into
a 15-minute show.

We also spoke about how they would each feel about filming in public. Because Ben had spent so long trying not to draw attention to himself, I anticipated that he might find this public exposure too anxiety-
provoking. I was wrong. Both boys were enthusiastic about the project and, like many adolescents, were looking forward to becoming
neighborhood celebrities.

A week later the tape was done, and I previewed it for ways to use
it to teach reading. There were many good shots of new words to
learn, nearly 150 in all. I decided to edit the tape into four segments:
at home, in a restaurant, in school, and on the road. Each section had
a list of sight-words associated with it, complete with an introduction
of each word, highlights of its use and context, exercises, and reviews.

Improving Personal Hygiene

I was reluctant to bring up Ben's personal appearance as an issue in
therapy, assuming that he had more than enough reminders at home
to tuck in his shirt and comb his hair. I had noted, in fact, that Ben's
grooming had improved over the last several months, as he viewed
himself more and more on videotape. While watching the tape that
Ben and James had taken, a part of which showed Ben dressing in the
morning, I realized that this segment might provide a good opportunity to reinforce his new interest in grooming.

Everyone agreed that Ben looked great on the day he and his
brother went out to film. That morning, while getting ready, Ben
hammed it up in front of the camera. He shaved with the eloquence
of a dancer, scrubbed his hair until every follicle glistened, and used
his soap unmercifully. When he adjusted his tie in the mirror, he
shone.

In editing this segment of the tape, I decided to emphasize Ben's grooming by slowing the action down and interjecting positive reinforcements that I thought Ben might find amusing and flattering. I taped one of Ben's favorite TV shows (about three beautiful female detectives) and chose several sequences which showed closeups of the women talking. I then asked three women to lip sync comments flattering Ben's appearance onto the tape. On the final version of the tape, there were just three 10-second segments of reinforcement for Ben's grooming, but these seemed to be enough. He was overjoyed with his new image and the humor of the tape, and watched this segment at least a dozen times. One day he brought two of his friends over to watch and they all had a good laugh. I couldn't help but notice that I had never seen Ben look so good.

CHAPTER 8

THE SOCIAL SYSTEM MODALITY

My definition of short-term therapy comprises two major directions of the treatment: to help the child develop inner resources to cope with inner or external conflicts and to help change the child's environment to be more responsive to his or her needs. A child's social system, the context in which the presenting problem exists, includes everyone he or she comes in contact with: siblings, parents, teachers, extended family, babysitters, and others. In writing a short-term therapy treatment plan, I view each of these people as part of a possible solution to the child's immediate problem. In my initial assessment, I list every important person in the child's life and rate them as to their potential to participate in the treatment plan.

The criteria upon which I rate them include:

- Availability
- Nurturing qualities
- Cooperativeness
- Interest in the child's improvement
- Degree to which they will directly benefit from the child's improvement
- Identification with the child
- Sympathy or empathy with the child's problem
- Consistency in the child's life
- Interest or compatibility with a specific treatment technique

Once I have identified the people who can help carry out the treatment plan, I also identify the people who can be most resistant to change, whether consciously or unconsciously. For example, there was the father who hated all psychologists and made no effort to hide his disdain for my ideas. And there was the mother who said all the right things and showed an interest in helping her son deal with his encopresis, but also admitted that she liked when her 10-year-old "baby" needed her to stay home with him because of his soiling. As family systems theories tell us, each system is unique, with many forces conspiring to keep things just as they are. It is up to the therapist to determine how to modify the social system so that these forces are interrupted and redirected towards the child's growth and development.

Volumes have been written about interventions which can be used to help children by restructuring the system in which the problem exists. The model of short-term therapy described in this book is not a family therapy model (where the whole family is the patient), but it acknowledges the importance of intervening in the child's system to effect both immediate and sustained therapeutic change. Short-term and other therapists must also acknowledge the importance of the child's peer system. School-age children typically spend more time with their peers than with their families, and for many of the children referred for psychotherapy, this time may unfortunately be very difficult. In the following paragraphs, I will review a variety of approaches to making the child's social system—family, peers, community—more conducive to steering the child towards healthier functioning and development.

Social Skills Training Through Games

In many cases it is possible to involve parents and teachers in a social skills program aimed at teaching the child very specific social behaviors which will enhance their relationships with both adults and other children. There are several games which can be played to teach children of different ages these important social behaviors (see *The Book of Psychotherapeutic Games,* Shapiro, 1994, for in-depth reviews):

> **Harvest Time (Ages 3-7):** This was one of the first and most successful of the cooperative games invented by Jim Deacove of Family Pastimes. Cooperative games form a unique category of therapeutic games because they can't be played unless the players cooperate—either everyone wins or everyone loses. In this simple game for young children, players must gather their vegetables before winter comes (a fall scene is covered by a puzzle depicting a winter scene.) Each player has his or her own garden, but *everyone's* garden must be harvested before winter, or the game is lost. When a player has harvested his or her garden he or she may help other players their turns.

> **You & Me (Ages 4-10):** This game teaches simple

social skills by asking children to pantomime, draw, or verbally respond to questions such as: "Act like the person you like most!", "Draw something your Mom worries about", or "Why do grown-ups get angry when children talk back?" Players earn chips which can be pooled for a common social reward, like going to the movies or sharing a plate of cookies.

Communicate Jr. (Ages 6-10): In this cooperative game, players earn invitations to a party by responding correctly to questions about social situations. But the party doesn't begin until all the players earn their invitations, reinforcing the social learning by all group members. The game addresses 12 social skill areas including: body language, hygiene, facial expressions, time and place, sharing and taking turns, conversations, ignoring, manners, voice, following rules, eye contact, and listening.

The Social Skills Game (Ages 7-14) is designed to teach children attitudes and behaviors that will lead to positive and rewarding interactions with their peers. The game is based on a cognitive behavior modification model and encourages players to learn to make positive self-statements that will lead to changes in behaviors in the areas of making friends, responding positively to peers, cooperating with peers, and communicating personal needs. The game manual includes a social cognition inventory, which provides pre- and post-game measures of the child's attitudes and thoughts regarding social interactions.

Communicate (Ages 12-18) was one of the first games to promote social communication skills. Originally designed for learning disabled children or other children with specific cognitive or learning deficits, this game has proven to be popular and effective with a wide variety of young adolescents. The object of the game is to obtain *Good Communicator* cards by responding to questions such as: "Tell about your most recent conversation", "Demonstrate good eye contact when you tell the group about your favorite pizza," or "How do you feel about a person

who is always complaining about everything and anything?" The appropriateness of answers is determined by a designated Judge. If a player doesn't
answer correctly, the group must discuss the answer
before play resumes.

Games are important vehicles for teaching children social skills,
whether these are communication skills, behavioral skills, or skills
which provide them with new social experiences. The three pencil-
and-paper games in Figures 8.A, 8.B, and 8.C (from the *Building
Blocks of Self-Esteem,* Shapiro, 1993) are examples of these three
game functions. These types of pencil-and-paper game are very effective when used as therapeutic homework. The activities can be done
with parents, teachers, or other children, providing opportunities to
discuss social skills within a social context.

Nonverbal Social Training

Recently, attention has been paid to children who have difficulty in
getting along with other children because they are unable to read
nonverbal cues. In their book *Helping the Child Who Doesn't Fit In*
(Peachtree Publishers, 1992), Dr. Stephen Nowicki, Jr. and Dr.
Marshall Duke address the problem of children who do not effectively interpret facial expressions, gestures, tone of voice, posture,
interpersonal distance, and other forms of nonverbal communication.
Referring to these children as *dyssemic,* the authors consider this
problem to be a type of language deficit: an inability to process nonverbal communication. The authors hypothesize that many children
who are rejected by their peers may be having social difficulties
because of this typically-unrecognized problem; fortunately it can be
relatively easily corrected.

Nowicki and Duke assert that there are six channels of nonverbal
communication:

1. Rhythm and the use of time
2. Interpersonal distance (space) and touch
3. Gestures and postures
4. Facial expressions
5. Paralinguistic (voice tone, pitch, etc.)
6. Objectics (style of dress)

Dyssemic children may have difficulty in understanding nonverbal
communication in several or all of these channels. The authors sug-

Figure 8.A
Saying the Right Things

There is a new kid in your classroom. Can you think of some things that you can say to make her feel welcome? Write them in the "speech balloons."

Figure 8.B
Everybody Likes Betty

Betty is one of the happiest and best-liked kids we know. What is it about Betty that makes her so popular? Let's follow her through one day and see what she does. Below each picture, write down what Betty is doing to make other people like her.

Figure 8.C
Creating a Club

Mary and her friends wanted to start a club. Mary was a very organized person, and she made a list of six things that needed to be done. But when she was telling her best friend Sheila about the list, she realized she had left it at home. Mary could remember what was on the list, but she couldn't remember the correct order of the things that had to be done!

Can you help her by putting her ideas in the correct order? Put the correct number (1 - 7) by each picture showing the correct order of the steps to start a club.

gest that adults (therapists, teachers, parents) can tutor these children and teach them to discriminate nonverbal cues, understand their meaning, and apply this understanding to social situations. They support activities such as:

1. Teaching children to estimate and maintain proper distance from other people
2. Giving children exercises in which they practice estimating time, so they are more likely to be at the right place at the right time
3. Teaching children, through observation, how various forms of touching can be misinterpreted
4. Playing games like Feelings Charades to learn about posture and body language
5. Developing a dictionary of facial expressions by mounting photographs or magazine pictures on cards
6. Developing an audio dictionary of voice tones that reflect various and attitudes

Values Clarification Therapy

Values Clarification Therapy, whether used as part of an individual treatment program or as part of a classroom's affective curriculum, consists of a series of exercises designed to encourage children to explore who they are. Raths et al. (1966) suggest the valuing process is composed of seven sub-processes, including: prizing and cherishing one's beliefs and behaviors; publicly affirming this pride in appropriate forums; learning to choose from alternatives based on one's beliefs and behaviors; considering the consequences of alternatives; learning to choose freely; learning to act on one's values; and integrating one's values, choices, and actions into a consistent pattern.

Values Clarification techniques can be effective because they are simple and nonthreatening. While they open up channels to the child's feelings, attitudes, and beliefs, they can also enrich the relationships between the child and other people involved in the child's life. There are many books on Values Clarification techniques, such as Simon et al.'s classic *Values Clarification: A Handbook of Practical Strategies for Teachers and Students* (1972). A sampling of these activities include:

Rating Scales: Rate how you feel about the following things from 1 to 10: Dogs. People getting angry at you. Ice cream.

Forced Choice Exercises: If you were on a desert island and could take only three people and three objects with you, whom and what would you choose?

Diagrams and Charts to Explore Relationships: Family tree collages, sociograms, etc.

Self-Concept Projects: Design and build a model car that expresses five things about your interests.

Exploring Beliefs and Attitudes: Role playing.

Interpersonal Exchanges: Make a collage for your best friend showing everything you like about him or her.

Community Projects: Since you believe that having a clean environment is so important, what can you do about it? List 10 projects that would help improve your neighborhood's ecology, and pick the one or two that you think you would like to do.

These are just a few of the infinite number of techniques that can be used.

Self-Help Groups

Americans are known as a fiercely independent people who like to help themselves, and so it is no surprise that self-help groups are an important part of our national culture. For the short-term therapist, referring a parent or an adolescent to a self-help group may seem to be a simplistic intervention, but there are many times that a support group can fill a need in a particular child's social system and have profound and lasting effects.

Self-help groups serve a variety of purposes. They stress a positive identify for their members, reframing a "problem" into a "difference" that makes the member feel unique rather than different. Secondly, the majority of self-help groups provide an educational forum for members, in many cases providing information more specialized and up-to-date than any professional can provide. For many people self-help groups provide a place to belong. Parents of children with disabilities or special needs may themselves feel different from other parents they come in contact with; indeed they are. Parents of a mentally handicapped child, a child with Cerebral Palsy, or who is deaf, or blind, certainly have different experiences from other parents. Self-help groups can help these parents feel part of a group where they can get support for their difficult work as parents, and then in turn provide more nurturance to their children.

Many self-help groups which consist of parents of special children serve an important lobbying function, both in terms of how these children are perceived as well as the actual laws which may affect the education of these children. CH.A.D.D. (Children with Attention Deficit Disorders) is a self-help group of this type.

Family Token Economy Systems

Another way to help the people in a child's social system change is to involve them in the same strategy that the child is using to change. Most parents readily understand that the child will change more quickly (presumably making life more easier for everyone) if they cooperate in the therapy. With this understanding, I explain to the family that there are certain behaviors that they can observe which will make the therapy process advance more quickly. But I emphasize that change can be difficult for them, just as it is for their child. Perhaps I want a mother to use a time-out procedure with her defiant son, but she finds this very difficult to do. Or I want to have a whole family play a particular game with a child, but Mom and Dad and the older siblings are very busy with their own activities and find this a chore. When I must ask a particular family member to change a behavior (or a whole family for that matter), I explain to them that behavioral change can be made easier for them, just like it can be made easier for the child in treatment. I recommend that the significant adults and siblings go on a token economy system along with the child in treatment, with each person earning points for a specified reward when they perform a behavior which will affect the family system, but which they would rather not perform (see Figure 8.D).

Figure 8.D
Family Point Chart

Directions: Put a "+" for each task each person accomplishes each day.

	M	T	W	Th	F	Sa	Su	Ind. Total
Susie								
Nate								
Mom								
Dad								
Daily Family Total								
Totals								

Communicating Solutions

Dr. William Hudson O'Hanlon of the Hudson Center for Brief Therapy is a proponent of Solution-Oriented Brief Therapy and stresses the use of therapeutic communication to help people see the solutions to their problems. As short-term therapists working with children, we have many opportunities to help the adults in a child's life view problems in more positive and helpful ways. From the first call about a referral, to communication with teachers, to scheduled sessions with the parents, the effective therapist should view every word spoken as an opportunity for treatment. Therapists and counselors working within a school, hospital, or other institutional setting, should be particularly aware of the pressure to scapegoat children whose behavior is making life difficult for teachers, child care workers, and other personnel. While they may have the best of intentions, there is a tendency to let off steam and commiserate about how difficult a child is being. In many staff lounges, I've heard comments like: "Wait until you see Teddy today. You might as well take your aspirin now!" or "Mary looks so pathetic, I could just cry when I see her."

These comments may be made in jest or even in sympathy, but

they are not therapeutic: they do not help the child. And although it
may seem awkward at first, particularly if the therapist or counselor
has a peer relationship with these other professionals, the therapist
should make it a point to *always* communicate in ways which help the
people in a child's life see the child's positive aspects. Just a few of
the ways that Dr. O'Hanlon suggests to communicate solutions
include:

• Creating an expectation for change
• Suggesting changes in how the problem can be viewed
• Identifying the first signs that indicate movement towards a thera-
peutic goal
• Listening for and reinforcing comments that indicate things are
changing for the better
• Reinforcing people's competence and skills to help with the child's
problem

Creating a Double-Bind to Ensure Therapeutic Success

I often create a double-bind for the parents or the child to force
them to be accountable for a specific change that I deem to be pre-
requisite to the success of the therapy program. In creating a double-
bind, we give the people in the system only two choices; either choice
will move the therapy in the appropriate direction. In every case of a
double-bind however, one choice is less preferable to the child or to
his system, so it is most likely that the road that will be taken will be
the one the therapist indicates.

I treated David, who had become school phobic after a short stay
in the hospital for minor surgery. The surgery was followed by a one-
month recuperation period, but when David was ready to go back to
school, his school was closed due to a severe snowstorm. Although
the weather let up intermittently and school reopened, David continued to find reasons why he couldn't return to school. He had a cold.
His leg hurt him. He had stomachaches, headaches, and dizziness.
His pediatrician declared these illnesses to be minor, but David insisted that he was too sick to study. On the few days that he went to
school, David complained so loudly to the school nurse that she sent
him home by midmorning.

By springtime, David's parents had given up trying to get their son
to go to school. A tutor was coming to the house; the parents reasoned that at least David was getting some education. They were

concerned that David was becoming more and more isolated from his friends and the community, but they seemed powerless to do anything about it.

In June, David's parents finally sought psychotherapy. They saw that David was determined to stay in the house and were concerned that he would never want to go back to school. (I learned subsequently that there was a history of agoraphobia in the family that went back three generations). When I met with David, he seemed more angry than depressed. I made it clear from our first session that I was there to help him get back into a normal school routine, and David made little effort to hide his disdain for my intentions. Still, we played and talked for sessions on four successive days, and by the end of the week, we were beginning to enjoy each other's company. David was usually early for his appointment, and his mother reported that she never had to ask him twice to get ready.

In our fifth session, I presented my plan to David to help him be ready to go back to school by September. A token economy system would reinforce his doing more physical activities. Relaxation training would help him deal with headaches. A game he could play with his family would help them all talk more openly about their feelings. All these things would make him feel better about re-entering school in September, but I explained that it was, after all, up to him:

> But you do have to go to school. You can choose to go back to your old school, where your old friends go, or if you think you are too sick, you can go to a school in a hospital or to another school I know which is in a different state, but treats children who are too sick to attend regular classes. Of course this is entirely up to you. But you do have to go to school somewhere. That is the law.

David listened to this speech impassively. Perhaps he expected some trick like this. Perhaps he didn't think I was serious. But I *was* serious and I made this clear to David's parents in our next meeting. I told them, just as I had told David, that the law required him to go to school. There was no other option. I said that I thought that it was very unlikely that David would choose not to go back to his old school, but that they needed to be prepared for him to live away from home as an alternative. I insisted that they talk to their insurance company about funding his hospitalization and visit the residential school as well. I explained that they had to go through every detail of planning for David to go to school in a residential setting, or I couldn't continue to see David in treatment. I insisted that this was the only solution to their problem.

With this explanation the double-bind was in place. The only two choices moved David toward the therapeutic goal of returning David to school. How he and his parents chose to meet that goal was entirely up to them. David *did* return to school that fall, but if he had decided to opt for hospitalization or residential treatment, this would have been all right too. As therapists, it is our job to point out the way to achieve more functional and productive behavior, but we cannot force people to take the shortest or the easiest route.

Bibliography

Adams, Patricia, and Marzollo, Jean. *The Helping Hands Handbook.* New York: Random House, 1992.

Azrin, Nathan, and Nunn, Gregory. *Habit Control in a Day.* New York: Pocket Books, 1977.

Beck, Aaron. *Cognitive Theory of Depression.* New York: The Guilford Press, 1979.

Biffle, Christopher. *A Journey Through Your Childhood.* Los Angeles: Jeremy P. Tarcher, Inc., 1989.

Bloch, Douglas. *Positive Self-Talk for Children: Teaching Self-Esteem Through Affirmations.* New York: Bantam Books, 1993.

Brown, Barbara. *Stress and the Art of Biofeedback.* New York: Bantam Books, 1977.

Bry, Adelaid. *The T.A. Primer.* New York: Harper and Row, 1973.

Burns, Robert and Kaufman, S. H. *Kinetic Family Drawings.* New York: Brunner/Mazel, 1970.

Canter, Lee, and Canter, Marlene. *Assertive Discipline for Parents.* New York: Harper Collins, 1982.

Clark, Lynn. *SOS! Help for Parents.* Bowling Green, KY: Parents Press, 1985.

Crary, Elizabeth. *Pick Up Your Socks!* Seattle: Parenting Press, 1990.

Dayton, Tian. *Daily Affirmations for Parents.* Deerfield Beach, FL: Health Communications, 1992.

de Shazer, Steve. *Keys to Solution in Brief Therapy.* New York: W. W. Norton & Co., 1985.

Eysenck, H. "A Mish-Mash of Theories." *International Journal of Psychiatry,* 70:140-146.

Faber, Adele, and Mazlish, Elaine. *How to Talk So Kids Will Listen and Listen So Kids Will Talk.* New York: Avon Books, 1980.

Feder, Elaine and Feder, Bernard. *The Expressive Arts Therapies.* Englewood Cliffs, NJ: Prentice-Hall, Inc., 1981.

Freed, Alvyn M. *T.A. for Kids (and Grownups Too).* Sacramento, CA: Jalmar Press, 1971.

Freed, Alvyn M. *T.A. for Teens and Other Important People.* Sacramento, CA: Jalmar Press, 1976.

Freed, Alvyn M. *T.A. for Tots.* Sacramento, CA: Jalmar Press, 1976.

Garber, Stephen, Garber, Marianne D., and Spizman, Robyn A. *Good Behavior Made Easy.* Fallbrook, CA: Family Life Productions, 1993.

Gardner, Gail. "Hypnosis with Children." *International Journal of Clinical and Experimental Hypnosis,* 22 (1974): 20-38.

Gardner, Richard A. *Conduct Disorders of Childhood.* Cresskill, NJ:

Creative Therapeutics, 1994.

Gardner, Richard A. *Psychotherapeutic Approaches with the Resistant Child.* New York: Jason Aronson, 1975.

Gardner, Richard A. *Self-Esteem Problems of Children.* Cresskill, NJ: Creative Therapeutics, 1992.

Gardner, Richard A. *The Boys and Girls Book About Divorce.* New York: Bantam Books, 1970.

Gardner, Richard A. *The Parent's Book About Divorce.* New York: Bantam Books, 1977.

Gauchman, Ruth, and Wong, Abiel. *The A.D.D. Tool Kit.* King of Prussia, PA: The Center for Applied Psychology, Inc., 1994.

Greelis, Michael, and Haarmann, Betsy. *The ABC's of Video Therapy.* Novato, CA: Academic Therapy Publications, 1980.

Haley, Jay. *Problem-Solving Therapy.* San Francisco: Harper Colophon Books, 1976.

Haley, Jay. *Uncommon Therapy.* New York: W.W. Norton & Co., 1973.

Harris, Thomas. *I'm OK, You're OK: A Practical Guide to Transactional Analysis.* New York: Harper and Row, 1969.

Ingpen, Robert and Mellonie, Bryan. *Lifetimes.* New York: Bantam Books, 1983.

Kids' Random Acts of Kindness. Oakland, CA: Conari Press, 1994.

Lange, Arthur, and Jakubowski, Patricia. *Responsible Assertive Behavior.* Champaign, IL: Research Press, 1976.

Lazarus, Arnold. *Multi-Modal Therapy.* New York: Basic Books, 1980.

Levick, Myra, et al. "The Creative Arts Therapies." *Handbook for Specific Learning Disabilities.* Edited by Adamson and Adamson. New York: Gardner Press, 1979.

Lewis, Barbara. *The Kid's Guide to Social Action.* Minneapolis: Free Spirit Publishing, 1991.

Nowicki, Stephen and Duke, Marshall. *Helping the Child Who Doesn't Fit In.* Atlanta: Peachtree Publishers, 1992.

Olness, Karen and Gardner, Gail. "Some Guidelines for Uses of Hypnotherapy in Pediatrics." *Pediatrics,* 62 (1978).

Quinn, Patricia O. and Stern, Judith M. *Putting on the Brakes: Young People's Guide to Understanding Attention Deficit Hyperactivity Disorder (ADHD).* New York: Magination Press, 1991.

Raths, L. et al. *Values and Teaching.* Columbus, OH: Charles E. Merrill, 1966.

Shalov, Jeanette. *You Can Say NO to Your Teenager.* Addison-Wesley, 1990.

Shapiro, Lawrence E. *Games to Grow On: Activities to Help Children Learn Self-Control.* Englewood Cliffs, NJ: Prentice-Hall, Inc., 1981.

Shapiro, Lawrence E. *Interviews with Experts in Child Psychotherapy.*

King of Prussia, PA: The Center for Applied Psychology, Inc., 1994.

Shapiro, Lawrence E. *Jumpin' Jake Settles Down.* King of Prussia, PA: The Center for Applied Psychology, Inc., 1993.

Shapiro, Lawrence E. *The Book of Psychotherapeutic Games.* King of Prussia, PA: The Center for Applied Psychology, Inc., 1993.

Shapiro, Lawrence E. *The Building Blocks of Self-Esteem.* King of Prussia, PA: The Center for Applied Psychology, Inc., 1993.

Simon, Sydney et al. *Values Claification: A Handbook of Practical Strategies for Teachers and Students.* New York: Hart Publishing Co., Inc., 1972.

Slap-Shelton, Laura. *Child Therapy Today.* King of Prussia, PA: The Center for Applied Psychology, Inc., 1994.

Smith, Sally. *No Easy Answers: Teaching the Learning Disabled Child at Home and School.* New York: Bantam Books, 1980.

Zeigler, Robert. *Homemade Books to Help Kids Cope: An Easy-to-Learn Technique for Parents & Professionals.* New York: Magination Press, 1992.

Zisfein, L. and Rosen, M. "Personal Adjustment Training." *Mental Retardation,* 11 (1971): 16-20.

Zswerling, Israel. "The Creative Arts Therapies as 'Real Therapies.'" *Hospital and Community Psychiatry,* 30 (Dec. 1979).